The Gender Impact of
Social Security Reform

The Gender Impact of Social Security Reform

ESTELLE JAMES,
ALEJANDRA COX EDWARDS,
AND REBECA WONG

The University of Chicago Press
Chicago and London

Estelle James is professor emerita at the State University of New York, Stony Brook, and consultant to the World Bank and other organizations. Alejandra Cox Edwards is professor of economics at California State University, Long Beach. Rebeca Wong is professor of population economics at the University of Texas Medical Branch/Galveston, director of its WHO/PAHO collaborating Center for Pan American Aging and Health, and research associate of the Population Studies Center at the University of Texas at Austin.

The University of Chicago Press, Chicago 60637
The University of Chicago Press, Ltd., London
© The International Bank of Reconstruction and Development/The World Bank Group
All rights reserved. Published 2008
Printed in the United States of America

17 16 15 14 13 12 11 10 09 08   1 2 3 4 5

ISBN-13: 978-0-226-39200-4 (cloth)
ISBN-10: 0-226-39200-7 (cloth)

Library of Congress Cataloging-in-Publication Data

James, Estelle.
    The gender impact of social security reform / Estelle James, Alejandra Cox Edwards, and Rebeca Wong.
        p. cm.
    Includes bibliographical references and index.
    ISBN-13: 978-0-226-39200-4 (cloth : alk. paper)
    ISBN-10: 0-226-39200-7 (cloth : alk. paper) 1. Social security.
    2. Women—Pensions. I. Edwards, Alejandra Cox, 1954– II. Wong, Rebeca. III. Title.
    HD6080 .J36 2008
    331.25'22082—dc22
                                                                    2007046726

♾ The paper used in this publication meets the minimum requirements of the American National Standard for Information Sciences—Permanence of Paper for Printed Library Materials, ANSI Z39.48-1992.

CONTENTS

ACKNOWLEDGMENTS

This project was supported by the Economics and Gender Trust Fund at the World Bank, for which we express our appreciation. An earlier abbreviated version of parts of this study was published in James, Edwards, and Wong (2003) and James, Edwards, and Wong (2007). Permission to reuse material from these papers has been granted by Cambridge University Press, Oxford University Press, and the Pension Research Council of the University of Pennsylvania. For previous papers coming out of this project on Chile and Argentina, see Edwards (2000, 2001a, 2001b, 2002); on Mexico, see Parker and Wong (2001) and Wong and Parker (2001). The authors wish to thank Gustavo de Marco, Rafael Rofman, Hermann von Gersdorff, Augusto Iglesias, and David Madero Suarez for their helpful comments on earlier versions and for answering our endless questions. We owe a special debt to Maria Correia for her enthusiastic encouragement and to Edward Whitehouse for sharing with us his model for deriving actuarial factors, used to convert accumulations to annuity payouts. We are grateful for support we have received from the Social Security Administration through the Michigan Retirement Research Center for our work on gender and social security, as well as other ongoing work on pension reform.

INTRODUCTION

The majority of old people are women, and poverty among the old is concentrated among very old women.[1] Women live longer than men, on average, but often have smaller lifetime incomes. Therefore, in designing a social security system and social security reform, which are meant to safeguard the living standards of the elderly, it is essential to account for the gender impact. Pension systems and their reforms may have different impacts on men and women because of their differing employment histories and demographics. These employment and demographic differences may be offset or exacerbated by particular design features in the systems. This book examines alternative social security systems, their disparate impact on men and women, and the key policy choices that determine gender outcomes. (Henceforth, we use the terms "social security system" and "pension system" interchangeably.)

Social security systems around the world differ in many ways that affect women. In some cases, benefits are closely tied to work and contributions, while in other cases the connection is tenuous if it exists at all. In some cases benefits are targeted toward poverty prevention, while in other cases they are intended to replace wages, including high wages. In some cases generous benefits are provided to surviving spouses who have not worked in the marketplace, while in other cases survivors' benefits are meager and women are expected to finance their own benefits as workers. In this study we compare the impact of two types of social security systems: traditional, publicly managed, pay-as-you-go defined benefit plans versus newer multipillar systems that are partly pay-as-you-go and partly funded. We also analyze the particular design features that will make each type of system more beneficial to women and the impact of these features on the broader economy.

We start by defining a few terms that we will use many times in the course of this book. First, what do we mean by a pay-as-you-go defined benefit plan? In a *defined benefit (DB) plan*, a formula determines the pension promise that is made to each worker. Usually the pension depends on years of work and wages, but in some cases it depends simply on age and/or marital status. In a *pay-as-you-go plan*, these benefits are financed by payroll contributions from current workers rather than funds saved by the retirees while they were working—thus, no saving, no investment earnings. Today's workers must contribute enough to cover the benefits that were promised to retirees many years ago, or else the system is in financial trouble. In principle, benefits received by retirees are often linked to contributions they made previously, but in a very loose way. Sometimes women gain from this process, and sometimes they are hurt. All these systems now face fiscal strain, as the number of older individuals with pensions has grown relative to the number of workers who must finance them.[2]

During the past two decades, new *multipillar systems* have swept through Latin America, the transition economies of eastern and central Europe and the former Soviet Union, and many Organisation for Economic Cooperation and Development (OECD) countries.[3] These new systems were designed to reduce the government's fiscal obligation and to eliminate undesired redistributions and incentives as well as misallocated capital in public pension plans. The new systems contain two separate mandatory "pillars," or financing arrangements—hence the term "multipillar."

One part is a privately managed, defined-contribution, funded plan that handles workers' retirement saving. In a *funded plan*, enough money is saved and invested to cover the future benefits. In a funded *defined contribution (DC) plan*, workers are required to contribute a specified amount to their retirement accounts—that is where the savings are kept—but the benefits are uncertain a priori; they depend strictly on contributions plus investment earnings that accumulate through the workers' lifetime. In the new systems, the money in the accounts is invested by private fund managers chosen by workers—hence this is often called the private pillar—under regulations established by the government. The object is to avoid politically motivated investments, which are often found in publicly managed pension funds.

The second part of the new systems is a publicly managed, tax-financed defined benefit plan that is much smaller than the traditional DB plan. Its main objective is to avoid poverty in old age for low earners and to offset some of the risk they face that their investments will do poorly or they will outlive their savings. It provides a redistributive social safety net. Because its function is narrower than in traditional systems, the hope is that its redistributions will be more transparent and better targeted. The fact that the public tax–financed part is relatively small relieves the government of a large future financial obligation, making these plans very popular among policy planners. However, they have become controversial because the defined contribution part passes investment and longevity risk on to retirees and may result in low pensions for those who have not contributed. Both these pillars—the private and the public—are mandatory in the new systems.

In the course of this controversy, critics have argued that defined contribution plans will produce lower pensions for women, who have worked and contributed less than men. In contrast, supporters argue that the new systems remove biases in the old systems that favored men and discouraged work by women. For example, in most old systems widows could not get their own pension if they received a survivor's benefit, which may have discouraged work by women, while in the new systems women can generally keep both pensions, which may encourage their participation. Supporters also hypothesize that women will benefit disproportionately from the new public pillar, which usually has the limited objective of preventing poverty and redistributing to low earners.

Since theoretical arguments push in both directions, they can never resolve the issue. This book aims to throw empirical light on this debate, a goal that becomes particularly important as multipillar systems spread throughout the world. We draw on the experience of three countries with multipillar systems—Chile, Argentina, and Mexico—to analyze in detail the impact on the two genders of traditional pay-as-you-go systems versus new multipillar systems. Because none of these countries has yet had a full set of retirees with the new systems, we use simulations as our basic analytic tool. Using household survey data, we construct several representative men and women with typical employment histories in these three countries. We then simulate the pensions that these individuals would have received under the rules of the new versus the old systems. For example, the new systems generally require that the money in the accounts be withdrawn gradually after retirement, in the form of a joint pension that covers both spouses, so we incorporate this joint pension into our analysis. Most important, we include benefits from both the public and private parts of the new systems, rather than looking at the defined contribution part alone.

The three countries we analyze have in common the use of privately managed defined contribution accounts. However, their public safety nets differ considerably in terms of size, degree of targeting, eligibility conditions, indexation provisions, and incentives generated. We chose them as our main sample countries precisely because they allow us to demonstrate how variations in the public pillar have a particularly strong influence on the well-being of women. We further broaden the sample by presenting evidence on the gender impact of reforms in several OECD countries (such as Sweden and Australia), as well as the transition economies of eastern and central Europe. In some of these countries survivors' benefits have been eliminated, again having a special impact on women. This variety of experiences enables us to investigate how specific design features affect men versus women. They point, in particular, to the nature of the public pillar and the joint pension requirement in the private pillar as key policy choices that determine gender outcomes.

The United States is sometimes given as an example of a country with a multipillar system, as funded DC plans are common. However, they are not mandatory, hence they are not part of the country's social security system. Instead, they are a voluntary supplement, which makes them quite different. In mandatory systems, coverage, especially of women, is likely to be greater, regulations are more restrictive, and the public benefit is constructed with the assumption that most people will have a retirement savings account. The countries discussed in this book all include mandatory defined contribution plans as part of their social security systems. Thus, they provide insights into the issues and outcomes that would become relevant if retirement savings accounts became mandatory in the United States or elsewhere. Moreover, much of our analysis is directly applicable to reforms of traditional pay-as-you-go systems.

Gender impact can have many different meanings. We ask the following questions to determine its significance:

1. What are the relative monthly and lifetime benefits of men versus women in the new systems?
2. How do their replacement rates (pensions/wages) compare?
3. Which gender receives net redistributions (lifetime benefits minus lifetime contributions or taxes), and which gender pays for these redistributions?
4. What are the relative gains or losses of men versus women due to the shift from the old to the new systems?
5. Which subgroups within each gender gain or lose the most from the reform and from redistributions under the new systems?
6. What are the incentive and disincentive effects and potential behavioral changes stemming from these redistributions?

Pension analysts have disagreed on whether the reforms are good or bad for women partly because of the paucity of careful quantitative evidence and partly because different studies have focused on different gender indicators instead of looking at the whole picture.[4] For example, looking at monthly versus lifetime benefits will produce different results because women live longer. Looking at redistributions gives us yet another perspective, because women may receive net transfers even though their gross benefits are lower. Looking only at the benefits from the private accounts rather than the sum of all benefits from both pillars will also yield a different story. Putting together all the indicators listed above forces us to think through which gender outcomes we care about most and how we can best design the new public and private pillars to achieve them. Our objective is to connect the dots between the key policy choices and the outcomes.

Most of the analysis is positive—comparing gender indicators and the policies that generate them. However, as part of the benefit is tax financed and involves redistributions, it is impossible to avoid value judgments. Should public benefits depend on market income and contributions, and if so, how? Should those who work more get larger public benefits, or should these benefits be targeted toward low earners, whether or not they have worked in the marketplace? Should society compensate those who have worked in the home raising children by giving them a pension to which they have not contributed? How redistributive should the system be? Which group should receive the subsidies, and which group should be forced to finance them? Even in the private pillar, value judgments must be made that involve distributional effects. Should husbands and wives be required to purchase joint annuities that protect both spouses? Should insurance companies be required to use unisex mortality tables so that women get the same monthly payouts as men from similar accumulations, even though they will live longer and therefore receive more over their lifetime? Later in the book, after the positive analysis has been presented, we address these value judgments in greater detail.

Finally, our analysis is based on the assumption that the individual recipient of benefits and payer of taxes matters. If we had hypothesized instead that all family income goes into a big pot and all family expenditure comes out of that pot, regardless of the identity of the earner or spender, gender policies would matter much less, because the welfare of men and women would depend on household resources rather than individual resources. To some extent, families do share incomes and costs of living. Many spouses take into account the current and future needs of their partner, and many old people live in extended family arrangements with their children. Nevertheless, in some marriages the distribution of consumption is unbalanced between the participants and depends in part on the income that each brings to the table. Even if both spouses care about the welfare of the other, each one may plan for and care primarily about his or her own lifetime. Since husbands, on average, die before their wives, this approach may leave many widows in a difficult financial position. "Myopia" may deter sufficient saving and insurance both for men and women, but older women are likely to be the ones left after the household savings have run out. Moreover, changes in the wife's household status midway through life, such as through divorce, may abruptly make previous expectations about joint support irrelevant. In all these cases, the public and private pension entitlements of men and women as individuals become important in determining their relative standard of living and the incidence of poverty between them.

What do we find? In a nutshell, we show that details matter a lot. In Latin America, women's relative position improves because of the detailed arrangements in those countries' systems. A joint annuity requirement, which provides survivors' benefits, and a public benefit that redistributes toward low earners, play key roles here. But in other regions, where these detailed provisions are absent, women have not fared so well.

Because of women's lower lifetime earnings, the accumulations in their accounts and the pensions that they generate are much smaller than those of men, as will be the case in any system that closely links benefits with contributions. Women manage to save only 30 to 40 percent as much as men.

But this annuity from their own accounts is only the beginning of the story. The public benefits in the Latin American reforms are targeted toward low earners, and low earners are disproportionately women. Low earners often do not earn enough to consume adequately when they are young, not to mention save for the days when they are too old to work productively. The public benefit in the new systems has the limited objective of remedying this deficiency—and does so more effectively than the public benefit in the old system, which was meant to serve everyone. Restrictions on payout provisions from the private accounts, particularly requirements that married men purchase joint pensions that will cover their wife after they die, also improve the position of women in the new Latin American systems. Widows are permitted to keep both their own pension and the joint pension, so formal labor market work is not discouraged, as it was in the old systems, which forced them to choose between the survivor's benefit and their own benefit. Countries in other regions have not adopted the joint pension requirement, a major reason why women do not fare as well there.

The net result of these public and mandatory private arrangements in our three countries is that total lifetime retirement benefits for the average married woman are projected to reach 70 to 90 percent those of men, and for the "full career" married woman they are projected to exceed those of men. Women get positive transfers, from the public treasury and/or from the family, which means they get back more than they have paid in. In fact, it turns out that female/male ratios of expected lifetime retirement benefits in the new systems exceed those in the old systems in all three Latin American countries that we have studied and also exceed gender ratios of lifetime earnings during the working stage.

But which subgroups of women gain the most varies by country, mainly because of variations in the design of the public benefit. It emphasizes poverty prevention and low tax costs in Chile; work incentives and equalization in Mexico; and broader access to benefits, with less regard for costs or work incentives, in Argentina. Consequently, women who work in the labor market fare well in Mexico, while those who spend most of their adult lives at home get the best return on their contributions in Argentina; women Chile fall in between. As policy makers in other countries evaluate their options, they need to decide which women and families have priority needs on public resources, which needs can best be accommodated by private resources on a mandatory or voluntary basis, and which incentives they want to include in their old age systems.

Chapter 1 provides an overview of demographic and labor market differences between men and women and generates hypotheses about how men and women might be affected differentially by pension systems and reforms. Chapter 2 summarizes the living arrangements of older women and men and how the standard of living of the two genders compares in old age. Chapter 3 sets forth the methodology we use in this study. Chapters 4 through 6 examine in detail the recent multipillar reforms in Chile, Argentina, and Mexico, respectively, including the expected pensions for men and women from the new private accounts, and how this expectation is modified by public transfers and annuitization rules. We evaluate which subgroups gained and lost the most from the shift to a new system, and which behaviors were rewarded by the new system. Chapter 7 contrasts the Latin American situation with that in selected transition and OECD economies, where the policy choices and gender implications have been quite different.

Chapter 8 returns to the need to make the value judgments raised above and asks, What are the key objectives and trade-offs of a gender-sensitive social security system, and what are the key policy choices that determine these outcomes? Drawing on recurring issues in our case studies, we ask, Should eligibility for the public benefit be based on contributory history, or simply on age? If contribution based, how many years of work should be required for eligibility, or should the link be proportional? How targeted should the public benefit be toward low earners or other groups; that is, how redistributive, and to whom? Should low labor force participation be the basis for subsidization? Should marital status matter? Should the public benefit be price indexed or wage indexed? With regard to the private benefit, we ask, What policies should be adopted to deter unwise portfolio choices during the accumulation stage? Should retirement age be equalized for both genders? Should annuitization be required? Should joint annuities and survivors' benefits be required? Should annuities be price indexed? Should unisex mortality tables be used for determining annuity payouts? What should be done in the case of divorce? The book's conclusion summarizes lessons for policy makers. Since old people are disproportionately women, a system that does not protect women can hardly be said to protect the old. We hope this study will help policy makers design their reforms with this thought in mind.

CHAPTER ONE

Why Do Social Security Systems and Social Security Reforms Have a Gender Impact?

Most public pension programs—both the traditional defined benefit and the newer multipillar plans—are contributory; that is, they are financed by payroll taxes, and they pay out benefits the amount of which depends on wage history, years of work, or, more directly, on contributions. These contributory schemes are sometimes supplemented by a uniform or means-tested pension that is more universal, based only on age and residence and financed by general revenues. But the contributory part of the program usually dominates.

Contributory social security systems have developed for a variety of reasons:

- Pensions are viewed as a source of income that replaces part of the wage when old age makes work difficult or less productive; hence a connection between pension benefits, wages, and payroll taxes seems logical.
- If benefits are linked to contributions, workers may be willing to contribute over and above the taxes they would otherwise pay for public services, as they perceive this as a payment for services that are specifically earmarked for them rather than a tax for the general treasury.
- Workers who evade these contributions pay the price in terms of forgone benefits, rather than passing this cost on to the common pool—this distinction is particularly important in developing countries with weak tax-enforcement mechanisms.
- Basing the tax on payroll rather than general income limits the redistribution involved and therefore increases the political support of high earners for the plan.
- Payroll taxes from large employers are relatively easy to collect.

However, these arrangements pose a problem for women, who are likely to have worked and contributed for fewer years; have earned lower wages when working; and outlive their husbands, who provide the family's monetary income. As a result of these socioeconomic and demographic differences, the same pension policy may have different effects on men and women, and pension reform can have important gender effects. Moreover, social security systems often include rules that explicitly differentiate between men and women. This chapter reviews these labor market and demographic differences and the issues they raise for pension policy.

Differential Labor Market Histories

Labor Force Participation Rate

Women traditionally have less continuous labor force attachment than men. The intrafamily division of labor has typically resulted in men working in the market and women working in the home. Even when women work in the market, this attachment tends to be temporary and part time. It is more likely to be in the informal sector, which is not covered by formal social security schemes. Women's work may be interrupted by childbearing and rearing, caring for elderly parents or sick members of the family, and so forth. Consequently, women, especially married women with children, are in the system for far fewer years over their lifetime—roughly 50 to 70 percent as many years in our three sample countries (see tables 4.3, 5.3, and 6.3 later in the book).

A large gender gap persists in industrial countries too, even though it has been declining in the last two decades. In the United Kingdom, Canada, and Australia in 2000, the female labor force participation rate was still 10 to 15 percent below that of men (compared with 25 to 35 percent in 1980). In Organisation of Economic Co-operation and Development (OECD) countries as a whole, the gender gap is only 12 percent for women without children but jumps to 32 percent for women with two or more children; the latter group, however, is becoming smaller as fertility rates fall in these countries. And much of the work women do is part time: On average in OECD countries, 26 percent of women, but only 7 percent of men, work part time. In Switzerland, Norway, and the United Kingdom, more than 40 percent of women, but less than 10 percent of men, work part time (OECD 2003).

In the United States, women's labor market experience is converging with that of men, and younger cohorts are more likely to remain in the labor force throughout most of their adult lives, but a gap still exists. In 1960 the female labor force participation rate was less than 50 percent that of men, in 1980 it was 75 percent, and in 2000 the percentage had risen to 87 percent (U.S. GAO 1997; OECD 2003). However, the convergence process is very gradual and the growth in female work propensities seems to be slowing down. In the transition economies of eastern and central Europe, female work propensities are actually declining and the gender gap is increasing (Woycicka et al. 2003). Traditional roles continue to dominate in most developing countries.

The lower work propensities of women raises a key policy question: to what extent should public benefits compensate for the lower employment-based pension rights that they accumulate, or should family support be required for this purpose, in return for the nonmarket work that women perform? We will return to this issue in chapter 8 after discussing how the old and new systems in our sample countries have handled this question.

Wages

Women typically earn less per week or per year of work than men, even after controlling for age and education. This may be due in part to their lower labor force attachment (past experience and expected future tenure), in part to occupational segregation, and in part to social norms that condone lower pay to women. In our three sample countries, at age twenty women earn almost as much as men, but the disparity increases with age, and by age fifty they earn only 60 to 70 percent as much per month of work (see tables 4.5, 5.5, and 6.5 later in the book).

The gender gap in work and pay is smaller, but still significant, in higher-income countries. For example, in the United Kingdom, Canada, and Australia hourly wage rates for women are 15 to 30 percent less than those of men (Ginn, Street, and Arber 2001). Much of this gap may be due to differential experience in the labor market—at any given age women have less work experience than men and less assured continuity of future work, which in turn influences the jobs they choose and are chosen for. In the United States median earnings for full-time employed women are 70 percent those of men, and the gap is cut in half when age, education, work effort, and other relevant variables are controlled (U.S. GAO 1997). Nevertheless, the earnings differential and much-noted "glass ceiling" remain. Thus any pension system that links benefits to earnings or contributions is likely to produce lower benefits for women, even if they worked the same number of years as men. Should old age systems include a component that is not contributory and does not depend on earnings?

Front-Loading Women's Earnings

Women tend to concentrate their total earnings at an earlier age than men. This occurs because they work when young but frequently drop out of the labor market when bearing and rearing children. Even if they reenter the labor market, their age-earnings profiles are less steep than those of men, in part because of interrupted careers. This means that their contributions are in the system longer and do not reflect the productivity growth that is embodied in the earnings and contributions of older men. A system that bases the pension on nominal earnings without adjustment for economy-wide price and wage growth therefore disadvantages women, while a system that places heavier weight on early contributions, as through a compounded rate of return, benefits women.

Provisions in Old Age Systems that Augment or Diminish These Labor Market Effects

PROVISIONS THAT OFFSET LOW WORK PROPENSITIES AND EARNINGS Most systems contain provisions that mitigate the impact on pensions of women's interrupted careers, part-time work, and low earnings. For example, the contributory occupational plan in the Netherlands is accompanied by a flat public benefit based mainly on residence, not employment. Individual accounts in Argentina are supplemented by a flat benefit that depends on employment, but with only a ten-year eligibility requirement. Australia features a broad-based means- and asset-tested public benefit that most old people receive, in addition to its defined contribution plan. Many countries (including Chile, Kazahkstan, and Poland) have a minimum pension guarantee that underlays the other parts of their system and protects women with limited work histories. These flat and minimum pensions are often set at 20 to 30 percent of the average wage. In the United States and Switzerland, a progressive benefit formula gives a high rate of return to women with partial careers. Most OECD countries (except for the United States) give credits toward their public benefits for years spent caring for their children. Most countries have a ceiling on earnings counted toward benefits.

These measures reduce the gender gap in pensions due to low labor force participation and earnings of women, but they do not eliminate it completely. Minimum pensions increase the female/male ratios at the low end of the earnings spectrum, benefit ceilings increase it at the high end, and flat benefits tend to equalize in the middle as well. As we shall see later, their effectiveness depends in large part on eligibility conditions and indexation rules. Mexico's minimum pension guarantee seems at first to favor women until it becomes clear that very few women contribute long enough to become eligible. Exactly which measures are used can have a large impact on women's incentives to work and build their own pensions.

PROVISIONS THAT AUGMENT LOW WORK PROPENITIES: EARLY RETIREMENT AGE FOR WOMEN Rules of the system sometimes allow women to retire earlier than men, thereby exacerbating the gender-pension differential. For example, women are permitted to retire five years earlier than men in Chile and Argentina. In most transition economies of eastern Europe and the former Soviet Union, women can retire three to five years earlier than men. This enables them to retire at the same time as their husbands, who tend to be several years older. It is sometimes argued that working women have two jobs—one at home and a second in the market—so they are "entitled" to retire earlier as compensation. But this is a costly compensation, to the women and to the economy. Early retirement may seem to be a privilege—appreciated by women who do not enjoy their work and prefer leisure—but they pay the price later on in terms of lower pensions. A policy allowing early retirement may also discourage employers from hiring or promoting older women for fear they will retire soon. Further, the loss of experienced labor reduces the country's gross domestic product.

In traditional defined benefit systems women were often permitted to retire early without an actuarial penalty—this meant that early retirees were subsidized by others. In contrast, in "actuarially fair" systems workers who retire early get a lower monthly pension to compensate for the larger number of years they will be receiving it. Annuitization arrangements in most new defined contribution systems are actuarially fair and require retirees to live within their own retirement accumulations; this means that early retirees receive a lower annual pension than they would if they retired at a later age. This cost may not be fully realized until the woman is too old to reverse her decision to retire early. Should retirement ages be equalized for men and women to avoid such myopic choices?

Less Education, Lower Productivity, and Pensions for Girls in Low-Income Countries

In low-income countries, children of both genders often do not attend secondary school or even complete primary school. However, girls are less likely to do so than boys. Families are more likely to invest in the schooling of their sons because of the expectation that sons will use these skills in the labor market and will become the future financial supporters of the extended family, whereas girls are expected to marry, leave their parents' home, bear and raise children, and provide household services to their future husbands and their parents. The lack of schooling for girls inhibits their ability to work productively in the labor market even if they should wish to do so.

In the process of economic development, this attitude toward women's education changes, and schooling tends to be equalized between the two genders. For example, comparing mean years of schooling for urban men and women in Mexico in 2000 across age groups, we see that men had at least one year of schooling more than women (roughly a 20 percent increment) for all ages over thirty-five. However, for younger ages the schooling differential declined and reached virtual equality for men and women under twenty-five. Years of schooling had increased for both genders for successively younger birth cohorts, but much more so for women, who thereby caught up to men (Mexican Census 2000, accessed through IPUMS). Similarly, in Chile in 2000 among urban women in the age group fifty-six to sixty-four (just prior to retirement) only 11 percent had a university degree, compared with more than double that number—23 percent—for men. But the proportion of younger women receiving higher education trebled by the cohort age fifteen to twenty-six (just entering the labor force), while for men the increment was very small, so currently there are more young women than men in the top educational categories (University of Chile 2000).

We know that the labor market returns to education are high and, moreover, that females' labor market participation is strongly correlated with their education (much more so than that of males). If schooling raises their potential market wages faster than the value of their household production, it follows that more educated girls will face incentives that make it attractive for them to work. In contrast, those without schooling will find it more advantageous to stay at home. In the following chapters we present empirical evidence of higher labor force participation rates among more educated women on a cross-sectional basis as well as evidence of rises in aggregate female participation rates over time as education among females has increased in the three countries we studied.

Here we simply note that decisions made by families about the education of their girl children leave a long legacy—it affects the girls' employment prospects and work propensities in adulthood and their pension prospects in retirement fifty to sixty years later. The differential labor market role and pension access among older men and women in middle- and high-income countries today is due in part to family decisions made many years ago, and this effect will persist until the new generations of females with greater schooling fully replace the cohorts with lesser schooling in the economically active and retirement stages of life. The gradual positive change we observe now in women's market role is due in part to this transition to higher education. (And, of course, the growing expectation of families that their girl children will work adds to their willingness to educate these girls—causation runs both ways, reinforcing both trends, in the process of economic development). The future gender gap in pensions is likely to fall as a result of increasing educational equality in the recent past.

Demographic and Biological Differences

Longevity

In most countries, women at age sixty have a life expectancy that is three to five years greater than that of men. From this vantage point, women should retire later, not earlier. In Chile, a sixty-year-old woman is likely to live another twenty-three years, while a sixty-year-old man lives another nineteen years and a sixty-five-year-old man lives only an additional fifteen-and-a-half years. A woman who retires at age sixty has a future lifespan that is 7.5 years longer than her husband's when he retires at age sixty-five. This is a typical retirement-period differential in Latin America and the transition economies.

The disparity in life expectancy increases with age. In the United States the ratio of females to males still alive at age fifty-five to sixty-four is 1.1, at seventy-five to eighty-four it is 1.5, and above age eighty-five it is 2.5 (U.S. Census Bureau 2001). The gender disparity has also been growing over the past half-century. Increasingly, very old people are women.

Women who have specialized in home work rather than market production face a particular problem as they age: they may become less productive in the home but have no monetary savings of their own to live on or to contribute to the family in lieu of in-kind services. Thus, they are more dependent on the accumulated "goodwill" of the family for many years of old age. What steps should public policies take to reinforce this goodwill or substitute for it in cases when it fails?

For women who have worked in the market and have acquired retirement savings, annuitization—which provides longevity insurance—is a valuable option. When a retiree purchases an annuity with these savings, he or she gets a monthly pension for life in return. Since women live longer than men on average but face a large variation around the mean, this lifetime protection is particularly important to them. Defined benefit systems pay a lifetime benefit that is like an annuity. In a defined contribution plan the accumulation in the individual's account can be turned into an annuity upon retirement, and this is sometimes required.

However, because women live longer, any given retirement accumulation yields lower annual benefits to them if gender-specific mortality tables are used to calculate the monthly payout, as in Latin America. In contrast, defined benefit systems implicitly use unisex tables (acting as if men and women have the same expected lifetimes), since they generally do not use gender-differentiated rules to determine benefits. A key policy choice must be made: should annuitization be required for the individual accounts to provide lifelong income security, and should gender-specific tables or unisex tables be used by companies issuing the annuities? As we shall see, different countries have answered these questions very differently.

Widowhood

The greater longevity of women also means that they are more likely to become widows than men are to become widowers; hence survivors' pensions are of key importance to women. The social custom for husbands to be older than wives exacerbates the importance of survivors' benefits. In Chile, 41 percent of women over age sixty, but only 14 percent of men in this age group, are widows, and the numbers are similar in Argentina and Mexico. In Chile, women in urban areas are almost as likely as men to receive a pension. However, for women the pension is a widow's or social assistance pension in almost half the cases, while for men it is almost always an own-earned pension. In Mexico the disparity is even greater (see table 2.2 later in the book). Without survivors' benefits, nonworking widows are likely to find themselves without monetary means, and even widows who have a pension of their own find their household income cut by far more than their cost of living when their husband dies, due to household economies of scale (see chapter 2). In a group of nine OECD countries, for women age sixty-five to seventy-four, becoming widowed implied a fall in income of 20 to 33 percent (Casey and Yamada 2002). As a result, poverty among the old tends to be concentrated among very old women, many of whom are widows. In the United States in 1997, poverty rates were less than 5 percent for elderly women in married couples but 18 percent for widowed women, who constituted 45 percent of all women over age sixty-five (NEC 1998).

Survivors' benefits are often included in social security systems, but the precise arrangements vary. Publicly provided survivors' benefits are being reduced or phased out in central and eastern Europe. Joint annuities play a major role in the new Latin American systems. Two key questions arise:

(1) Who should finance the widow's benefit—the state or the husband? (2) If a woman has worked in the labor market, should she have to give up her own pension when she gets the widow's benefit? In the old systems, survivors' benefits were financed out of the common pool and typically women had to give up their own benefit to receive it. This was regressive because widows of high earners got the largest benefits, for which neither they nor their husbands paid. At the same time, the opportunity cost was especially great for women with high education and high potential productivity. If they worked they would have to make relatively large payroll contributions, but they would get little or no incremental benefit because the widow's benefit usually exceeded their own benefit. This may have discouraged them from working. In the new systems, survivors' benefits are often required to be purchased by spouses, and women can keep their own pension as well. This increases women's incentive to work in the labor market and increases their standard of living in very old age.

Decision-Making Power within the Household about Survivors' Benefits

Can countries rely on husbands to voluntarily provide life insurance for survivors? Part of the family's income during the retirement period does indeed come from voluntary saving and insurance. The amount of saving and insurance then depends on the expected lifetime of the decision maker. The distribution of decision-making power within the household determines whose lifetime enters into this calculation. Recent evidence indicates that the individual who generates the most income also has the most decision-making power. This is usually the husband. If he takes into account primarily his own expected lifetime in making saving and insurance decisions for the family, this may lead to undersaving and underinsurance in younger years and underconsumption for widows in later years, leaving the widow poor and sometimes a burden on the public treasury (Bernheim et al. 2003; Friedberg and Webb 2006).

This issue does not arise in defined benefit social security systems, which mandate the contribution and payout rate as well as the existence or nonexistence of survivors' insurance—the individual has no choice. It does arise in voluntary retirement saving plans and in mandatory defined contribution plans that give retirees a choice of payout modes. A husband may not voluntarily finance a pension that includes survivors' benefits, which will not pay off until after his death. To avoid this problem, some countries with individual account systems require that payouts take the form of joint annuities or gradual withdrawals spread over the lifetimes of both spouses.

Divorce, Cohabitation, and Single Parenthood

While widowhood is the greatest problem for older women in traditional societies, in richer countries divorce and cohabitation without formal marriage are becoming increasingly common. In both cases, women may allocate part of their time when young to bearing and raising children with the expectation that their partner will provide their financial support when old—they may think an intertemporal trade has been made. But the partner may not fulfill his part of the bargain if divorce occurs or if the cohabiting arrangement is broken. Older women bear much of the financial risk of divorce.

Public programs sometimes include provisions for these situations. For example, in Switzerland and Canada pension credits are split upon divorce. In the United States marriages lasting ten years generate a spousal and survivor's benefit for the divorced woman whether or not there is a subsequent wife. In Chile survivors' benefits and the minimum pension guarantee cover the nonmarried mother of a man's children (as well as his spouse). But many countries overlook these groups. In the new systems, where funds build up in accounts, countries must decide whether spouses and partners are required to split these assets when the relationship dissolves. Mexico and Argentina have no regulations governing such situations. Chile, which has just legalized divorce, is grappling with this problem now.

How Do These Forces Change over the Process of Economic Development?

As countries develop, the labor force role of women tends to grow closer to that of men. This trend is accentuated by the fact that women's work propensities and earnings are closely linked to education, and their education increases dramatically as economies grow, while for men labor force participation rates are largely independent of their education. These educational and labor market changes operate to narrow the gender gap in pensions as countries develop. However, lower marriage rates, higher divorce rates, greater longevity (especially for women), and hence the reduced relevance of the nuclear family and the breakdown of the extended family, work in the opposite direction to maintain the gender gap. While women are having far fewer children in rich countries, they continue to hold the childbearing and most of the child-rearing responsibilities, which cuts into their labor market responsibilities. How should social security policy respond to these diverse conditions? Policy choices will ultimately depend on value judgments and trade-offs among objectives, but understanding the variety of options and their consequences is an important input into this process.

CHAPTER TWO

Living Arrangements and Standards of Elderly Men and Women

Before focusing on the pension system, we survey the living arrangements and standard of living of elderly men and women. The striking point is that, except in a small number of rich industrial countries, most elderly men and women live with others in a variety of household structures, so their living standards depend on these living arrangements and the income of the other people in the household, as well as their own income. For married women in traditional societies, the income of other family members—first the husband and later the children—is even more important than their own income. If the family support system works well, the formal pension system plays a less important role for these women. But the family system breaks down in the process of urbanization, worker mobility, and economic growth. Moreover, women without an extended family are likely to be disadvantaged financially, especially when they grow old. Mandatory old age programs are, in part, a response to an unreliable family old age system.

How Household Structure Affects Living Standards of Women versus Men

The Nuclear Family in Old Age

As men and women enter old age, typically they are married and living in a nuclear family structure (i.e., a family with a "head," a spouse, and possibly their children). At this point, the husband is generally the main source of monetary income, earning much more than the wife, but this becomes "household income," for both spouses. The wife's standard of living depends on the husband's income, whether or not that income is divided equally. This is clearly true of the three Latin American countries we have studied, which have traditional family structures, and it remains true in many industrialized countries.

Widows and Single Women

The husband, however, is likely to die before the wife, so she becomes a widow. In each of our three countries, women are much more likely to be widows than men are to be widowers (table 2.1, panel A). In Chile, 41 percent of women over age sixty, but only 14 percent of men this age, are widows. In Argentina and Mexico the proportion of widows is even higher—45 percent and 47 percent, respectively—while the proportion of widowers remains 13 to 15 percent. Elderly women are also more likely than men to be single or divorced (10–11 percent for men, 11–13 percent for women). This disparity also holds in other countries, and it grows with age. In the United States, 34 percent of women but only 7 percent of men, age sixty-five to sixty-nine are widows, while in the eighty to eighty-four age group these numbers are 72 percent and 27 percent, respectively. In the eighty-five and older age group, 48 percent of men, but only 9 percent of women, are living with their spouses (Posner 1995, 139, 277). Thus the majority of elderly women are

Table 2.1: Living Arrangements of Men and Women Age 60+

	Chile		Argentina		Mexico	
	Men	Women	Men	Women	Men	Women
A. Marital Status (%)						
Married	76.5	46.3	76.4	42.0	74.2	42.6
Widowed	13.6	41.3	12.5	45.4	15.0	46.7
Single and divorced	9.9	12.4	11.1	12.6	10.8	10.7
B. Household Structure (%)						
Nuclear	50.1	34.5	69.2	41.7	56.6	41.5
Extended	42.8	52.5	22.3	36.6	34.4	45.6
Uniperson	7.1	13.0	8.4	21.7	8.9	12.9

Sources: For Chile, data in all tables in this book are for urban areas. Unless otherwise noted, they are authors' calculations from the micro data set Caracterizacion Socioeconomica Nacional (CASEN), a nationally and regionally representative household survey for 1994 (Universidad de Chile–Santiago 1994). Data for Argentina are authors' calculations based on the micro data set of Encuesta de Ingresos y Gastos, a nationally and regionally representative household survey for 1996–1997 (Ministerio del Trabajo y Prevision Social 2004). Data for Mexico are national averages for urban areas. They are authors' calculations based on the National Income and Expenditure Survey, 1996. The Mexican Health and Aging Study (Soldo et al. 2003) is also used for data on household structure. For more details on data in this table, see Edwards (2000, 2001a, 2001b) and Wong, Espinoza, and Palloni (2007).

without spouses and the material and moral support that spouses bring, while three-quarters of elderly men still have their partners (and most live in nuclear families with them).

Extended Families

When the husband dies, household costs fall because they are now incurred by only one person, but household income falls further because the wife's own income is usually far less than that of her husband. If no other factors intervened, the woman's standard of living would fall. But the widow's children (if she has them) can limit this fall by making interhousehold transfers while she lives alone or by incorporating her into their extended households. In Mexico 18 percent of elderly women (15 percent of men) receive family transfers, and 46 percent of women (35 percent of men) live in extended families. In either case, a widow's standard of living now depends on the income of her children and not simply on her own income.

Among elderly women who are no longer in a nuclear family, the vast majority live in extended family arrangements (table 2.1, panel B). On the one hand, if the per capita income of young families is relatively high, the standard of living of the widow will now be relatively high—perhaps even higher than before when she lived in a nuclear family. This might occur because younger people have skills that are highly valued in the labor market in a context of recent rapid educational and economic growth. On the other hand, if the per capita income of young families is relatively low, the standard of living of the widow will also be relatively low—perhaps lower than it was before. This might occur because the main breadwinners of young families are at a low point on their age-earnings profiles and they have many children who must share the family income.

Diversity in Uniperson Households

However, all widows with children do not move into extended families—some have other options. The extended family arrangement benefits from scale economies and easy exchange of nonmonetary services, but at a cost in terms of lost privacy to both sides. We expect that widows with children are more likely to opt for uniperson households if they are members of wealthy families that can afford to spend money on privacy and services. This subgroup might have an above-average expenditure level due to selection of wealthy women into uniperson households (and vice versa for poor women selecting into extended families).[1]

Another subgroup of women live alone because they have no choice. This subgroup consists of widows without children and those who never married. Living alone is much more common for the elderly than for prime-age adults, and it is especially common for women. Those who live alone because they have no choice are likely to have below-average income and expenditures due to their lower personal income and the loss of spousal income.

Thus, uniperson households consist of two disparate groups: those who choose to live alone because they can afford to do so comfortably and those who have no such choice, despite being uncomfortable. When mixing these two groups, we do not know which will dominate and are therefore unable to predict the relative position of the group as a whole. We would expect, however, to find a pocket of poverty here—the subgroup with no choice will be relatively poor.

Women who actually become very old are more likely to come from the wealthy subgroup, given the positive correlation between longevity and income or wealth. Thus, in a cross-sectional analysis, selection reinforced by survival bias could cause very old women living alone to appear to have relatively high standards of living, on average. But the pockets of poverty may deepen at the same time for the small group of low-income elderly women who have survived. They will have used up any savings; they will be unable to work; and their pensions, if any, will become smaller relative to growing wages around them.

Elderly Men versus Elderly Women

The biggest difference between the living arrangements of elderly men and elderly women is that the men live predominantly in nuclear households that they head, while many women live in extended families headed by younger members. Consequently, the relative well-being of elderly men versus women (as measured in terms of family income per capita) depends intrinsically on the intergenerational comparison between "old" and "young" households, even more so than on the personal incomes of men versus women in the same generation.

To the degree that women share in the standard of living of their households, we would expect to find two alternative patterns:

1. If young households are poorer than old households, elderly women (many of whom live with their children in extended families) are likely to appear poorer than elderly men (who tend to live in their own nuclear households).
2. If young households are richer than old households, elderly women are

likely to be at least as well off as men because they benefit from the higher consumption standards of the extended families with which they live.

In addition, for reasons given above, we would expect to find pockets of wealth (selection and survival bias) and poverty (own-income effect) among elderly women living alone.

Empirical Evidence—Methodological Issues

Equivalency Scales when Family Size and Composition Differ

With household structure as background, we proceed to examine the standard of living of elderly men and elderly women as measured by the per capita income of the households in which they are living. Our empirical task is complicated by these different living arrangements.

When more than one person lives in a household, some of their consumption goods are, in effect, "public" goods, of which everyone in the household partakes. For example, the dwelling may have one kitchen and one bathroom, which everyone uses. These public goods create household economies of scale, which enable two persons to maintain a given living standard for considerably less than double the amount it would cost one person to maintain that same level of comfort.

But part of the family's consumption consists of private goods, which only one person can consume. When one member of a household eats an apple, another cannot eat the same apple. The division of household consumption between public goods and private goods may differ systematically by size of family and age of members, so calculations of average standard of living per family member (total household income or expenditure divided by the number of household members) requires an adjustment for these factors using *equivalence scales*. These scales give us an adjusted number of equivalent full cost family members by attributing different marginal costs to incremental members depending on their age and family size, while assuming that all members enjoy the same standard of living.

Exactly how this adjustment should be made is far from clear. The fact that small children may consume less food and space than adults often leads to a lower weighting for children in calculating the adjusted number of family members. However, if the mother works in the labor market, the advent of a child may impose large monetary expenditures for child care and other household services. In such cases, one might argue that children, especially the first child, should be weighted more heavily than adults, but this is rarely done. For similar reasons, very old people are sometimes weighted less heavily than prime-age adults. However, it is also possible that the elderly will incur large medical or custodial expenses that are not covered by insurance; in these cases, it might be appropriate to weight old people more heavily than young people.

As a result of these and related issues, several equivalence scales exist. The *modified OECD scale*, which is often used, weights the first adult as 1, additional adults as .5, and children younger than fourteen years of age as .3. The *square root scale* takes the square root of the number of family members as the divisor to determine adjusted per capita income (OECD 1982; Hagenaars, De Vos, and Zaidi 1994). The modified scale implies that the cost of maintaining a given living standard is 67 percent as much for a uniperson household as it is for a couple, while the square root scale implies it is 71 percent as much. When an old person joins a household that consists of two prime-age adults and one child, the net addition to household adjusted members is .5/1.8, so total household income must go up by 28 percent to enable other family members to maintain their previous standard of living according to the modified scale. In contrast, according to the square root scale, total cost rises from 1.7 to 2, or 16 percent. Both numbers are smaller than the required increase of 33 percent in unadjusted per capita income because they take household economies of scale into account. Other scales weight older people differently from prime-age adults. Clearly, calculations of the relative well-being of people with different living arrangements and of young versus old households will be very sensitive to choice of equivalency scale (see Deaton 1997; Deaton and Paxson 1997; Deaton and Meullbauer 1986; Whitehouse 2000; Lanjouw, Milanovic, and Paternostro 1998). Our figures on per capita income and poverty rates rely primarily on the modified OECD scale, in which children are weighted less heavily than adults (see table 2.3 below).

Bargaining Power and Nonmonetary Services

In addition to these accounting issues, we do not really know how the private goods in the family are divided among its members. The equivalence scales discussed above may not correspond to the actual bargaining power of diverse family members. In some traditional cultures, old people own the family wealth and dictate the division of family consumption, so the elderly of both genders fare better than indicated by these equivalence scales. But in modern societies the fact that prime-age males are usually the major breadwinners may give them predominant control over what is purchased and for whom, so the elderly may fare less well. Elderly men contribute more money than elderly women, so they may have greater bargaining power than women—both in extended and nuclear families. The likelihood that private goods will not be divided equally among household members due to differential bargaining power means that all members do not end up with the same "average" standard of living—but usually we can only observe the average.

Additionally, nonmonetary household services contributed by family members are not included in these analyses. Women contribute more nonmonetary services than men, which may raise the living standards of households with elderly women, as well as the bargaining power of these women. Similarly, the elderly who live in extended families may receive nonmonetary services, such as custodial care, from their children, which raises their standard of living. As women grow very old they are more likely to require than to provide such services, and they are less likely than men to be able to contribute monetary wealth to the household. This may place them at a disadvantage in the family's pecking order. Data are usually not available on nonmonetary services, but those services undoubtedly play an important role.[2]

Empirical Evidence—Results

Comparisons of Personal Income

As expected, based on their own income, older women are much poorer than older men (table 2.2). Although relatively few people of either gender show evidence of saving, women are less likely to have saved (which would produce interest or rent) than men in all three countries. In urban Chile, only 11 percent of women, compared with 38 percent of men, have some wage income, and among these the average amount is 60 percent greater for men. Men are also more likely to own their own housing (imputed rent). Pensions are the largest source of personal income for the elderly. Men are more likely to have old age pensions (62 percent, versus 31 percent for women), while women are more likely to receive survivors' benefits or Pensiones Asistenciales (PASIS, the means-tested social assistance pension for the elderly), both of which are much smaller than male pensions. Taken together, 74 percent of all old women and 98 percent of all old men in urban areas have some source of personal income, but the average amount is more than twice as large for men. These disparities are even greater in rural areas, where almost one-quarter of all elderly women qualify for PASIS.

Table 2.2: Personal Income of the Elderly by Gender, 2002 (in 2002 US$)

	Men		Women	
	% with Income	Average Amount (US$)[a]	% with Income	Average Amount (US$)[a]
A. Chile				
Salary	37.8	275	11.2	169
Imputed Rent	72.2	65	37.7	56
Pensions (all)	70.1	224	59.7	129
Old age and disability	62.0	240	30.9	141
Disability	5.6	116	4.5	87
Survivors (widows)	1.2	227	19.4	139
PASIS (social assistance)	3.2	28	6.2	28
Total	97.6	407	73.5	195
B. Argentina				
Salary	19.1	128	8.0	75
Interest and Rent	3.4	79	2.5	50
Family Transfers	7.7	29	6.2	35
Pensions	49.7	68	48.3	51
Total	66.5	99	54.7	63
C. Mexico				
Salaries	21.3	358.9	3.3	257
Self-Employed	40.1	489.9	13.6	147
Interest and Rent	4.0	484.5	2.4	531
Family Transfers	15.0	251.2	17.5	185
Pensions (all)	19.4	260.2	9.0	140
Old age and disability	19.4	260.2	3.0	n.a.
Survivors (widows)	0	n.a.	6.0	n.a.
Other	.7	299.7	1.0	562
Total	79.5	488.5	36.9	271

Sources: Edwards (2000, 2001a, 2001b, table 11); Parker and Wong (2001, tables 8.14 and 8.9). Estimates based on 1994 data for Chile, 1996 data for Argentina, and 1997 data for Mexico, transformed into 2002 US$.

[a] Monthly amounts for those who have this income source.

The same story applies to Mexico. There, only 17 percent of older women, but 61 percent of older men, have some salaried or self-employment income (and for women this is mainly low-paid self-employment). Nine percent of women, but 19 percent of men, receive a pension, which is mostly an old age pension for men and a smaller widow's pension for women. In contrast, more women than men receive intrafamily transfers. Analysis of the distribution of these transfers shows that they go predominantly to those who do not receive a pension, providing crude evidence of crowd-out.[3] Interestingly, transfers are an equalizing force between the genders—they are the only income source that goes more heavily to women. Altogether, 37 percent of older women, but 80 percent of older men, receive some personal income, and, among these, the average amount is almost twice as large for men.

A similar picture emerges in Argentina, although the disparity is not as striking: In urban areas, 67 percent of older men and 55 percent of older women report some personal income, and the average amount is 50 percent greater for men. About half the elderly receive pensions. Consistent with the description of Argentina's old age system that follows (especially the role of the flat benefit), the proportion is the same for both genders and the amounts are less disparate than in the other two countries.

Living Standards in Young versus Old Households and Implications for the Gender Gap

As we have seen, in the presence of the extended family, the lower personal income of women does not mean that they have a lower standard of living than men. In Chile, households without any elderly members have lower per capita incomes than households with elderly numbers when using the OECD scale (table 2.3, panel A). The former are probably households with young adults at the start of their careers and with many small children. Families with two elderly—which tend to be nuclear families—have the highest incomes. Many of these are families just past the peak of their earnings, possibly with some savings, and with a high permanent income that is signaled by their longevity. Similarly, families without elderly members are most likely to be living in poverty, while nuclear families of two elderly are least likely to be below the poverty line (table 2.3, panel B). Families with one elderly member (usually elderly women) are in between. These relative positions are important when deciding on the importance of public subsidies to the elderly as a group versus young families with children. If the objective is poverty alleviation, targeting subsidies toward families with children may make more sense than targeting them toward the elderly.

Above, we conjectured that if young families had relatively low incomes, this would lead older women to have lower incomes and higher poverty rates than older men. And that is exactly what we find in Chile (table 2.3, panel C). According to the OECD scale, poverty rates for elderly women are 50 percent higher than for men in urban areas (150 percent higher in rural areas). Poverty is concentrated in very old women living in extended families

Table 2.3: Income per Capita and Poverty Rates in Urban Areas by Age, Gender, and Household Structure Using Equivalence Scales

Elderly in household	Chile Unadjusted	Chile OECD Scale	Argentina Unadjusted	Argentina OECD Scale	Mexico OECD Scale
A. Monthly income per capita by number of elderly in household (2002 US$)[a]					
0	167	270	64	95	n.a.
1	197	278	66	87	n.a.
2	214	313	60	112	n.a.
B. Poverty rates among households by number of elderly in household (%)[b]					
0	28.9	10.1	24.3	8.0	27.2
1	17.2	6.1	14.1	5.8	36.9
2	13.5	3.5	17.3	6.7	42.4
C. Poverty rates among individuals by age and gender (%)					
0–17 M + F	40.1	13.4	45.3	14.3	40.0
18–59 M	24.6	7.5	25.5	7.9	29.4(M + F)
18–59 F	26.6	8.5	24.5	7.8	
60+ M	14.4	3.8	16.4	6.1	40.2
60+ F	15.6	5.5	14.7	6.0	39.0
70+ M	13.1	3.2	14.2	6.6	44.0
70+ F	15.4	6.1	14.2	6.6	42.8
D. Poverty rates for elderly individuals by living arrangement and gender (%)					
Males					n.a.
Uniperson	6.6	6.6	7.1	7.1	
Nuclear	8.7	2.6	14.8	5.4	
Extended	22.2	4.8	25.4	7.8	
Females					n.a.
Uniperson	7.7	7.7	5.6	5.6	
Nuclear	4.9	2.5	14.4	5.3	
Extended	22.4	7.0	21.3	7.1	

Sources: Edwards (2000, 2001a, 2001b, tables 5, 6, 7, 8, 10); Parker and Wong (2001, tables 8.3, 8.4).

Note: M = male; F = female.

[a] 1 elderly in household refers to uniperson or extended family household; 2 elderly usually refers to a nuclear family of elderly. For Mexico this category includes a small number of households with more than two elderly.

[b] Poverty lines are used here to compare the relative positions of different groups within a given country. They should not be compared across countries because they were taken from different sources that used different definitions. Chile poverty line and numbers are from World Bank (1997). Argentina poverty line and numbers are from Lee (2000). Poverty level in Mexico is defined as per capita income below the 30th percentile using the OECD equivalence scales.

(with low-income children) or living alone (because they have no children); it is very gender specific rather than being widespread among the elderly (table 2.3, panel D).

In contrast, in Mexico, families with young members tend to have less poverty than those with older members. Above, we predicted this intergenerational pattern would cause the gender gap to disappear among the elderly, as older women benefit from the higher incomes of their children. And again, this is exactly what we find. In fact, poverty rates are slightly higher for elderly men than women. Argentina falls between the two opposite cases of Chile and Mexico. However, in Argentina, as in Chile, poverty among the elderly is highest for the very old, who are mostly women, and lowest in nuclear families, where most men reside (table 2.3, panels C and D).

Do Elderly Members Raise or Lower Living Standards in Extended Families?

As we saw above, many old people bring some income of their own into the household. For Chile, we compared elderly people's own income with household income to see if they represent a net benefit or a net cost to the household. To accomplish this comparison, we calculated unadjusted per capita family income with and without the addition of the older member(s). In Chile, where income is relatively high among the elderly, older men increase family per capita income in 85 percent of the cases, while older women increase it in only 44 percent of the cases. Moreover, the typical increase by women is much lower (and the typical decrease much larger) than for men. On average, adding an elderly man to a household without one raises its per capita income by 23 percent, while adding an elderly woman decreases it by 5 percent (table 2.4).

This outcome, of course, is a function of the larger personal incomes of men, and it may give men greater bargaining power to secure a larger share of total household resources. If men have saved some of their past income and plan to leave it in bequests to heirs of their choice, this too increases their bargaining power. At the same time, women make larger direct contributions to nonmonetary household income, which do not show up in these data. As women grow very old their ability to contribute current nonmonetary services decreases, and such services cannot easily be saved for later delivery or bequests, as men can do with their monetary income. Therefore, the gender disparity in contributions to household income is expected to increase in very old age, which may decrease the power of very old women to bargain for their share of family resources.

Table 2.4: Older Members' Effect on Living Standards of Their Extended Family Households in Chile[a]

	Households in Each Category (%)	Average Monthly Change[b]
Male elderly		
Increase	85	$58
Decrease	15	–$25
Female elderly		
Increase	44	$34
Decrease	56	–$45

Source: Edwards (2000, 2001a, 2001b, table 13). Based on unadjusted household per capita income.

[a] Original data are based on CASEN 1994. The values are reported here in 2002 US$.

[b] These changes should be compared to typical per capita monthly household incomes of about US$200 in Chile in 1994.

Summary

1. Older men have higher personal incomes (wages and pensions) than older women. Men are likely to live in nuclear families, where this income is shared between husband and wife.

2. Older women are likely to become widows, and widows are likely to live in extended families in Latin America, so their standard of living is determined by the income of the family with which they live. If the income of young families is relatively high (as in Mexico), this narrows average measurable gender differentials in living standards among the elderly, while if young families are relatively poor (as in Chile), gender differentials persist. However, measurable differentials may differ from actual differentials that depend on the bargaining power of various household members, and the bargaining power of very old women may be relatively low.

3. Although survival effects push in opposite directions from personal income effects (because wealthy people are likely to live longer than poor people), poverty among the elderly tends to be highest among the very old, who are mostly women, and lowest in nuclear familes, where most men reside.

Women in old age live with and are protected by their extended families, far more than men. This may be considered a consequence of the informal family contract—traditionally, women have worked in the home providing nonmarket services, while their husband and subsequently their children provide monetary support for them. So long as this system works, it keeps older women who have not worked in the market out of poverty and with reasonable living standards compared with others in society.

But the family system, of course, does not always work, which raises a number of questions for pension policy that we shall return to in the following chapters: If the public pillar is targeted to the poor, as in means-tested programs, should it take individual or family income into account in allocating subsidies? If the former, it may spend large amounts redistributing to women, whose standard of living is actually quite high ex ante because of family support. If the latter, it may discourage families from supporting their older members. The informal family contract is difficult for older women to enforce on their own. Should public policies be designed to enforce and formalize it by requiring family support for older women? Such arrangements may be criticized as creating a relationship of dependency—but dependency will disappear only when women's labor market roles converge with those of men so that women become financially independent. In the meantime, what happens to those who do not have welcoming families—who are single, divorced, widowed, with no children, or with poor children? And what will happen if the family system breaks down before the labor market and social norms have equalized personal incomes for men and women? How can social security policies plan for and alleviate these potential issues?

CHAPTER THREE

How Do We Measure the Impact of Social Security Systems and Reforms?

To investigate more precisely the impact of pension design and reform on men and women, we carried out detailed simulations of the old and new systems in three Latin American countries: Chile, Argentina, and Mexico. The old systems in all three countries were pay-as-you-go, defined benefit schemes that paid a benefit to workers based on their years of work and average wage during the last few years. Projected revenues were far less than expenditures in these systems, so they had to be changed. In addition, inequities, negative impacts on the broader economies, and distrust of politically motivated schemes led to a major institutional reform. Chile was the pioneer, and other Latin American countries, as well as countries elsewhere, followed.

The new systems were adopted for pressing economic and political reasons, and their differential impact on women and men was hardly given any thought. The loose connection between benefits and contributions in the old systems favored women in some ways but hurt them in others. Critics claimed that the closer connection in the new systems would disadvantage women because of their lower contribution histories. But this argument overlooks important features of these systems, such as the public benefit and the joint pension requirement. The net impact of the change is ultimately an empirical issue, which we proceed to analyze in this book.

Main Features of the New Multipillar Systems

The new systems are multipillar schemes that feature a mandatory defined contribution plan—individual retirement accounts that are fully funded and privately managed, hence not dependent on government promises. Workers are required to contribute to these accounts and have limited discretion over the choice of investment manager and strategy. Upon retirement, these savings are turned into annuities or other forms of pensions. We expect that individual accounts will produce lower personal pensions for women than for men, because women typically have less continuous employment histories, lower wages, earlier retirement, and longer life expectancy. Of course, in pure defined contribution plans the lower pension is directly attributable to lower contributions; in this sense, lower pensions for women may be interpreted as "neutral treatment." However, it also may signal a very low standard of living for older women, which social security was designed to avoid.

Defined contribution plans have an *accumulation stage*, during which the individual is contributing and savings are building up, and a *payout stage*, during which the individual has retired and is drawing down these savings. Mandatory defined contribution plans in Latin America and elsewhere contain elaborate restrictions at the payout stage, which redistribute between the genders. For example, in our sample countries, most withdrawals must take the form of annuities or gradual payments, and husbands are required to purchase pensions that spread their payouts over their wife's lifetime as well as their own. We hypothesize that the common requirement of survivors' benefits and joint annuities will generate an important intrafamily redistribution toward women, including women who have not worked in the formal labor market. In the United States, unisex tables are required to be used by insurance companies offering employment-related annuities so that women are not penalized for their greater longevity. They are not required in Latin America. To what degree do these payout restrictions equalize pension amounts of men and women? Do joint annuities and unisex tables have similar effects?

In part to mitigate the uneven pension size stemming from the defined contribution plan, even after these payout restrictions, all multipillar systems contain a publicly managed defined benefit plan, usually financed by general revenues. These take the form of a minimum pension guarantee (MPG) in Chile, a "social quota" plus an MPG in Mexico, and a flat benefit in Argentina. The public benefits have several functions: The most limited function is to avoid poverty by raising pensions for the lowest income group; Chile's MPG does little beyond that. But Mexico's social quota and Argentina's flat benefit reach many more workers; hence they equalize more broadly between genders and across income groups, besides avoiding poverty. Additionally, by diversifying retirement income sources, they also reduce risk. We hypothesize that public benefits that redistribute to lower income groups will generate transfer payments that favor women.

Detailed arrangements in the public pillar, such as degree of targeting to low earners, eligibility rules, retirement age, and indexation provisions, dictate which women benefit and how much. We chose these three countries in part because their public benefit schemes vary greatly according to their distributional effects, incentives, and costs. This variation allows us to address two important policy questions: who should be subsidized by the public pillar, and which behaviors should it encourage?

We pay particular attention to the impact of the public and private pillars on work incentives, because it affects the broader economy as well as women's ability to achieve financial parity. In general, both pillars in the new systems contain more positive work incentives than the old systems, especially for women.[1] The fact that contributions made early in life earn many years of compound interest creates a positive reward to women who work when young, before having children. Later on in life, workers who postpone retirement are rewarded with much larger monthly pensions because their accumulations grow and their payouts have to cover fewer years; this particularly benefits full-career women. Married women can keep their own pension in addition to the widow's pension, so they are not penalized for working in the formal market as they were in the old systems, where they often had to choose between the two benefits. In some cases payroll taxes were reduced, thereby increasing net wages. But moving in the opposite direction, the new systems continue the earlier normal retirement age for women than for men, and workers (most often women) who reach the eligibility point for the public benefit in Chile and Argentina face a disincentive for marginal work. In general, given the greater variability in their behavior, women may be more sensitive to these incentives than men, and systems that allow them to receive the full market compensation for their work are likely to achieve greater gender equality in earnings and pensions.

Methodology

Methodological Problems

Analysis of how women fare relative to men in the new and old social security systems is difficult for a number of reasons. First, the new systems have not been in effect long enough to be mature. That is, current retirees in Chile and Argentina are subject to a mixture of old and new system benefits, and we do not know how someone will fare in the future who is fully covered under the new system. In Mexico almost everyone has retired under old-system rules, given the short period for building up individual accounts and the option current workers have to revert to the old system upon retirement.

Moreover, in all three cases we do not know what the rate of wage growth and rate of return on investments will be in the future, and these factors determine how rapidly retirement funds will accumulate in the new system. Along similar lines, longitudinal data from the past are not available. Thus, we could not use actual employment histories of current retirees and workers to estimate their new-system benefits. Finally, we do not know what the old-system benefits would have been in the future because they were financially unbalanced and had to change.

Construction of Synthetic Men and Women: Education and Marital Status

We solved some of these problems by constructing synthetic men and women using cross-sectional data on current behavior of people at different ages, education levels, and marital status to proxy the lifetime employment, wage, and contribution histories of "typical" persons in each category. We then simulated how the average man and woman in each category, if entering the labor force today, would eventually fare under the rules of the old and new systems.[2] While we focus on the average person in each category, we also make some attempt to estimate the dispersion within each cell. Five education levels are presented, ranging from incomplete primary education to several years of postsecondary education. The modal group has full secondary education in Chile, incomplete secondary education in Argentina, and primary education in Mexico (table 3.1). With the exception of young women in Chile, fewer than one-quarter of our sample had any postsecondary education. We use education as a proxy for permanent income.

Our representative men and women are assumed to be single until the median age of marriage in each country, and married thereafter. They marry within their education class, and the average husband is three years older than the average wife. We also make some attempt to show the wage and work profiles for single women, but this is difficult because of the small sample size of single women and our inability to distinguish between those who are never married versus those who are widowed or divorced. Our simulation procedure is discussed further in appendix 1.

Age Effects versus Cohort Effects: The Impact of Rising Education for Women

This methodology assumes that age-specific labor force participation and wage rates will remain constant through time for each schooling level (except for secular wage growth, which we impute). We treat behavioral differences across age groups as *age effects* (behavior due to age and differences

Table 3.1: Distribution of Sample by Schooling at Selected Ages[a]

Chile—Urban Areas

Age	Incomplete Primary	Incomplete Secondary	Secondary	4 Years Postsecondary	5+ Years Postsecondary
Males					
31–35	12.85	28.04	31.94	14.76	12.41
46–50	34.64	16.23	23.43	13.63	12.07
61–65	56.92	12.76	17.86	4.39	8.07
Total	26.33	24.53	26.45	14.07	8.62
Females					
31–35	9.01	22.21	33.21	23.13	12.43
46–50	35.45	16.33	20.1	17.67	10.45
61–65	64.76	8.49	13.69	7.68	5.38
Total	24.58	19.09	26.61	20.88	8.84

Argentina—Full Labor Force

Age	Incomplete Primary	Incomplete Secondary	Secondary	Some Postsecondary	University Degree
Males					
31–35	7.18	49.70	19.78	14.65	8.7
46–50	15.1	51.60	14.24	10.01	9.05
61–65	24.28	52.01	12.40	5.27	6.04
Total	11.65	52.95	17.00	12.37	6.03
Females					
31–35	5.93	36.21	19.04	28.48	10.34
46–50	13.88	42.80	17.51	15.07	10.74
61–65	34.04	46.78	8.30	8.78	2.11
Total	9.88	40.65	18.61	23.58	7.29

Mexico—More-Urban Areas

Age	0–5 Years	6–8 Years	9 Years	10–12 Years	13+ Years
Males					
31–35	8.49	21.85	20.23	23.33	26.10
46–50	20.66	29.55	11.61	13.43	24.75
61–65	43.48	32.97	5.71	6.70	11.14
Total	13.75	25.68	18.78	19.69	22.09
Females					
31–35	9.60	20.22	12.61	28.79	28.78
46–50	22.45	32.24	8.42	23.35	13.54
61–65	57.50	17.86	3.13[b]	7.31[b]	14.20[b]
Total	14.35	22.47	13.79	28.42	20.97

[a] As percentage of the total in each age/gender group.

[b] Estimated on cell sample size < 30.

across age groups remain constant through time) rather than *cohort effects* (behavior due to birth year; differences across age groups will change through time as each cohort ages). However, in reality cohort effects are undoubtedly involved, and failing to take them into account may have led us to underestimate future work proclivities and pensions of women. We seek to understand the degree and source of possible cohort effects.

One reason to believe that cohort effects are involved is that aggregate female labor force participation (averaged over all schooling groups) has been rising—by 15 to 30 percentage points, implying increases of 35 to 90 percent relative to the initial rates—over the past thirty years in the three countries studied. Men's behavior, however, has not changed much over this period. We also observe that participation rates are much higher for young and middle-age women than older women. We analyze two possible causes for these changes and differences: (1) rising female education—in the course of economic development, women's educational levels rise toward equality with those of men, and women's work propensities are strongly correlated with education—and (2) changing social norms and declining fertility rates among younger women, both of which make it more acceptable to work.

If the changing behavior is due primarily to increased education, age-specific behavior will remain constant within each schooling group. Our results will continue to be valid for younger cohorts within each schooling category, even though the aggregate will change as more women shift into higher educational levels. In contrast, if the changing behavior is due primarily to new social norms, age-specific behavior will change and our results will underestimate future labor force participation even within each schooling group. Therefore it is important for us to investigate which of these is the dominant force.

To make this determination, we decomposed the total change in aggregate female labor force participation over the past thirty years and found that one-third to one-half of this change was due to increased education of women, the remainder to changing work proclivities within a given educational category—new norms of behavior. The new norms will probably lead today's young women to stay in the labor force as they age and to end up contributing more than we have projected. Therefore the gender gap in pensions will probably be smaller than we have estimated, even when we hold education constant. However, the disparity within each schooling category will not be as great as that suggested by the aggregate data. In the aggregate, women's contributions will increase more because of the shift toward higher schooling categories, which has been much greater for women than for men. Worker and pensioner groups will increasingly be populated by women with secondary school and higher education, equalizing the behavior and pensions of men and women overall. Our decomposition of behavioral change into parts due to rising education versus changing social norms is discussed in greater detail in appendix 2.

Moreover, work incentives in the new pension systems may alter work habits endogenously in the future. The new pension systems tend to reward work more than the old systems. For example, the fact that married women do not have to give up their own annuity to get the widow's benefit increases the old age income of working women and may lead them to stay in the labor market. For all these reasons, our calculations based on status quo behavior probably overstate the future gender gap in pensions.

Representative Women: Average, Ten-Year, and Full-Career Women

While we do not take these potential changes in age-specific female labor force participation rates into account directly in our simulations, we do so indirectly by our choice of representative women. In addition to the "average" woman in each education group, we also calculate pensions for "ten year" women, who work full time from age twenty-one to thirty prior to childbearing and then withdraw from the labor market, and "full career" women, who have the same labor force participation and retirement age as men. Average women in older cohorts, who are retiring today, probably look like ten-year women with primary or incomplete secondary education, while average women in younger cohorts will probably look more like full-career women with some higher education.[3] Similarly, the working time of single women, especially those who never married, is much closer to that of men and may be approximated by our full-career women (table 3.2).[4]

Thus, altogether, we model five categories of men (by education grouping) and fifteen categories of women—five education groups and three levels of labor force attachment—and we also make some distinctions between single and married people for each gender. Additionally, at various points we analyze differences among individuals who retire early and late, and individuals with regular and irregular contributory histories—variables that turn out to play an important role in the new systems.

Data

In constructing our synthetic men and women, we used national data sets for urban areas (see appendix 1). The "average person" in these countries is quite different from the "average person in the social security system," and

Table 3.2: Lifetime Years of Work of Single and Married Women Relative to Representative Women[a]

Chile

Education Groups	Incomplete Primary	Incomplete Secondary	Complete Secondary	Up to 4 Years Postsecondary	5+ Years Postsecondary
Married women	0.77	0.78	0.94	0.98	0.95
Single women	1.73	1.68	1.54	1.33	1.13
Average men	1.54	1.57	1.43	1.18	1.08

Argentina

Education Groups	Incomplete Primary	Incomplete Secondary	Complete Secondary	Some Postsecondary	Univesity Degree
Married women	0.98	0.97	0.84	1.02	0.94
Single women	1.28	1.64	1.44	1.18	1.06
Average men	2.17	2.09	1.70	1.33	1.19

Mexico

Education Groups	0–5	6–8	9	10–12	13+
Married women	0.78	0.78	0.83	0.94	1.01
Single women	1.87	1.99	1.89	1.73	1.28
Average men	3.30	2.96	2.59	2.18	1.56

Source: Calculations by authors based on CASEN 1994 (Universidad de Chile–Santiago 1994) for Chile, ENGH 1996–1997 (Ministerio del Trabajo y Prevision Social 2002) for Argentina, and Mexican Census (2000) Sample, IPUMS for Mexico.

[a] Estimated lifetime years of work must be viewed with caution since these tables are based on cross-sectional data, not longitudinal data. Representative woman and average man are defined as single until median age of marriage, then married thereafter. Single woman is never-married woman in Mexico and never married, widows, separated, and annulled in Chile and Argentina. In the latter two countries the never-married group cannot be separated from the others.

we are primarily interested in the latter. We focus on urban workers because social security coverage in rural areas is very limited; men and women in these areas are still heavily dependent on the extended family system. (*Urban* is only a rough proxy for *coverage*, as some social security affiliates live in rural areas while some urban residents are not covered by social security). In Chile our data cover only those affiliated to social security, which means they were in the system at some point in their life. In Argentina and Mexico, all urban workers are included in our sample. This difference in sample helps explain why the labor force participation rates of women appear to be higher in Chile. Also in Chile the wage and work data primarily cover full-time workers, while in Argentina and Mexico they cover full-time and part-time workers. Part-time workers are predominantly women, are low paid, and often do not contribute to social security. These factors suggest that our data may understate wages and work of women who were covered by social security and therefore overstate the pension gender differential in Argentina and Mexico. At the same time, they remind us that many workers are not in the system at all, and these are probably disproportionately women.

Contributing Time versus Working Time: Density of Contributions

Our cross-sectional data give us working years, but this measure may be quite different from contributory years. In many low- and middle-income countries the density of contributions—the proportion of potential working time that affiliates contribute—is quite low because many affiliates spend considerable time unemployed, self-employed, or in the informal sector, where contributions are not required or where governments cannot enforce the requirement. In Chile, affiliates contribute about 80 to 90 percent of the time that they work, and the proportion seems to be even lower in Argentina and Mexico (Arenas de Mesa, Behrman, and Bravo 2004; Arenas de Mesa et al. 2007; Berstein and Tokman 2005; Bertranou and Sanchez 2003; Sinha and Yanez 2007). In addition to calculating pensions for men who generally contribute when they work, we also show results for "low density" men who contribute only 60 percent of the time that they work. Our ten-year women approximate women with average work propensities but low contribution densities.

While the available data are incomplete, they indicate that gender differences in density of contributions are not large once working time is controlled. Thus density of contributions while working does not have a large impact on the relative size of pensions for men and women from the defined contribution plan. It does, however, influence the absolute size of the pension and eligibility for the public benefit for both genders. The combination of low work years and low density of contributions while working makes many women ineligible for the full public benefit.

Assumptions for Simulations

In chapters 4, 5, and 6 we use these employment histories to simulate the accumulations, private pensions, and public benefits that different groups of men and women can expect under the new systems. Accumulations and pensions in defined contribution plans are very sensitive to rates of return on investments and rates of wage growth. In our baseline simulations, we assume a *moderate growth* scenario in which economywide real wage growth is 2 percent per year and the real net rate of return is 5 percent prior to retirement. The return during the payout stage is assumed to be 3.5 percent, given the likelihood that many will choose a low-risk or fixed rate annuity, which pays a lower return (James and Song 2001; James and Vittas 2001; James, Martinez, and Iglesias 2006). (In reality, average annual real rates of return exceeded 9 percent in the early years in all three countries, although this is not expected to continue in the long run). Sensitivity analyses assuming a 3 percent real rate of return during the accumulation stage, a 1.5 percent real rate of return during the payout stage, and a 0 rate of wage growth were also carried out. The gender implications of this "slow growth" case were very similar to the baseline, except that the relative role of the public benefit increases dramatically.

Some evidence from the United States and other countries indicates that women may choose less risky portfolios with lower expected rates of return than men, in which case their accumulations and pensions would end up lower. However, in Latin America regulations and limited financial markets have meant that workers had little portfolio choice during the first twenty years of the new systems. They could choose an asset manager, but all managers offered very similar portfolios. Thus, little opportunity has been available for gender differences in portfolio risk and return. This may change in the future, as Chile in 2002 started allowing differentiated portfolios and other countries will probably follow. Portfolio choice is likely to be an issue in the United States. Here we simply note that even in the United States this observed gender differential is reduced once earnings differentials are controlled and may disappear once women acquire more financial experience. Moreover, the differential return would be much smaller if measured in risk-adjusted terms. That is, women may get lower expected returns, but for the same reason they face lower financial market risk and may fare better than men if rates of return drop unexpectedly. We return to the policy implications of this issue in chapter 8, but in our computations we abstract from gender differences in response to financial market risk in the new systems and political risk in the old systems.[5]

Administrative fees could reduce these returns. In the case of Chile, these fees are paid for out of an additional contribution, set by each pension fund, beyond the mandatory amount that goes into the account. Thus these fees do not enter into our simulations of accumulations from the mandatory contributions. In Mexico and Argentina the fees are subtracted from the mandatory contribution, which leaves less for the accounts in our simulations. In absolute amounts, fees per account have been increasing slowly over time, but relative to wages and assets they have been falling and likely will continue to do so due to scale economies and competition. In our simulations, we use the fees that were in effect in the late 1990s, which overestimates future fees and underestimates the eventual accumulations and pensions of young workers today. However, because administrative fees affect both men and women proportionately, this underestimate should have little impact on gender ratios, upon which we focus.

Although both gradual withdrawals and annuities are permitted at the payout stage, to impute a stable annual flow for purposes of this analysis we assume that these accumulations are fully annuitized upon retirement. For transforming the accumulations into annuities, we apply actuarial factors based on a 3.5 percent real interest rate and the World Bank mortality tables for the cohort retiring in 2040 for each country (see appendix 1). These tables build in projected improvements in life expectancy, so they yield a smaller annuity than today's mortality tables would. This approach affects the annuity size but not the gender ratios, so long as projected improvements are proportional for both sexes. Life expectancies for annuity calculations are differentiated by gender, except in the sections and tables that deal with the unisex issue. We know that, in general, mortality rates are highly correlated with income and education, but we have no data that allow us to make this differentiation in our three countries. Thus our results probably understate the ratio of lifetime annuities between high and low earners and overstate the redistributive impact of the public benefits. Men and women are assumed to annuitize at the normal retirement age that is specified in each country—lower for women than for men in Chile and Argentina—but we also explore the impact of early retirement, which is common. We pay particular attention to the influence of type of annuity, especially the joint annuity, which is required for married men.

To a limited extent we compare the results of these simulations with data based on actual experience of the new system. We can do this particularly for Chile, the only county whose new system is old enough (twenty-six years as of 2007) to have a substantial body of pensioners.

The Many Dimensions of Gender Equality and Inequality

Female/Male Ratios in New Systems

We use several alternative gender indicators in this analysis, as each tells us something different about the relative position of men and women. For all the reasons we have just given, we expect *monthly personal annuities* of women from the defined contribution plans in the new systems to be much lower than those of men. This measure tells us how much income in old age men and women have from their own retirement savings. The differential will be somewhat smaller, but still quite substantial, when we add the public benefit, telling us how much monthly income men and women have from a *combination of the public and private pillars.*

We expect the male/female differential to become much smaller and possibly to disappear when we discuss the *replacement rate,* the monthly pension/monthly reference wage, which tells how much of the worker's wage is replaced by the pension and the degree to which men and women will be able to maintain their previous standard of living after retirement. In discussions of replacement rate, the reference wage in the denominator is sometimes final-year salary and sometimes average annual earnings over some longer period, such as the last five years or the worker's entire lifetime. We present two different estimates of replacement rates, based on two different concepts of the reference wage: (1) the average monthly full-time wage during ages fifty-one to fifty-five (after age fifty-five our data are biased by the selection of workers into early retirement) and (2) the average amount earned during ages fifty-one to fifty-five, which equals the monthly full-time wage multiplied by the proportion of time the average individual actually worked during that same age interval. We would expect men to have a higher monthly pension relative to monthly full-time salary than women, as men have worked and contributed much longer to build their pensions. But the monthly pension relative to average amount earned may be very similar for men and women because the most important source of the differential, time worked, has been controlled, reducing the denominator of this ratio for women.

While we start by comparing monthly benefits, for the analysis of transfers and systemic change we shift to a comparison of *lifetime benefits,* as retirement age and age of death vary by gender, by country, and as a result of the reform, and benefits from the joint annuity start flowing to widows late in old age. We convert expected monthly flows into *expected present value (EVP) at age sixty-five* using the same discount rate as was assumed for annuity calculations—3.5 percent. We expect the gender gap in expected lifetime present values to become much smaller than the gap in monthly pensions, because women live longer than men, often they are permitted to retire earlier than men, and hence they collect benefits for more years. The lifetime pension captures these extra years. Additionally, this measure includes widows' benefits and joint annuities, which provide a major boost for married women and often equalize lifetime incomes for men and women.

The defined contribution plan is, by definition, nonredistributive (aside from the transfer from husband to wife through the joint pension), because the lifetime pension equals lifetime contributions plus investment earnings, on average. In contrast, redistributions almost inevitably occur though the public defined benefit plan. We investigate who gets positive transfers and who pays. However, often we do not know the future cost of the public benefit and how this cost is allocated, as it is financed, in whole or part, out of general revenues. Our method for imputing the tax cost of each subgroup, described in detail in appendix 3, is based on the simplifying assumptions that each cohort covers its own bill and, within each cohort, the tax burden is distributed proportionally to lifetime earnings.

We use *three pension redistribution indicators*: net public benefits (lifetime public benefits minus imputed lifetime taxes paid), money's worth ratios for the public benefit (lifetime public benefits divided by imputed tax cost) and money's worth ratios for the public plus private benefit (lifetime public plus private benefits divided by imputed lifetime taxes plus contributions). In contrast to the monthly and lifetime benefit indicators just discussed, redistributions are likely to favor women—in fact to be positive for women and negative for men—due to the targeted public benefit and the joint pension that is often required. Thus the imputed money's worth ratio will be greater for women than that for men.

Finally, we examine *which subgroups of women benefit the most* from these redistributions and *which behaviors are thereby encouraged*. Individuals with low wage rates are disproportionate net beneficiaries in all three systems. Additionally, the net public benefit goes disproportionately to women who have worked and contributed for only a small part of their adult lives in Argentina, but it is more closely tied to working time, continuously in Mexico and discontinuously in Chile. These redistributions create differential incentives for women to enter and remain in the formal labor market and gain financial independence.

Men and Women in the New versus Old Systems

While most of this book is about the gender impact of the new systems, we also compare the new systems against the old systems. This comparison introduces an additional set of methodological problems. The old systems were financially unbalanced, with future expected revenues lower than future obligations, so they could not have delivered their promised benefits in the long or medium term. Argentina was already defaulting on its payments to pensioners. We cannot compare the new systems with the nonsustainable old systems. What, then, is the counterfactual? What system would have prevailed in the absence of reform? Whose benefits would have been cut or whose taxes increased to make the old system solvent?

We avoid this problem by focusing on relative rather than absolute gains and losses to different gender-education groups. We ask, Which groups gained or lost in relative position due to the reform? Did gender ratios improve or deteriorate? Implicitly, then, the counterfactual is the old system, with benefits squeezed down or taxes increased enough to achieve fiscal balance in a distributionally neutral way. That is, we assume equiproportional benefit cuts or tax increases for each group, which would leave relative positions unchanged. Essentially, we are comparing gender positions in the actual reform with some other potential reform that is solvent and in which each group retains the same relative position that it had in the old system.[6]

Even this comparison is sometimes difficult to define, as the old systems were fragmented: different rules applied to different occupations, and these rules often changed or were unevenly implemented due to political and fiscal pressures. The new systems, too, have been undergoing change. In chapters 4, 5, and 6 we describe the new and old systems that we use for our main analysis, which are generally the initial reformed system compared with the main system that existed just prior to the reform. We also examine new rule changes and behaviors that are likely to have an important gender impact— for example, the tendency of men to retire early in Chile and the eased eligibility requirement for the public benefit in Argentina. It turns out that these adaptations generally tend to equalize pensions between the genders.

In general, the old systems provided a benefit of the following sort:

$$B = a\text{YS and/or Surv}$$

where

B = annual pension benefits
a = incremental benefit per year of work
Y = number of contributory years
S = average salary during last few years of work
Surv = survivor's benefit

This formula typically provided a generous benefit for women who worked for only a short time and then withdrew from the labor market, because a was often very high for the first ten years of work. In all three countries, the first ten to twenty years of contributions seemingly produced

Table 3.3: Basic Demographic and Economic Data

Summary Data	Argentina		Chile		Mexico	
	Men	Women	Men	Women	Men	Women
1. Among Working Age Population (16–65)						
% currently employed	70.8	40.0	75.2	38.0	83.7	44.1
% ever employed	n.a.	n.a.	89.8	70.5	92.6	78.5
% affiliated to social security	75.5		66.6	41.6	31.6	14.6
2. Among Older population (60+)						
% who receive own pension	49.7	48.3	67.6	35.4	30.5	5.4
% who receive other pensions		4.4	25.6	.03	9.4	
% who live in extended families	22.3	36.6	42.8	52.5	35.9	44.6
% who get monetary transfers from extended family	7.7	6.2	n.a.	n.a.	15.0	17.5
3. Life Expectancy						
At age 60 (gender specific)	20.0	24.5	21.2	25.3	19.7	24.1
At age 65 (gender specific)	16.2	20.2	17.3	20.9	15.9	19.7
Unisex at age 65	18.3	18.3	19.2	19.2	17.9	17.9
4. Wages and Pensions						
Average monthly wage (2002 US$)	$661	$445	$335	$245	$401	$285
Minimum wage (as % of average)	30.3	44.9	37.6	51.4	33.1	46.3
Minimum or flat pension (as % of average wage)	30.3	44.9	27	37.2	33.1	46.3
Social assistance pension (%)	n.a.	n.a.	12.8	17.6	n.a.	n.a.
Poverty line (as % of average wage)	23.6	35.1	21.8	29.9	n.a.	n.a.

Note: For section 1, numbers are for urban population in household surveys described in appendix 1. Data are from 1994 (Chile), 1996–1997 (Argentina), and 1997 (Mexico). Male-female breakdowns of affiliation are not available for Argentina. For section 2, data are from surveys described in appendix 1. For Argentina, the breakdown between own and other pensions is not available. For Mexico, data are from Parker and Wong (2001), using household survey data for the country as a whole. Own pensions refer to old age, disability, and severance; other pensions refer to widows' and survivors' benefits. For section 3, data are for the population as a whole, from World Bank mortality tables for the cohort retiring in 2040, used in our simulations. These are cohort tables that incorporate projected mortality improvement factors. Today's life expectancy in period tables based on cross-sectional data would be about 10% less. For section 4, data refer to our sample and sample dates, as described in appendix 1 (minimum wage and flat benefit decline through time as % of average wage due to wage growth). As of 2002, Argentina and Mexico had no social welfare program targeted toward the elderly.

a high benefit rate. Women were more likely than men to work for ten to twenty years and then leave the formal labor market. Married women got a widow's benefit that was 50 percent of their husband's pension in Chile, 75 percent in Argentina, and 90 percent in Mexico—and this benefit was usually larger than their own pension. Implicitly, unisex tables were used. Women could retire five years earlier than men with no actuarial penalty in Chile and Argentina.

In contrast to these provisions that favored women, the old systems based their benefits on wage rates during the last few working years, which favored men. A woman who worked during ages twenty to thirty, before childbearing, would earn no interest on her contributions and would find her pension based on wages that would appear to be very low compared with prevailing wages when she retired at age sixty to sixty-five. In addition, using final-year salary as the reference wage especially favored workers with steep age-earnings profiles, who tended to be highly educated men. For example, a Chilean woman with secondary education who worked from age twenty-one to thirty would have had a pensionable wage base of US$205, while her male counterpart who continued working to ages fifty-five through sixty-five would have had a pensionable wage base of US$375 with 0 economywide wage growth or $750 with 2 percent economywide wage growth. Thus, his base salary would have been two to four times as great as hers.[7] In contrast, under the new system, with her contributions earning a 5 percent real rate of return, they would have quadrupled over this period, greatly narrowing the gender pension gap.

In the old systems benefits were not automatically indexed for inflation. This especially hurt women, who live longer and see their pensions dwindle in real value. In contrast, indexation for inflation is common in the new systems.[8]

Furthermore, in Chile and parts of the Argentine system women had to give up their own pension to get the widow's pension, so women who worked much of their lives in the labor market got little or no incremental benefit. Their contribution was a pure tax—a tax that cut their lifetime income and may have deterred them from working. If they had been allowed to keep both benefits, it would have greatly increased the costs and insolvency of the old systems. Under the new systems, women get both but without imposing a double cost on the common pool.

The reforms eliminated all the biases mentioned above—both those that helped and hurt women. We evaluate whether, on balance, this made women better or worse off. (For details of the old and new systems, see tables 4.1, 5.1, and 6.1 later in the book. For basic demographic and economic information about Chile, Argentina, and Mexico, see table 3.3.)

CHAPTER FOUR

Chile

In 1981, Chile replaced a mature, traditional, government-run, pay-as-you-go defined benefit system with a new multipillar system that included a defined contribution plan along with a public benefit in the form of a minimum pension guarantee (MPG). The old system was insolvent, having promised benefits that increasingly exceeded contributions. Many workers and employers evaded the payroll tax, exacerbating the fiscal problem. The objectives of the reform were to make the system largely funded and therefore fiscally sustainable; to manage the funds privately in order to avoid political manupation; to link benefits more closely with contributions, thereby reducing the tax element and the vulnerability of the system's finances to evasion; and to make the redistributive element explicit and better targeted. The potentially divergent impacts on the two genders was not a big factor in the policy choice, but it is a bigger factor in the present reevaluation. In this chapter we analyze whether women in Chile were helped or hurt by this reform.

The Old and New Systems and Our Data for Comparing Them

The Old System

The old Chilean system had a 26 percent contribution rate and a typical defined benefit formula: the annual pension benefit equaled 50 percent of the reference wage for the first ten years of work and 1 percent per year thereafter, up to a maximum of 70 percent.[1] Workers who contributed for less than ten years got nothing, but those who contributed ten years got a high replacement rate due to the high accrual rate for the first ten years. Most of these short-term workers were women. A minimum benefit applied after twenty years of work. The pensionable salary was the average of the last five years' salary, of which the last three years were indexed up for inflation. Women whose work was done many years earlier, prior to childbearing, had a low reference wage base and a low pension relative to contemporary wages, due both to inflation and real wage growth in the interim. After retirement the initial benefit was not indexed for inflation, although the inflation rate was high. Ad hoc adjustments usually lagged the actual inflationary process. Married women whose husbands were in the system were entitled to a widow's benefit that was 50 percent of their husband's pension—but they had to give up their own pension to receive it. This rule benefited women who did not work in the labor market, but those who did work got no incremental benefit for their contributions. Men could retire at age sixty-five and women at age sixty, but earlier retirement was possible and common.

The New System

Chile's new system is a multipillar system that includes a defined contribution plan (an individual account for each worker) buttressed by a public benefit in the form of a minimum pension guarantee. Mandatory payroll contributions are paid to private investment management companies (*administradoras de fondos de pensiones*, or AFPs), which compete for worker-affiliates, rather than to a public fund. These contributions are 10 percent of payroll for investment plus 2.5 percent for administrative fees and requisite premiums for disability and survivors' insurance.[2] Normal retirement age continues to be sixty-five for men and sixty for women. Upon retirement, workers can draw upon their accumulated savings in the form of gradual withdrawals or an annuity that must be joint for married men. However, workers are allowed to stop contributing and start withdrawing their money whenever they meet the early retirement preconditions. Until recently they could do so as soon as their accounts were large enough to purchase a pension that was 110 percent of the MPG and 50 percent of their average wage. These requirements are now scheduled to rise to 150 percent of the MPG and 70 percent of their own wage. Both these conditions are more easily met by high earners, especially men. All medium- and long-term financial transactions, including annuitization, are price indexed in Chile, and many indexed instruments are traded in the stock and bond markets.

Those who have contributed for at least twenty years are guaranteed a minimum pension. If the pension from the worker's private retirement savings does not reach the MPG level, the government provides a subsidy. For retirees who have annuitized, the government tops up the annuity to the MPG

Table 4.1: Main Features of Old and New Systems in Chile[a]

	Old System	New System
Structure	Pay-as-you-go defined benefit	Private pillar: funded individual accounts Public pillar: MPG
Contribution Rate	26%	12.5% to private pillar;[a] MPG financed from general revenues
Benefits	50% of base salary + 1% for every year > 10 up to maximum of 70% of base salary	Private pillar: annuity or programmed withdrawals from accounts Public pillar: MPG
Base Salary	Average of last 5 years (final 3 years indexed)	n.a.
Pensionable Age	Men = 65; women = 60	For annuity or programmed withdrawals: 65 for men, 60 for women, or earlier if meet conditions; For MPG: 65 for men, 60 for women
Years for Eligibility	10 years	20 years for MPG; no minimum for pension from accounts
Pension if Worked Fewer Years	0	Pension from account
Indexation Provisions	No automatic indexation	Price indexation of annuity; MPG price indexed but has risen faster, roughly on par with wages ad hoc
Minimum Pension	Ad hoc minimum after 10 years, no indexation	MPG (about 27% of average male wage) after 20 years' contributions
Widows	50% of husband's pension *or* own pension	60% of husband's pension (joint annuity) + own pension

[a] Contribution rates given for individual accounts for Chile include roughly 2.5% of payroll for survivors' and disability insurance plus administrative costs. The old system described here is the Servicio Seguro Social (SSS).

level. Retirees who have chosen a gradual withdrawal must withdraw the minimum pension from their account until it is exhausted, at which point the state pays the whole minimum pension thereafter. This public benefit is financed from general revenues. Qualification for the MPG is based purely on the individual's own income and does not take other family income into account. (For a summary of the old and new systems, see table 4.1.)

As of the date of the reform, affiliation with the new system became mandatory for new employees in the formal labor force, and it was voluntary but encouraged for employees already in the labor force.[3] Self-employed workers

Table 4.2: Contribution Factors in Chile

A. Affiliation and Propensity to Contribute among Chilean Workers (by employment status and gender, 1994)

Status	Employment Distribution (%)	Total Employment	Affiliates among Employed (%)	Contributors among Working Affiliates (%)	Contributors among Employed (%)
Males					
Employer	4	107,027	61	86	52
Self-employed	22	603,020	44	61	27
Employee	71	1,968,742	89	95	84
Domestic	.1	3,866	83	87	72
Other	3	82,879	69	88	61
Total	100	2,765,534	78	90	70
Females					
Employer	2	36,757	60	88	52
Self-employed	18	275,358	33	65	21
Employee	59	912,578	89	96	85
Domestic	17	257,710	59	86	51
Other	4	60,573	45	75	34
Total	100	1,542,976	71	91	65

B. Propensity to Contribute

	All, Ages 18 to 60 (%)	Workers (%)	Wage Workers (%)	Unemployed or Not in Labor Force (%)
Men	60	79	89	4
Women	43	82	91	3

Source for panel A: Calculations by the authors based on CASEN 1994 data (Universidad de Chile–Santiago 1994).

Source for panel B: Arenas de Mesa et al. (2007), based on EPS 2002 (Ministerio del Trabajo y Prevision Social 2002).

have the option to affiliate and pay contributions voluntarily, and about 25 percent of them do so (table 4.2, panel A). Among all Chilean workers in our sample, 70 percent of men and 65 percent of women contributed in 1994. This difference is not large. However, half the working-age women were not working in the formal market or contributing, while most working-age men were working.

Chile also offers a noncontributory social assistance program called Pensiones Asistenciales (PASIS), which pays about 50 percent of the MPG and is financed out of general revenues. PASIS is designed to keep out of poverty the elderly who are not eligible for contributory benefits. The number of eligible applicants exceeds the available money, so a long waiting list has developed. In this study we mainly analyze the contributory scheme, but it is important to be aware that many old people are not covered by it or receive only a minuscule benefit and a modest noncontributory scheme exists to help fill this gap. The vast majority of PASIS recipients are women living in rural areas. In chapter 8 we discuss the possible role of noncontributory schemes in providing support for older women.

Data

To investigate the impact of pension reform on men and women, we simulate pension benefits under the old and new systems. As discussed in chapter 3, we use cross-sectional data from household surveys to build a series of synthetic cohorts and project life-cycle contributions of "typical" individuals. Our key data source is the Caracterización Socioeconómica Nacional (CASEN) for 1994, a national household survey carried out by the National Planning Office (Universidad de Chile–Santiago 2004; hereafter referred to as CASEN 1994). This survey collects information on a variety of indicators, including demographic characteristics, labor force participation, earnings, affiliation to social security, and the answer to the question, "Are you currently a contributor to any of the social security systems?" Responses to the questions on affiliation and contributions and data on respondents' relationship to employment status are presented in table 4.2. We use observed work and earnings patterns by age in this survey to project contributions of an "average" twenty-year-old into the future.

The previous chapter discussed some of the pitfalls of this methodology. In particular, young women today are unlikely to behave as their predecessors did, particularly regarding labor force participation. One key factor driving this generational change is that younger cohorts have more schooling, and women with more schooling have more continuous work experience, a characteristic that they are likely to keep as they age. For example, in the Greater Santiago area, among women born between 1926 and 1930, 56 percent had six years or less of schooling, while this proportion had fallen to 8 percent for the cohorts born between 1961 and 1965 (authors' calculations from University of Chile household surveys). Therefore we divided the 1994 urban sample into five schooling categories: incomplete primary, incomplete secondary, complete secondary, up to four years of postsecondary, and five or more years of postsecondary education. We measure work propensities separately for each group. The pattern within each education group will be more stable over time than is the aggregate pattern, which is affected by shifting weights of higher and lower education. Still, changing social norms have been pushing fertility down and market work up within each schooling group, so we are probably underestimating the work proclivities of young women cohorts.

In these calculations, we assume that individuals are single until the median age of marriage in Chile, after which they are married. Comparisons with working patterns for individuals who remained single indicate that they work twice as much as married women at the primary and secondary levels, but married women tend to catch up at the university level (see appendix 2). Chile is still a very traditional society where most women marry. We could not model singles because of small sample sizes in some age-education cells.

To capture the impact on pensions of the heterogeneity among women in labor force participation, we simulate our results for three types of women:

1. Average women, who work at the average rate for females of their age
2. Full-career women, who adopt the labor force patterns of men, including a later retirement age
3. Ten-year women, who work full time from age twenty-one to thirty prior to childbearing and then withdraw permanently from the labor force

Our simulations for ten-year women probably apply to older cohorts who are retiring today. Our simulations for full-career women may apply to younger cohorts today, especially those with more education, and to the small group of single women. We focus on urban workers, because social security coverage in rural areas is very limited, for both men and women. Many women in rural areas receive support from the social assistance pension, PASIS.

Years of Work and Contributions among Affiliates

Affiliation is necessary to contribute and obtain benefits. Once a person affiliates to the system, he or she remains affiliated for life. In 1994, 67 percent of men and 39 percent of women in the working-age population were affiliated with the system, meaning that they were current contributors or had contributed at some point in the past (CASEN 1994). Affiliation is required for formal-sector employees, who comprise about two-thirds of urban workers. Of this group, 89 percent were affiliates, and 95 percent of working affiliates make contributions—evidence of high compliance, equally among both men and women (table 4.2, panel A).

Corroborating evidence is provided by a new retrospective survey of affiliates (Ministerio de Trabajo y Prevision Social 2002; hereafter referred to as EPS 2002). Overall, men and women contributed 60 percent and 43 percent, respectively, of all possible months between ages eighteen and sixty. However, among periods when they were workers, women contributed 82 percent of the time (compared with 79 percent for men) and, among wage workers, 91 percent of the time (compared with 89 percent for men). The difference in overall contributory rates is obviously due to the longer periods when women were out of the formal labor force or self-employed, a status that is not required to contribute[4] (see table 4.2, panel B).

We confine our sample to affiliates of the system. That is, our results apply to those who worked in the formal market and belonged to the social security system. This gives us a better estimate of the pension acquired by individuals who were in the system, but it overstates the work experience of the average individual in the population as a whole, and this overestatement is greater for women, who are less likely to work in the formal market and become affiliates.

Among affiliates, we calculate the average fraction of men and women who are workers in each five-year age cell and use this to estimate the average years of work within that age group. Men typically accumulate about thirty-eight years of contributions between ages sixteen and sixty-five. Women, especially those in the lower schooling categories, tend to have more interruptions, and their normal retirement occurs at age sixty. As a result, an average woman who completes secondary school accumulates only twenty-seven years of contributions, and at the incomplete primary level only twenty-two years of contributions, by the time she is eligible to retire at age sixty (table 4.3). However, a university graduate accumulates thirty-five years, almost as many years as men accumulate.

We also calculate the density of work, which we define here as the number of years worked divided by the potential years of work between age sixteen and normal retirement age. Male affiliates have an average density of 77 percent, while average density for women varies from 50 percent at the primary education level to 77 percent for university graduates. Women affiliates have fewer potential working years (because of their earlier retirement), and they contribute for a smaller proportion of these potential years. In addition, a larger proportion of women never affiliated with the formal system in the past, although that may be changing for younger cohorts. The density of contributions, which takes into account the probability of contributing while working, is about 80 percent of the density of work for affiliates.

Table 4.3: Estimated Years of Work among Affiliates, by Age, Education, and Gender in Chile[a]

Age	Education				
	Incomplete Primary	Incomplete Secondary	Complete Secondary	Up to 4 Years Postsecondary	5+ Years Postsecondary
Males					
16–20	3.37	3.02	1.65	1.28	0.00
21–25	3.65	3.89	4.19	4.07	2.79
26–30	3.63	4.13	4.49	4.32	4.46
31–35	3.84	4.29	4.70	4.70	4.87
36–40	3.97	4.30	4.69	4.62	4.90
41–45	4.40	4.35	4.53	4.47	4.75
46–50	3.89	4.24	4.12	4.23	4.71
51–55	3.74	4.20	3.97	4.01	4.77
56–60	3.03	3.32	3.70	3.83	4.66
61–65	2.46	2.31	2.25	3.34	3.06
Total 16–65[b]	35.98	38.05	38.29	38.97	38.97
Density of Work[c]	72%	76%	77%	78%	78%
Females					
16–20	3.64	2.85	1.39	1.21	0.00
21–25	3.20	3.66	3.92	3.91	3.26
26–30	2.96	3.52	3.33	3.78	4.61
31–35	1.64	1.92	2.94	3.74	4.23
36–40	2.35	2.83	3.37	3.71	4.82
41–45	2.44	2.91	3.37	4.37	4.61
46–50	2.09	2.21	3.38	3.36	4.65
51–55	2.54	2.31	2.47	3.44	4.63
56–60	1.63	1.85	2.38	4.16	3.96
61–65	0.93	0.11	0.25	0.24	1.28
Total 16–65	23.42	24.17	26.80	32.92	36.05
Total 16–60[b]	22.49	24.06	26.55	32.68	34.77
Density of work[c]	50%	53%	59%	73%	77%

Source: Calculations by the authors from data in CASEN (1994).

[a] Based on years of work for a cross-section of adults in urban areas who are affiliated with the social security system. See appendix 1 and text for more details on data and methodology.

[b] Total years of work to normal retirement age (60 for women and 65 for men).

[c] Density of work = total years of work to normal retirement age/total possible years from age sixteen to normal retirement age. We define "low-density worker" as one who contributes only 60% of working time.

Earnings

We estimate monthly wages for each age, sex, and schooling cell based on a sample that includes all full-time workers, whether contributing or not (table 4.4).[5] The resulting age-wage profiles that we build show how full-time wages rise with age for each gender and education level. This increase

Table 4.4: Estimated Average Monthly Wage among Full-Time Workers by Age, Education, and Gender in Chile (urban areas, 1994 data in 2002 US$)[a]

Age	Education				
	Incomplete Primary	Incomplete Secondary	Complete Secondary	Up to 4 Years Postsecondary	5+ Years Postsecondary
Males					
16–20	$103	$129	$152	$159	
21–25	$128	$152	$185	$248	$653
26–30	$141	$176	$225	$324	$747
31–35	$146	$198	$278	$408	$1,005
36–40	$159	$216	$316	$466	$1,093
41–45	$184	$241	$365	$518	$1,127
46–50	$196	$299	$461	$563	$1,341
51–55	$190	$267	$421	$516	$1,242
56–60	$193	$284	$413	$587	$1,132
61–65	$170	$256	$337	$502	$1,071
Females					
16–20	$101	$100	$131	$139	
21–25	$103	$127	$158	$199	$373
26–30	$111	$123	$172	$349	$484
31–35	$110	$138	$190	$272	$542
36–40	$109	$146	$224	$288	$635
41–45	$122	$166	$286	$375	$652
46–50	$127	$174	$281	$436	$443
51–55	$131	$158	$327	$322	$463
56–60	$133	$196	$352	$313	$591
60–65	$122	$131	$244	$328	$761

Source: Calculations by the authors based on data from CASEN (1994).

[a] Wage estimates are for full-time workers in urban areas. Monthly wages would be somewhat lower if part timers were included; however, most affiliates who work, work full time. For more details on data and methodology, see appendix 1 and text.

occurs through the lifetime of the average person, apart from any economy-wide wage growth. The economywide growth that we assume in our simulations raises earnings further for all age groups as time moves on.

Based on these cross-sectional data, it appears that age-earnings profiles in Chile have a concave shape: earnings grow fastest at the earlier stage of careers, grow more slowly after age forty, and often peak for men around age fifty (a bit later for women). The female/male full-time wage ratio for most cells is 60 to 80 percent, falling with age, as women's age-earnings profiles are flatter than men's. The lowest gender ratio is for people with five or more years of postsecondary schooling. Although this group of women works almost as much as men, their wage rates are only half as much; women's returns to higher education are much lower than those for men.

How Women Fare—Accumulations and Pensions from Their Own Accounts

How Much Do Men and Women Accumulate?

We assume that workers in a given schooling and gender category contribute 10 percent of their wages, as required by law. We start with the average wage rate for each five-year age group. For our baseline scenario we add an economywide real wage growth rate of 2 percent per year until retirement age is reached—an increase that is roughly similar to Chile's experience during the last twenty-five years and projections for the future. This growth rate is in addition to the age-earnings wage growth implied by our cross-sectional wage data. The two together add up to an annual growth rate above inflation of approximately 4 percent per year for the average male, as he gains work experience and the economy grows. We further assume the real interest rate is 5 percent during the accumulation stage and 3.5 percent during the annuitization stage. Both of these percentages are far lower than the actual rate of return (10 percent per year above inflation) that accounts have received in the new system, but they are closer to assumptions that are usually made for long-term returns to a mixed investment portfolio of stocks and bonds. We also estimate a slow-growth scenario in which economywide real wage growth is 0 and real interest rates are 3 percent and 1.5 percent for the accumulation stage and the annuitization stage, respectively. The accumulated pension savings for each gender-education group at point of retirement depends on these assumptions, the work histories of the group, and the retirement age. Since all AFPs followed very similar investment strategies, participants had practically no choice over portfolios (at least until the system was modified in 2002), so gender differences did not arise as a result of different rates of return and risk-return trade-offs that may exist between men and women.

Table 4.5 reports simulated fund accumulations for men and the three types of women described above, and figure 4.1 compares gender ratios. We show accumulations for individuals who contribute regularly when they work and also for low-density workers who contribute only 60 percent of the time that they work. The first point to note is that women have substantial funds in their own name—which may be the first time this happened to many of them. An average woman retires at age sixty with a savings account of $11,700 to $87,400, depending on education level (all values given are in 2002 US$) (table 4.5, row 2). Of course, these accumulations are much smaller than those of men as a result of women's lower wage rates and labor

Table 4.5: Gender Differences in Fund Accumulation in Chile: Decomposition of Male/Female Differences[a]

	Education				
	Incomplete Primary	Incomplete Secondary	Secondary	Up to 4 Years Postsecondary	5+ Years Postsecondary
Accumulated funds at retirement (2002 US$000)					
1. Woman retiring at 60 with 10 years' contributions	7.0	8.3	10.8	17.2	27.6
2. Average woman retiring at 60	11.7	16.3	28.8	47.5	87.4
3. Average woman retiring at 65	15.3	20.9	36.9	60.9	114.6
4. Full-career woman retiring at 65	23.6	31.8	51.5	70.8	121.7
5. Man at 65	32.4	46.9	69.9	97.4	224.4
6. Low-density man	19.4	28.1	41.9	58.4	134.6
Fund ratios of women relative to men retiring at 65 (%)					
7. Woman retiring at 60 with 10 years' contributions	22	18	16	18	12
8. Average woman retiring at 60	36	35	41	49	39
9. Average woman retiring at 65	47	45	53	63	51
10. Full-career woman retiring at 65	73	68	74	73	54
11. Full-career woman retiring at 65, male wages	100	100	100	100	100
12. Man at 65	100	100	100	100	100
13. Low-density woman at 60/low-density man at 65	36	35	41	49	39

Source: Calculations by the authors.

Note: This table gives projected fund accumulations at retirement for young workers entering the labor force today. Women with 10 years of contributions are assumed to work for 10 years from ages 21 to 30. Average woman retiring at 65 works as average woman to 60, then keeps money in account until pensioning at 65. Full-career women are assumed to have the same participation rate as men, work to 65, but earn the same wage rate as other women. Normal retirement age for women is age 60. Normal retirement age for men is 65. Accumulations are also given for low-density men who contribute only 60% of their working time.

[a]Based on 1994 data and assumptions of 5% real return, 2% real wage growth.

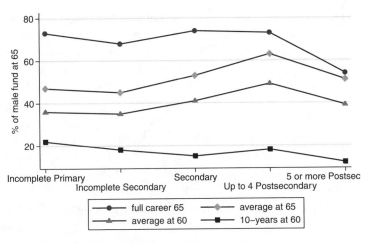

4.1. Female/male ratios of accumulation at retirement, Chile. More work and postponed retirement would increase female/male ratios of accumulations in Chile.

force attachment. Estimated funds for the average woman are 35 to 49 percent of male funds (row 8). If these women postpone retirement to age sixty-five, the additional interest earned would allow their funds to grow by about 30 percent, even if they did not work (row 3 vs. row 2). Full-career women, who have the same labor force attachment as men and retire at sixty-five, accumulate about 70 percent as much as men (rows 4 and 10). The incremental effect of full-career work is most significant among the least educated women, who work the least in the baseline average scenario. The remaining gender gap in fund accumulations is due to the wage rate differential, and it is the largest among the most highly educated women, where the wage differential is greatest.

Of course, women who contribute for just ten years accumulate much less than any other group—only 15 to 20 percent as much as the average man (table 4.5, rows 1 and 7). Low-density men and women also accumulate much less, but gender ratios are unchanged if they both contribute the same proportion of working time.

Expected Pension Benefits

We now proceed to estimate the pensions that men and women derive from these accumulations. Chilean law allows a choice between "programmed withdrawals" and annuities. For programmed withdrawals the retiree continues to invest the money and takes a scheduled amount out each month, according to a formula that is set by the regulator. For annuities, the retiree turns the entire accumulation over to an insurance company that provides investment and longevity insurance in the form of a guaranteed monthly payout. More than two-thirds of all current pensioners have chosen to annuitize. The price for the annuity is determined in the market, but prior analysis has shown that insurance companies return the entire accumulation to annuitants when future payouts are discounted at the risk-free rate of return, which roughly corresponds to our 3.5 percent assumed rate (James and Vittas 2001; James and Song 2001; James, Martinez, and Iglesias 2006; Edwards and James 2006). Insurance companies are permitted to use gender-specific tables with different survival tables for men and women. To simplify the exposition we assume that the entire accumulation is annuitized.

Chilean law requires a married man to purchase a joint pension that covers his wife at a level at least 60 percent as great as his own pension, upon his death. The law does not require or even allow a married woman to provide for her surviving husband, unless he is handicapped. To calculate the payouts a joint pension produces, we assume (based on CASEN 1994 data) that the average man is married to a woman who is three years younger than he is and in the same education category. He retires at the normal retirement age of sixty-five and purchases a joint annuity based on his own and his wife's expected lifetimes. A single man purchases an individual annuity at age sixty-five, as does an average woman at her normal retirement age of sixty.

Our comparisons of pension estimates for married men and women show clearly the lower annuities received by women and the key role played by their earlier retirement age in producing this disparity (table 4.6). Individual annuities for the average female are about one-third of the corresponding joint annuity purchased by males at the normal retirement age (table 4.6, row 8). Despite the dampening effect on men's pensions of the joint annuity, the gender differential in annuities is larger than the accumulation differential because of the earlier retirement age of women—the same accumulation has to last longer.

Once retirement age for women is raised to sixty-five, the monthly pension and gender ratio rise by almost 50 percent (table 4.6, row 9). The increase in monthly pension is greater than the increase in accumulation at sixty-five, because there are five fewer payout years. A recent analysis based on data from EPS (2002) yields a consistent picture (Berstein and Tokman 2005). The estimated gender gap in pensions is shown to exceed the gender gap in earnings, but this result is reversed if women's retirement age is increased to sixty-five. If policy makers want to increase the monetary incomes of older women, raising their normal retirement age to that of men would

Table 4.6: Simulated Monthly Annuities from Individual Accounts in Chile[a]

	Education				
	Incomplete Primary	Incomplete Secondary	Complete Secondary	Up to 4 Years Postsecondary	5+ Years Postsecondary
Average married males, monthly annuity (2002 US$)					
1. Annuity at 65	179	259	386	538	1,240
2. Annuity at 60	120	174	261	356	826
3. Low-density man at 65	107	155	232	323	744
Females, monthly annuity (2002 US$)					
4. Average woman at 60	59	83	146	241	444
5. Average woman at 65	88	121	213	351	661
6. Full-career woman at 65	136	183	297	408	702
7. Ten-year woman at 60	36	42	55	87	140
Female annuity as % of annuity of average married man at 65 (%)					
8. Average woman at 60	33	32	38	45	36
9. Average woman at 65	49	47	55	65	53
10. Full-career woman at 65	76	71	77	76	57
11. Ten-year woman at 60	20	16	14	16	11
12. Average woman at 60/ average man at 60	50	48	56	68	54

Source: Calculations by the authors.

Note: This table gives projected annuity at retirement for young workers entering the labor force today. For notes, see appendix 1 and text. The MPG ($78 monthly) is not included in this table. Married men are assumed to purchase joint annuity with 60% to survivor. Females purchase individual annuities. Gender-specific World Bank mortality tables for the cohort retiring in 2040 are used. Men are assumed to retire at normal age of 65, except for rows 2 and 12. Low-density men and women contribute only 60% of the time that they work.

[a] Based on 1994 data and assumptions of 5% real return in accumulation stage, 3.5% in annuity stage, 2% real wage growth.

seem to be an effective way to accomplish this. Of course, their higher income would come at the price of less retirement leisure than they had before but would still result in more leisure than men have, given their greater longevity.

Ironically, the opposite seems to be happening: instead of women retiring later, men are retiring earlier. The vast majority of men take advantage of the early retirement provisions in Chile and start their pensions before age sixty-five, many even before age sixty. This enables them to stop contributing, and, if they stop working as well, it represents a trade-off between future retirement income and current leisure. A much smaller percentage of women start their pensions early, because they are less likely to meet the early retirement preconditions. Thus, in reality, average pension age for both men and women is now around fifty-nine. This has an equalizing effect on gender ratios—by reducing men's pensions rather than raising women's pensions (see table 4.6, row 12).

Other conclusions that emerge from our pension estimates are as follows:

1. Gender differentials are reduced as schooling rises, but then increase again for the most highly educated women (table 4.6, rows 8 and 9). This is because labor force attachment rises with education but the most educated women face the largest wage differential compared with their male counterparts.
2. The gender gap is reduced considerably for women who adopt the labor force participation patterns of men. But even for full-career women, a pension gap of 25 to 30 percent remains for most groups due to the wage gap, and the pension gap is largest for the women with the most education, where the wage gap is greatest (row 10).
3. Women with less than ten years of accumulated contributions receive a small annuity, as opposed to no benefit at all in the old system (row 11).
4. The differential between workers at the top and those at the bottom of the education spectrum is greater than the differential between men and women. Workers with primary education get only 14 percent as much as those with a university degree (rows 1 and 4). One should not lose sight of the many dimensions of inequality, as this bears on the issue of which subgroups should be targeted as priorities for subsidies.

The Minimum Pension Guarantee

Who Gets It?

Many countries have a minimum pension guarantee, so it is important to understand how it works. Its equalizing role depends crucially on its level, eligibility criteria, and indexation provisions.

Chile's MPG in 1994 was equivalent to $78 (2002 US$) per month, which was about 27 percent of the average male wage, 37 percent of the average female wage, and 125 percent of the poverty line. Older retirees received more—an additional 9 percent at age seventy, and more recently, another 5 percent was added at age seventy-five. Twenty years of contributions are needed for eligibility. The MPG was linked to prices, moving together with the price index; thus it would stay at this real level indefinitely. This amount is far below the estimated personal annuity for all male groups and all but one of the female groups. Only average women in the bottom education group fall below the MPG level, and they receive a top-up that adds about 31 percent to their own annuity (table 4.7, row 6; figure 4.2).[6]

Table 4.7: Simulated Impact of Public Pillar on Gender Ratios of Monthly Pensions, Chile (in 2002 US$)[a]

	Education				
	Incomplete Primary	Incomplete Secondary	Complete Secondary	Up to 4 Years Postsecondary	5+ Years Postsecondary
Married men					
1. Average man, annuity	179	259	386	538	1,240
2. Low-density man, annuity	107	155	232	323	744
3 Low-density man, annuity + MPG if wage indexed	190	190	232	323	744
Women					
4. Average woman, annuity	59	83	146	241	444
5. Annuity + MPG	78	83	146	241	444
6. % increase, MPG	31	0	0	0	0
7. Annuity + MPG if wage indexed	172	172	172	241	444
8. Annuity + MPG at 80 if wage indexed	291	291	291	291	444
9. Full-career woman, annuity, 65	136	183	297	408	702
10. Full-career woman, 65, annuity + MPG if wage indexed	190	190	297	408	702
Average female/male ratios (%)					
11. Personal annuity	33	32	38	45	36
12. Annuity + MPG	44	32	38	45	36
13. Annuity + MPG if wage indexed	96	66	45	45	36
14. Annuity + MPG at 80 if wage indexed	100	100	75	54	36

Source: Calculations by the authors.

Note: MPG was $78 in 1994, in 2002 US$. It will retain same real value when young workers retire if price indexed. If wage indexed, it will be $172 in 40 years, when today's young average woman worker retires. It will be $291 20 years later if wage indexation continues to apply after the individual retires. If MPG is price indexed, it is not received by average or low-density man or full-career woman because their own annuities exceed MPG, or by ten-year woman because she does not meet the 20-year eligibility requirement. Except for full-career woman, we assume worker retires at normal retirement age, retiree annuitizes, and MPG is used to top up annuity, if appropriate. See appendix 1 and text for more details. For comparison, poverty line was $63 in 1994, in 2002 US$.

[a] Based on 1994 data and assumptions of 5% real return in accumulation stage, 3.5% in annuity stage, 2% real wage growth.

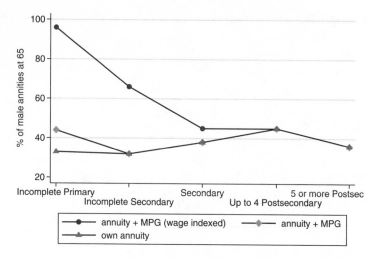

4.2. Female/male ratios of annuities plus MPG, Chile. Price-indexed MPG goes to lowest earners; wage-indexed MPG has much larger and broader impact in Chile.

Thus, the MPG truncates the pension distribution at the bottom end. Considering that the bottom end is mainly composed of women, the female/male ratio of pensions is raised at the primary education level by a modest amount. However, only 25 percent of our sample falls into the bottom education category, and this percentage falls to 9 percent for younger cohorts. The MPG becomes less relevant as more women obtain higher education. In contrast to this situation for average women, ten-year women and low-density women have pensions below the MPG through the secondary level of education. However, they do not meet the twenty-year requirement for eligibility.

Is twenty years a reasonable requirement for eligibility? Should measures be taken to bring noncontributing women and those in the middle education categories toward greater equality with men? Should subsidies depend on individual income or family income? Chile is now grappling with these issues.[7]

Insurance against Partial Careers and Moral Hazard—Disincentive to Marginal Work

The MPG insures low-earning women against the risk of career interruptions, to which they are exposed as a result of family obligations and social norms. However, because work is in part subject to the individual's control, the MPG also induces moral hazard (good behavior may be reduced if insurance offsets its negative consequences); it is a disincentive for them to work more than twenty years. If the average woman with least education postponed her pension until age sixty-five, her own annuity would be $88, only slightly higher than the MPG level. By postponing the pension she is mainly substituting her own contributions for the MPG. Low-earning women thus face a strong incentive to work up to the twenty-year point but a strong disincentive to work beyond that or to postpone retirement. In this way, the MPG may have a negative impact on the marginal labor supply of women and on the likelihood that they will become more independent. We return to this point below.

The MPG over Time: Wage versus Price Indexation

If the MPG is price indexed but real wages rise due to productivity growth, it applies to fewer and fewer people over time. Assuming a 2 percent annual real wage growth, the MPG that is 27 percent of the average wage will become only 13 percent of the average wage forty years from now, when today's young woman retires. The MPG will become practically irrelevant. Price indexation is the main reason it is received by so few pensioners in our simulations.

However, in reality the government has been raising the MPG almost every year on an ad hoc basis, faster than prices rise and roughly on par with wage growth. By 2005 the MPG already exceeded $100 (in 2002 US$). If the MPG were wage indexed (i.e., if it increased at the same rate as wages), it would be $172 when a young woman who entered the labor force today retires. Women would collect some subsidy even if they completed secondary school. The female/male pension ratio would rise substantially for this group (table 4.7, rows 7 and 13; figure 4.2).

Currently, increases in the MPG apply to the entire stock of retirees, not simply to new retirees. If this practice (as well as the upward adjustment at ages seventy and seventy-five) continues, the wage-indexed MPG would reach $291 by the time the woman was 80. Practically all women, as well as the bottom two categories of men, would then receive a large top-up in very old age. This means that men and women at the bottom end would receive exactly the same pension income in very old age (table 4.7, rows 8 and 14). From the viewpoint of reducing the gender gap (as well as the gap between high and low earners), this would obviously be much more effective than a price-indexed MPG.

But it would also cost much more. And it would induce more women to stop contributing to the system once they reached the twenty-year eligibility point. Additionally, some men in the lower education groups might switch to self-employed status and stop contributing after twenty years to receive the MPG. So the greater equality implied by a wage-indexed MPG is accompanied by higher fiscal cost and moral hazard problems. *Swiss indexation,* which is 50 percent price indexation and 50 percent wage indexation, is one possible compromise.

Chilean policy makers seem ambivalent about these trade-offs between equality, fiscal cost, and moral hazard, as evidenced by the fact that they are not required to wage index but have done so through ad hoc political decisions. Protection for future cohorts of very old women and low-income women will depend on the choices they make.

Insurance against Slow Growth

We also modeled a slow-growth scenario in which real wage growth is 0 and the real rate of return on pension savings is 3 percent per year (1.5 percent during the payout stage) (see appendix 4, tables A5 and A6). In this case, lifetime contributions are much lower, and so are the annuities that retirees can purchase with their own accumulations. As a result, the MPG floor protects average women through the secondary education level and even protects some full-career women and men. This scenario holds true even if the MPG is not formally wage indexed; in fact, its value is the same whether wage or price indexation is used when wage growth is 0. In effect, the MPG provides insurance against prolonged low rates of return. If the low-return scenario materializes, women are the major beneficiaries and gender differentials are narrowed substantially. Among women, the gap between those with higher and lower education is narrowed. Of course, in a slow-growth scenario, the government might have a hard time financing the MPG.

Simulation versus Experience: Wage Indexed MPG and Early Retirement

How do our simulated results compare with results from Chile's twenty-six years of experience with its new system? Although current retirees in Chile did not spend their full working lives under the new system, many of them contributed to their retirement accounts for ten to twenty years and retired under the new rules. (They received credit for pre-1981 work in the old system in the form of "recognition bonds," which they applied toward their pensions upon retirement.) How does the actual status of men and women pensioners compare in the new system? Two observations stand out: (1)

based on data from the system regulator, women are much more likely than men to have pensions at the MPG floor, which is consistent with our predictions, and (2) based on our analysis of a new retrospective data set of affiliates (EPS 2002), the average female pension is 80 percent of the average male pension, which is much higher than we would have expected under the initial plans for the system.

On the first point: as mentioned above, pensioners in Chile can retire at the normal age or earlier if they meet specified preconditions. Their pensions can take the form of annuities provided by insurance companies or programmed withdrawals, which follow a formula set by the regulator. Most retirees with small pensions are normal-age retirees who have taken programmed withdrawals rather than annuities; 79 percent of these retirees are either drawing down their own accounts at the MPG level or have already exhausted their accounts and are receiving their pensions from the state. Forty-two percent of all women pensioners, but only 18 percent of all men pensioners, fall into this high-risk group; most of them are already at the pension floor.[8] The female proportion would be even higher if we included widows—beneficiaries of joint pensions or survivors' insurance. Moreover, because women live longer than men and use up their money in the meantime, the female share of pensioners at the floor will increase as they grow very old.

On the second point: for individuals whose pensions exceed the floor, pensions of men and women are quite similar; however, a smaller proportion of women exceed the floor, so the gender ratio of the average overall is 80 percent. The new system has developed in two important ways that explain these outcomes: (1) the MPG has been rising with wages rather than prices (and these higher values apply to the entire stock of retirees, not simply the new flow); and (2) high-earning men have been retiring early, at the same age as women.

As discussed above, a wage-indexed MPG reaches many more retirees than a price-indexed MPG. Also, men who retire early accumulate much less and have smaller pensions than they would if they worked to the normal retirement age. Both of these factors have had a strong equalizing effect on gender ratios. The former equalizes at the bottom end by pulling up low pensions, which are received disproportionately by women, while the latter equalizes at the upper end by keeping the pensions of high-earning men lower than they would be otherwise (see table 4.6, row 12, and table 4.7, rows 13 and 14). As a result, we would expect to find many women at the pension floor while at the same time gender ratios would be much higher than the 32 to 45 percent that we started with in these simulations—and indeed this is the case. Wage linkage of the MPG and relative retirement ages of men and women play key roles in achieving this result.

Low Coverage under a Contribution-Based Safety Net

Recent studies have emphasized a third development, the high proportion of individuals who will have a small pensions because of low contribution densities (Arenas de Mesa, Behrman, and Bravo 2004; Arenas de Mesa et al. 2007; Berstein, Larrain, and Pino 2006). Analysis of EPS (2002) indicates that both genders contribute 90 percent of the time they are wage workers, but they are not wage workers much of the time. Consequently, men contribute only 60 percent of their potential time between ages sixteen and sixty and women in this age range contribute only 43 percent (table 4.2, panel B). Many low-density retirees of both genders—but especially women—will receive low pensions yet fail to meet the twenty-year requirement for the MPG. Some retirees who are now withdrawing money from their own accounts at the pension floor may find themselves without any retirement income when their accounts are depleted. Their families may step in to support them; recall from chapter 2 that this is common. But many will be poor in old age as a result of low contribution densities. This has become a looming social and political problem in Chile and elsewhere in Latin America.

Chile's president, Michelle Bachelet, has set out to address this issue by proposing to replace the MPG and the social assistance pension with a new means-tested public benefit. This benefit would go to all old people in the bottom 60 percent of households, based only on age and residence, with no contributory requirement. It would be gradually phased out as beneficiaries' own pensions grow, at the implicit tax rate of 37.5 percent (the public benefit would be reduced 37.5 cents for every dollar of personal pension until the phaseout is complete). It is much like the Australian means-tested flat benefit, discussed in chapter 7. As low earners, women would be disproportionate recipients. At the same time, to increase the density of contributions, affiliation would become mandatory for the self-employed, and contributions of low-earning young workers would be subsidized.

The new benefit would solve most of the problems discussed above. It would avoid old age poverty for women who have not worked much in the labor market as well as those who worked at low wage rates, and it would eliminate the discontinuous incentives at the twenty-year point that exist today. However, it would introduce new problems of its own. The general revenue needed to finance it would be much larger than the MPG requires, and higher income tax rates might discourage work and saving. The 37.5 percent implicit tax on personal pensions coupled with the prospect of a "free" public benefit might, ironically, drive women further away from formal-sector work and contributions. Mandatory affiliation for the self-employed would be difficult to enforce. The proposed new benefit would do nothing to reduce the gender gap for middle-income women who work and who would be left with little or no public benefit after the phaseout. No decision has yet been made on the crucial issue of price versus wage indexation. Interestingly, raising the retirement age for women—the most cost-effective way to increase their pensions—was too politically explosive to tackle.

Replacement Rates

Pensions are often evaluated according to the percentage of the wage that they replace—the pension/wage ratio. This ratio tells us the degree to which the worker can maintain his or her standard of living during retirement. Because living costs may fall after retirement (no children or work-related travel and clothing costs) and the individual may have some voluntary saving (e.g., a home with the mortgage fully paid), a replacement rate of 40 to 60 percent of wage is a common goal of mandatory pension systems. Gender ratios of replacement rates tell us whether the relative position of women to men is higher during the working stage or retired stage. If the female/male ratio of replacement rates is less than 100 percent, women's relative pensions are lower than their relative wages, so they will have a harder time than men maintaining their previous standard of living.

But replacement rate calculations can be misleading if not examined carefully. They depend heavily on definition of the reference wage and policies regarding retirement age and indexation. Sometimes final-year salary is used as the reference wage. Replacement rates then indicate the proportion of final wage that is replaced. However, this approach ignores the fact that work in the final year is often part time or inflated. Earlier wages, which determined the individual's long-term standard of living, may have been quite different. Using the longer-term average wage solves these problems but ignores real wage growth in the economy that has occurred in the meantime, raising expected living standards. As our reference wage, we start by using the full-time wage earned over the five-year period during ages fifty-one to fifty-five, which was close to the peak wage period for men and women and includes prior wage growth.

Using this reference wage, replacement rates in Chile for the average male retiring at sixty-five are projected to be around 50 percent, purely on the basis of his own annuity (table 4.8, row 1). (Replacement rates for low-density men or for an average man who retires early would be lower; see row 2.) We would expect the average woman to have a much lower replacement rate because of her shorter years of contributions and longer period of retirement. However, the replacement rate differential should be less than the annuity differential because it essentially normalizes by the wage differences that create part of the annuity gap. Indeed, replacement rates for average women retiring at sixty, based on their own annuities, are about 25 percent of the reference wage for those without postsecondary education—half as much as men. This percentage rises to 40 to 50 percent for those with postsecondary education who work more and therefore have replacement rates similar to those of men (rows 4 and 10).

The replacement rate for women depends heavily on pension policy regarding retirement age and indexation of the MPG. If the retirement age for women were raised to age sixty-five, their annuities and replacement rates would increase by 50 percent because the accumulation would grow for five more years and the annuity would have to cover five fewer years. Although their pensions would still be lower than those of men, replacement rates would now be closer to those of men for less educated women and greater than men for more educated women (table 4.8, rows 5 and 11). This indicates that their lower normal retirement age is a major reason why gender ratios of pensions are lower than gender ratios of wages.

The minimum pension guarantee raises replacement rates for those in the lowest categories, and this effect is much stronger if the MPG is wage linked. In fact, a wage-linked MPG causes women in the bottom two categories to have higher replacement rates than those of men, because the difference in their pensions (including MPG) becomes much smaller than the difference in their wages (rows 6, 7, 12, and 13).

Women's behavior also makes a big difference in replacement rates. Those who work full career have higher replacement rates than men (table 4.8, rows 8 and 14; figure 4.3). This is due mainly to the equalization of their retirement ages and secondarily to the fact that their wages do not grow as steeply as male wages. Male wages at ages fifty-one to fifty-five are roughly double what they earned at twenty-one to twenty-five, while female wages have grown only about 30 percent over this aging period. This reference wage is a formidable target for men to meet, because their contributions were based on much lower wages when they were young. It is an easier

Table 4.8: Simulated Replacement Rates in Chile (pension/reference wage)

	Education				
	Incomplete Primary	Incomplete Secondary	Complete Secondary	Up to 4 Years Postsecondary	5+ Years Postsecondary
Replacement rates for average married males (%)					
1. Annuity	49	50	48	54	52
2. Annuity for low–density man	29	30	29	32	31
3. Annuity/adjusted reference wage	66	60	60	68	54
Replacement rates for females (%)					
4. Annuity	24	27	23	39	50
5. Annuity at 65	35	40	34	57	74
6. Annuity + MPG	31	27	23	39	50
7. Annuity + MPG if wage indexed	68	57	27	39	50
8. Full-career woman at 65	54	60	47	66	79
9. Annuity + MPG/adjusted reference wage	61	58	47	57	54
Female/male replacement rate ratios (%)					
10. Annuity	48	54	49	72	96
11. Annuity if woman retires at 65	71	79	71	105	143
12. Annuity + MPG	63	54	49	72	96
13. Annuity + MPG if wage indexed	139	112	57	72	96
14. Annuity, full-career woman retiring at 65	110	120	99	122	152
15. Annuity + MPG/adjusted reference wage	93	97	78	84	99

Source: Calculations by the authors.

Note: Replacement rates are defined as pension/reference wage. Reference wage is defined as monthly full-time wage rate at ages 51–55. Wage is from table 4.4, indexed up by 2% wage growth to get the wage that a young worker entering the labor force today will receive when he or she is 51–55. Annuity is from table 4.6 and MPG is from table 4.7. For rows 3, 9, and 15, reference wage is adjusted by percentage of time individual worked at ages 51–55 to obtain a measure of actual earnings (monthly wage rate multiplied by % time worked). All replacement rates are given for men and women with average work history from table 4.3, who retire at normal retirement age, except that in rows 5 and 11 woman retires at 65 and in rows 8 and 14 she is a full-career woman.

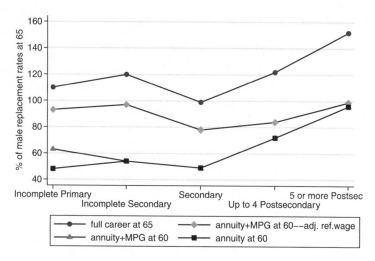

4.3. Female/male ratios of replacement rates, Chile. Replacement rate for women exceeds that of men for full-career women in Chile.

target for women, because their contributions when young were based on wages that were very similar to their peak. Then, if men and women work the same amount and get the same rate of return on their investments, women will receive a higher replacement rate. Does the higher female replacement rate mean that women are better off? It will be easier for them to use their pension to replicate the standard of living they previously supported out of their wages, but only because this standard was much lower for women than for men to begin with.

Finally, we examine the implications of a different definition for reference wage: actual earnings, which is the wage rate adjusted for the percentage of time actually worked. That is, we multiply the full-time wage by percentage of time worked at ages fifty-one to fifty-five. The rationale is that pensions are supposed to replace actual wage income, not some theoretical full-time wage rate that is not really earned. Because men (and women with higher education) work about 80 percent of the time, their replacement rates rise by only a modest amount when we adjust the reference wage for time actually worked (table 4.8, row 3). But the reference wage for women in the lower education categories is cut in half, so their replacement rates nearly double, bringing them to 55 to 60 percent, very close to those of men (rows 9 and 15). They receive a low retirement income, but their working income was also low, because their working time was low. If the purpose of the pension is to replace wage income, this is a reasonable definition of reference wage, and the pension is hitting the right target, for both men and women.

The Impact of Joint Annuities

So far we have worked with joint annuities for men, as married men are required to purchase joint annuities or other joint withdrawals. These annuities reduce the payout to the husband in order to leave a reserve to fund a survivor's pension that is 60 percent of his pension.[9] Single men, by contrast, have no obligation to provide for a widow's pension, so they would receive a higher annuity relative to their married counterparts. How much are married men's benefits decreased and widows' benefits increased by the joint annuity? How would the situation change if insurance companies were required to use unisex mortality tables? Unisex tables apply the average mortality of men plus women to both genders, in contrast to gender-specific tables, which apply different (higher) life expectancies to women.

Joint Annuities

Table 4.9 compares individual and joint annuities for men (retiring at sixty-five) and individual annuities for women (retiring at sixty) under the assumptions of gender-specific and unisex mortality tables. The largest monthly payouts are obtained by single men using male mortality tables to purchase an individual annuity (row 1). As a counterpart, single and married women use their own accumulation to obtain an individual annuity at age sixty using female mortality tables (row 5). This dual set of assumptions produces the largest gender difference in annuities.

If the man is married, he is required to purchase a joint pension that pays 60 percent of his benefit to his widow. Under the assumption that she is three years younger than he, this requirement reduces male payouts by about 17 percent (table 4.9, row 1 vs. row 3).[10] Widows receive the survivor's benefit after their husband dies, and this benefit is much larger than their own pensions, on average. It is also much larger than the MPG, so once a woman gets the widow's benefit she is no longer eligible for the MPG top-up. A joint pension must also be provided if a man is not married to but is cohabiting with a woman who is the mother of his children. Divorce only recently became legal in Chile. It is not clear whether the joint pension requirement will apply to divorced wives as well and, indeed, whether they will have any claims on their former husband's account before he retires, if he should die.

Table 4.9: The Impact of Joint Annuities and Unisex Tables in Chile (in 2002 US$)[a, b]

	Education				
	Incomplete Primary	Incomplete Secondary	Complete Secondary	Up to 4 Years Postsecondary	5+ Years Postsecondary
Males retiring at 65					
1. Individual, gender specific	$217	$314	$467	$651	$1,501
2. Individual, unisex	$200	$290	$431	$601	$1,385
3. Joint, gender specific[c]	$179	$259	$386	$538	$1,240
4. Joint, unisex	$175	$254	$378	$527	$1,215
Females retiring at 60					
5. Individual, gender specific[c]	$59	$83	$146	$241	$444
6. Individual, unisex	$63	$88	$156	$257	$472
7. Survivor's annuity	$107	$156	$232	$323	$744
8. Survivor's + own annuity	$167	$238	$378	$564	$1,188
9. Widow's pensions as % of husband's + wife's pensions[d]	70%	70%	71%	72%	71%

Source: Calculations by the authors.

[a] Based on 1994 data and assumptions of 5% return during accumulation stage, 3.5% during annuity stage, real wage growth = 2%.

[b] The MPG is not included in annuity calculations. Joint annuity assumes 60% to survivor.

[c] Corresponds to own pensions in table 4.6.

[d] Own annuity of wife plus survivor's annuity after husband dies relative to own annuities of husband plus wife while husband was alive.

Unisex versus Gender-Specific Tables

When unisex tables are used, monthly payouts to men from individual annuities decrease by about 8 percent, and those to women increase by 6 percent (table 4.9, row 1 vs. row 2, row 5 vs. row 6). But for joint annuities, payouts remain very similar whether unisex or gender-specific mortality tables are used (table 4.9, row 3 vs. row 4; figure 4.4). The basic reason is that both expected lifetimes are taken into account when determining joint annuity payments. The fewer years imputed to the widow under unisex calculations roughly offset the extra years imputed to the husband. Although the use of gender-specific versus unisex tables is highly controversial, apparently this choice has little impact on monthly payouts to either spouse under a joint annuity. In fact, joint annuities become relatively less expensive for men to buy if unisex tables are mandated (the reduction from row 2 to row 4 is smaller than the reduction from row 1 to row 3). However, the choice

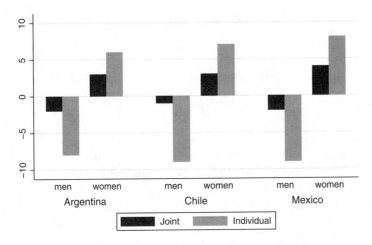

4.4. Impact of shift to unisex tables on men's and women's annuities (% gain or loss relative to gender-specific tables). Loss to men and gain to women from unisex requirement is much less for joint than for individual annuity.

of unisex versus gender-specific tables does make a difference (of 6 to 8 percent) for individual annuities, because those purchased by men cross-subsidize those purchased by women. Thus, the unisex issue becomes salient to single men and to women who purchase individual annuities.

Joint Annuities Avoid Poverty in Very Old Widows

Most important, the joint annuity is a major source of income for very old women, and it comes exactly at the right time of life, when household income would otherwise decline sharply. It protects very old women who have not worked in the labor market and have no income of their own. Even for women who have worked, the household income of a very old woman would fall to barely one-quarter of its previous value upon the death of her husband without the joint annuity. With the joint annuity, household income (from the survivor's pension plus her own pension) remains at about 70 percent of its previous value (table 4.9, row 9). As we saw in chapter 2, according to Organisation for Economic Co-operation and Development scales it will cost the widow in a single-person household 67 percent as much to live as it will cost the couple. Thus, the joint pension, together with her own pension, enables her to maintain her previous standard of living after her husband dies without imposing a cost on the public treasury. (The old systems, which required her to choose between her own pension and the widow's benefit, automatically reduced household income to about 40 percent of its previous value and resulted in the standard of living of widows falling dramatically.)

Lifetime Benefits, Imputed Taxes, and Redistributions

Comparisons of monthly annuities are of interest but ignore the fact that women are allowed to receive their pensions five years younger and typically live longer than men. In addition, the survivor's benefit begins much later in life than a woman's own benefit or MPG. To compare how much payout men and women receive over the course of their lifetimes, it is necessary to add up their full lifetime benefits in expected present value (EPV) terms. This also enables us to determine how these lifetime benefits compare with life-time costs. If benefits exceed lifetime costs, the worker has received a positive redistribution, a higher rate of return on costs than others, and vice versa. The difference between lifetime costs and benefits comes from two sources: the tax cost of financing the MPG and the joint annuity requirement, which imposes an opportunity cost on married men and a gain to their wives.

Gross Benefits

Table 4.10 presents the expected present value of the lifetime benefits from annuities and transfers, as evaluated at age sixty-five (with the 3.5 percent an-nuitization rate also serving as the discount rate). The expected lifetime ben-efit from the individual annuity for single men (row 1) equals the fund accu-mulations given for men in table 4.5. The expected present value of the MPG is 0 for the average man. The reduction in lifetime benefits for married men owing to the joint annuity mandate increases in absolute value with school-ing, but in each case it is 17 percent of the single man's lifetime benefits (row 2). These amounts become transfers to these individuals' spouses; the cost to the husband becomes a benefit to the wife. If the husband would have pro-vided equivalent insurance for his wife voluntarily, he does not really incur an extra cost—the mandatory insurance simply replaces the voluntary. But if the husband would have preferred to consume some of this amount dur-ing his lifetime, the joint annuity requirement becomes a real cost to him. (For empirical evidence on this point, in the context of the United States, see Bernheim et al. 2003.) Men with low density of contributions accumulate pensions that are much smaller than those of men who contribute regularly. Their pensions exceed a price-indexed MPG, but those with low education get a top-up from a wage-indexed MPG (row 4).

Turning to the case of women, we start with lifetime present values of the

Table 4.10: EPV of Gross Lifetime Benefits from Personal Annuities, Joint Annuity, and Public Benefits in Chile (2002 US$000 and %)[a]

	Education				
	Incomplete Primary	Incomplete Secondary	Complete Secondary	Up to 4 Years Postsecondary	5+ Years Postsecondary
	Average man				
1. Individual annuity	$32.4	$46.9	$69.9	$97.4	$224.4
2. Joint annuity	−5.6	−8.2	−12.2	−16.9	−39.0
3. Total—average married man	$26.8	$38.7	$57.7	$80.5	$185.4
4. MPG for low-density man if partly wage indexed	$9.7	$2.5	0	0	0
	Average woman				
5. Own annuity	$13.9	$19.4	$34.3	$56.5	$104.0
6. MPG (price indexed)	3.1	0	0	0	0
7. Joint annuity	6.3	9.1	13.5	18.8	43.3
8. Total (rows 5 + 6 + 7), married woman	$24.0	$28.5	$47.8	$75.3	$147.3
9. MPG, if partly wage indexed	18.5	14.6	4.3	0	0
10. % increase from price-indexed MPG	22	0	0	0	0
11. % increase from wage-indexed MPG	133	75	13	0	0
12. % increase from joint annuity	45	47	39	33	42
	Full-career woman				
13. Own annuity	$23.6	$31.8	$51.5	$70.8	$121.7
14. MPG, if partly wage indexed	$4.1	0	0	0	0
15. Total (row 7 + 13)	29.9	40.9	65.3	89.6	169.0
16. % increase from joint annuity	27	28	26	27	36
	Ten-year woman				
17. Own annuity	$8.3	$9.9	$12.9	$20.5	$32.8
18. Total (row 7 + 17)	14.6	19.0	26.4	39.3	76.1
19. % increase from joint annuity	75	92	105	92	132

(continued)

average woman's individual annuity (table 4.10, row 5). These values are larger than her fund accumulation at age sixty in table 4.5, because we are reporting the EPV as viewed at age sixty-five. Women are more likely than men to receive a positive present value from the MPG. If the MPG is price indexed, it is received only by women with the least schooling (table 4.10,

Table 4.10: *continued*

	Education				
	Incomplete Primary	Incomplete Secondary	Complete Secondary	Up to 4 Years Postsecondary	5+ Years Postsecondary
Married woman/average married man ratios (%)					
20. Average woman	87	73	83	94	79
21. Average, wage-indexed MPG	140	110	90	94	79
22. Full-career woman	112	105	113	111	89
23. Ten-year woman	55	49	46	49	41

Source: Calculations by the authors.

Note: EPV is given as of age 65. 3.5% rate is used to discount or compound all benefits to age 65. EPV of individual annuity for average men and full-career women are same as fund accumulations in table 4.5. EPV of annuities for average and ten-year women are larger than fund accumulations because EPV is given as of age 65 while accumulations in table 4.5 are given as of age 60. Husbands and wives belong to the same education group. Absolute amount of joint annuity benefit is same for average, full-career, and ten-year woman, but it varies as % of personal annuity. MPG varies by labor force attachment. For most rows it is assumed to be price indexed. For rows 4, 9, 14, and 21, it is assumed to be wage indexed up to the point when the individual retires, but price indexed thereafter. In Chile, MPG top-up for married women stops when MPG floor is reached due to joint annuity. Therefore, % increment from MPG for married women is less on lifetime than on monthly basis. Average men, full-career women, and ten-year women get no MPG if price indexed. EPV of loss through joint annuity to men is less than EPV of joint annuity benefit to women because EPV is measured as of age 65, which women reach 3 years later.

[a] Based on 1994 data and assumptions of 5% return during accumulation stage, 3.5% during annuity stage, 4% discount rate, real wage growth = 2%.

rows 6 and 10; figure 4.5). The value of the MPG is much larger and more widespread if it is wage indexed (table 4.10, rows 9 and 11). For the average married woman, the joint annuity increases her total expected lifetime benefits by 40 to 45 percent, even though she likely does not start receiving it until she is in her midseventies (table 4.10, rows 7 and 12; figure 4.6). This increment is much larger that that from the price-indexed MPG.

Full-career women get monthly annuities that are double those of average women, but because their pension begins at age sixty-five, the lifetime benefits of these two groups differ by only 25 to 70 percent (table 4.10, row 13 vs. row 5). Not surprisingly, the survivor's pension has a much smaller effect relative to personal annuity for full-career women than for average women. But it has a much larger effect for ten-year women, roughly doubling their income (rows 17, 18, and 19).

En toto, on a lifetime basis, average married women get 80 to 90 percent as much as average married men, most ten-year women get less than 50 percent, but full-career married women actually get more than comparable married men due to the combination of their own and the joint annuity

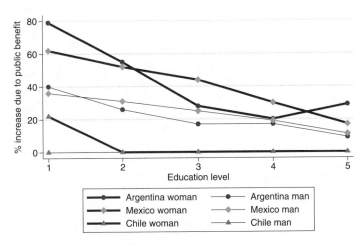

4.5. Increment to EPV from public benefit. Women and low earners get the largest percentage increment to EPV from the public benefit. (See tables 4.10, 5.10, and 6.10 for the definition of education levels 1 to 5 in each country.)

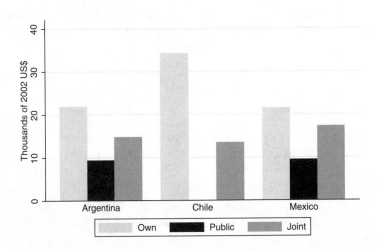

4.6. EPV of own annuity, public benefit, and joint annuity (married women with secondary education). Joint annuity adds more than public benefit to EPV of average woman.

(table 4.10, rows 20 through 23; figure 4.7). Single women obviously receive much less than married women with the same work behavior, but they are also likely to work more, having fewer family responsibilities keeping them at home. A single woman who works full career gets approximately the same lifetime retirement income as an average married woman.

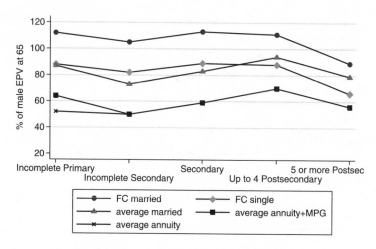

4.7. Female/male ratios in EPV of lifetime benefits, Chile. EPV of full-career married women exceeds that of men in Chile.

Note that lifetime gender ratios are much higher than monthly gender ratios, owing to the earlier retirement age and greater longevity of women, the MPG, and the joint annuity. Which matters the most? If we care about standard of living, monthly benefits are the key, but if we are measuring redistributions, lifetime benefits from all sources matter.

Imputed Net Benefits and Money's Worth Ratios

In a multipillar system, the private defined contribution plan is actuarially fair and does not redistribute (except for transfers between husband and wife through the joint pension requirement). All interfamily redistributions take place through the public benefit. We proceed, then, to assess redistributions from the MPG. We already know the gross EPV that each subgroup receives, from table 4.10. However, we do not know the tax cost paid by each subgroup, as the MPG is financed out of the government's general revenues. Intergenerational cost shifting is possible, and capital as well as labor income may be taxed. To obtain a rough estimate of the direction of redistribution, we make the simplified assumptions that (1) each cohort pays the full cost of its public benefits and (2) within each cohort taxes are distributed among education-gender groups proportional to their lifetime earnings. These assumptions allow us to solve for the uniform tax rate on earnings that will cover the total public benefit.[11] When this tax rate is applied to the lifetime earnings of each subgroup, we obtain its imputed tax amount (see appendix

3 for more details). For Chile, the imputed tax rate is neglibible—less than 0.1 percent of wages—if the MPG is price indexed, as assumed in this analysis. (If the MPG is wage indexed the imputed tax rate would be much higher because the benefit would be much larger and would reach more people.)

We use three measures of redistribution: (1) the net benefit from the MPG, which equals the EPV of the MPG top-up minus the imputed tax cost of financing it; (2) the money's worth ratio from the MPG (MWR_{pub}), which equals the EPV of the MPG top-up divided by the EPV of the imputed tax cost; and (3) the MWR from the public benefit plus private benefit ($MWR_{pub+pvt}$), which equals (EPV of MPG + own annuity)/(EPV of imputed tax cost + contributions). For women, we add a fourth measure—the MWR from public plus private benefit plus joint annuity ($MWR_{pub+pvt+jt}$), which includes the EPV of the joint annuity in the numerator.

A positive net benefit indicates that a subgroup is receiving more than it is paying, which means that some other group must be paying more than it receives, as, summed over all subgroups, net benefits cancel out to 0. In table 4.11 we see that only average women in the bottom education category receive positive redistributions from the MPG, financed by average men and full-career women whose net benefits are negative (rows 3, 9, and 16). Ten-year women also have small negative net benefits because they are not eligible for the MPG but pay some taxes to finance it.

Money's worth ratios are a common measure of return from annuities. An MWR of 100 percent indicates that the annuity is "actuarially fair" in the sense that the subgroup is getting back, in expected present value terms, exactly what it paid in, in taxes plus contributions. If the MWR is greater than 100 percent, the subgroup is getting back more than it paid; that is, it is getting a positive redistribution and vice versa. We see that the MWR_{pub} is 0 for average men, ten-year women, full-career women, and all upper education brackets because they receive no MPG. However, MWR_{pub} far exceeds 100 percent for average women in the bottom schooling groups, who receive a huge MPG benefit relative to their small tax cost (table 4.11, rows 4, 11, 17, and 23).

This extreme result is moderated when we measure $MWR_{pub+pvt}$. Most women and single men who do not get the MPG do receive their own annuity, which equals their accumulated contributions plus investment earnings minus the small tax they must pay to finance the MPG. Their $MWR_{pub+pvt}$ is almost 100 percent, indicating that they get back practically their full tax and contribution cost. In contrast, the $MWR_{pub+pvt}$ of average married men is only 82 percent because of the joint annuity that they must purchase for

Table 4.11: Expected Lifetime Public Benefits, Imputed Tax Cost, and Imputed Public and Private MW in Chile (2002 US$000's and %)

	Incomplete Primary	Incomplete Secondary	Complete Secondary	Up to 4 years Postsecondary	5+ year Postsecon
			Education		
Average man					
1. MPG	$0	$0	$0	$0	$0
2. Imputed tax cost	.04	.05	.08	.11	.27
3. Net benefit	−.04	−.05	−.08	−.11	−.27
4. MWR$_{pub}$	0%	0%	0%	0%	0%
5. MWR$_{pub+pvt}$, married man	82%	82%	82%	82%	82%
6. MWR$_{pub+pvt,}$ single man	99.9%	99.9%	99.9%	99.9%	99.9%
Average woman					
7. MPG	$3.1	$0	$0	$0	$0
8. Imputed tax cost	.01	.02	.04	.06	.11
9. Net benefit	3.09	−.02	−.04	−.06	−.11
10. Net benefit if MPG is wage indexed	18.1	14.0	3.2	−1.8	−3.3
11. MWR$_{pub}$	22745%	0%	0%	0%	0%
12. MWR$_{pub+pvt}$	122%	99.9%	99.9%	99.9%	99.9%
13. MWR$_{pub+pvt+jt}$	168%	147%	139%	133%	142%
Full-career woman					
14. MPG	$0	$0	$0	$0	$0
15. Imputed tax cost	.03	.03	.06	.08	.14
16. Net benefit	−.03	−.03	−.06	−.08	−.14
17. MWR$_{pub}$	0%	0%	0%	0%	0%
18. MWR$_{pub+pvt}$	99.9%	99.9%	99.9%	99.9%	99.9%
19. MWR$_{pub+pvt+jt}$	127%	128%	126%	126%	135%
Ten-year woman					
20. MPG	$0	$0	$0	$0	$0
21. Imputed tax cost	.00	.01	.01	.01	.02
22. Net benefit	−.00	−.01	−.01	−.01	−.02
23. MWR$_{pub}$	0%	0%	0%	0%	0%
24. MWR$_{pub+pvt}$	99.9%	99.9%	99.9%	99.9%	99.9%
25. MWR$_{pub+pvt+jt}$	176%	192%	205%	192%	232%
Female/married male ratios of MWR$_{pub+pvt}$					
26. Average woman	148%	121%	121%	121%	121%
27. Full-career woman	121%	121%	121%	121%	121%
28. Ten-year woman	121%	121%	121%	121%	121%
29. Average woman if MPG is wage indexed	283%	213%	136%	121%	121%

Source: Calculations by authors based on table 4.10 and assumptions described in text and appendix 3.

Note: MWR$_{pub}$ = MPG/imputed tax cost. MWR$_{pub+pvt}$ = (annuity + MPG)/(imputed tax cost + contribution). MWR$_{pub+}$ = (annuity + MPG + joint pension)/(imputed tax cost + contribution). Except for rows 10 and 29, MPG is price-indexed and imputed tax rate = 0.033 percent. MWR$_{pub}$ is very high for average woman in bottom educational categ because imputed tax is very low. In rows 10 and 29, MPG is wage indexed for successive cohorts but price indexed a age 60; imputed tax rate is 1 percent.

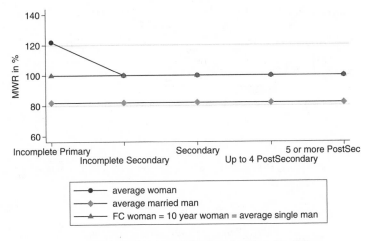

4.8. Money's worth ratios, public plus private benefits, Chile [(public + private benefits)/(tax + contributions)]. Low-earning average woman gets highest money's worth ratio in Chile.

their wives. And at the opposite end, the $MWR_{pub+pvt}$ of average women with low education, who get the MPG, is 122 percent (168 percent if we include the joint annuity they receive from their husband) (table 4.11, rows 12 and 13; and figure 4.8).[12] As a result of the tax paid by men and the joint annuity they must purchase for their wives, the average female/male ratio of $MWR_{pub+pvt}$ is well over 100 percent, especially for low earners. This effect is much stronger if the MPG is wage indexed (table 4.11, rows 26, 27, 28, and 29).

Marginal MRWs and Work (Dis)Incentives

Redistributions create incentives for behavior, particularly regarding work. We examine three types of individuals and the incentives they face from the pension system to work in or withdraw from the labor force: ten-year women who are considering taking on average employment practices, average women who are considering working full career, and low-density men who are considering more regular work and contributions. In table 4.12 we present the marginal net public benefits and marginal MWRs from incremental work for each of these groups. Marginal net public benefits are their increased MPG payments minus their increased tax cost, and marginal MWRs are their increased public plus private benefits relative to their increased tax cost plus contributions for their incremental work. Benefits from

Table 4:12: Marginal Net Benefits and MWRs for Incremental Work in Chile

	Education				
	Incomplete Primary	Incomplete Secondary	Complete Secondary	Up to 4 years Postsecondary	5+ years Postsecondary
Marginal net public benefit from incremental work (in 2002 US$000)					
1. Ten-year to average woman	3.09	–.01	–.03	–.05	–0.09
2. Average to full career woman	–3.11	–.01	–.02	–.02	–.03
Marginal net benefit if MPG is partly wage indexed (in 2002 US$000)					
3. Ten-year to average woman	18.24	14.20	3.41	–1.46	–2.72
4. Average to full career woman	–14.73	–15.03	–4.90	–0.43	–0.79
Marginal MWR$_{pub+pvt}$ for incremental work (%)					
5. Ten-year to average woman	155%	99.9%	99.9%	99.9%	99.9%
6. Average to full career woman	68%	99.9%	99.9%	99.9%	99.9%

Note: Marginal net public benefit from work level i to level j = $(MPG_j – MPG_i) – (T_j – T_i)$.

Marginal MWR$_{pub+pvt}$ from work level i to j = $((MPG_j – MPG_i) + (annuity_j – annuity_i))/((T_j – T_i) + (contrib_j – contrib_i))$.

MPG is assumed to be price-indexed except for rows 3 and 4 where partial wage indexation is assumed (see table 4.11 for definition).

joint annuities are not included in these calculations, as they do not change when women's work status changes and therefore do not affect marginal MWRs.

Most striking are incentives facing women in the bottom education category. They get positive incremental benefits if they shift from ten-year to average status, because this shift gives them access to the MPG. As a result, their MWR$_{pub+pvt}$ far exceeds 100 percent (table 4.12, rows 1, 3, and 5; figure 4.9). The system clearly gives ten-year women with low education an incentive to work about twenty years, like average women. However, if these average women go on to work full career they lose the MPG, so their marginal net public benefit becomes negative and their MWR for that decision becomes less than 100 percent (table 4.12, rows 2, 4, and 6; figure 4.10).[13]

These work disincentives become much smaller for women in the higher education groups, who never receive the MPG. Their own annuity yields a marginal MWR of virtually 100 percent. Based on these incentives we would expect less educated women to cluster around the twenty-year point, while highly educated women are more likely to work full career, giving them

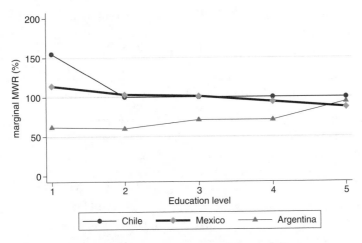

4.9. Marginal money's worth ratio for shift from ten-year to average woman [(change in public + private benefit)/(change in tax + contributions)] (%). Marginal money's worth ratio for shift from ten-year to average woman: high for low-earning women in Chile, low in Argentina. See tables 4.12, 5.12, and 6.12 for the definition of education levels 1 to 5 in each country.

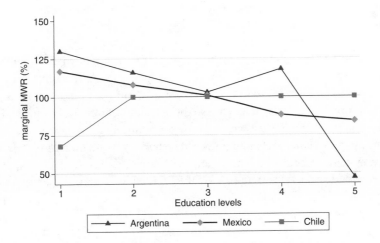

4.10. Marginal money's worth ratios for shift from average to full-career woman [(change in public + private benefit)/(change in tax + contributions)] (%).Marginal money's worth ratios for shift from average to full-career woman: low for low-earning women in Chile and high-earning women in Argentina. See tables 4.12, 5.12, and 6.12 for the definition of education levels 1 to 5 in each country.

greater financial independence.[14] Work incentives in Chile are high for more educated women, who also add the most productivity to the broader economy.

Who Gained or Lost Most from the Reform?

Comparison of the new and old social security systems in Chile is difficult because the old system was nonsustainable and unable to provide the promised benefits. Since we do not know what adjustments would have been made to make the old system solvent (higher taxes? lower benefit? whose taxes or benefits?), it is impossible to determine absolute gains or losses from the change. To avoid this problem we focus on relative changes in the position of men and women in different education–marriage status groups. In effect, we assume that the adjustment to achieve fiscal balance would have involved equiproportional tax hikes or benefit cuts for all groups under the old structure, leaving relative positions intact, and we compare these with relative positions under the new system. We ask the following questions: (1) Which education–marriage status–gender groups gained or lost the most from the reform? (2) Did the gender ratio get larger or smaller in the process of the reform? We carry out this analysis taking into account the full expected present value of lifetime benefits. We already have this value for the new system, and we apply the old defined benefit formula to obtain the promised benefits for the old system. (But bear in mind we do not assume that these promises would have been kept in an absolute sense, only that relative positions will be maintained.[15])

A priori, we can identify many reasons why the reform might have helped or hurt women. Women with less than ten years of contributions got no benefit at all under the old rules but receive an annuity in proportion to their contributions under the new rules, so their position should be improved. In contrast, women with just ten years of contributions got a favored accrual rate and replacement rate under the old system, while their pensions in the new system depend on the normal market rate of return, so their position may have deteriorated. Marginal benefits after ten years diminished sharply under the old system, so full-career women would be expected to gain from the reform. High final-year earnings were rewarded under the old system, while earlier earnings are rewarded (by compound interest) under the new system; this change benefits women who work while young. Women had to choose between their own benefit and the widow's benefit in the old system, but they can keep both in the new system. Finally, old system benefits were not automatically indexed for inflation. Annuities in the new system, in contrast, are fully indexed to prices and therefore insured against inflation. This provision helps men, but it helps women even more because they live longer.

Both systems have a minimum pension, but in the old system it was set on an ad hoc basis, while in the new system it is formally price indexed and, based on political decisions, has been rising even faster, with wage growth. This should benefit all pensioners, but women in particular, who are more likely to receive it. Since we do not know what the minimum pension would have been in the old system, we assume that it would have been set at the same level as the MPG in the new system. This introduces a bias in favor of the old system, because it ignores the fact that the old system did not provide inflation insurance.[16] This bias is particularly great for ten-year women, who were eligible for the minimum pension in the old system but not in the new system.

How Gender Ratios Changed due to the Reform

We proceed to compare the female/male ratio of lifetime benefits in the new and old systems (table 4.13). Ratios equal to 100 percent indicate that the expected present value of lifetime benefits for women equals the expected present value of benefits for men from the same schooling level. The top panel of the table pertains to gender ratios in the old system, the bottom panel relates to the new system. Based on information presented in the previous section, we would expect gender ratios to change in divergent directions for different subgroups, with the biggest gains going to working married women, and that is exactly what we find.

As expected, gender ratios for the average woman are higher in the old system when we look at personal pensions alone (table 4.13, row 1 vs. row 6). This is the situation for single women with average work experience. Adding the MPG raises the relative standing of women in the lowest education group, but all female/male ratios postreform remain below the ratios prereform if the MPG is price indexed (row 1 vs. row 7). If it is partly wage indexed, the positive effect becomes much larger for the bottom two schooling groups, but the other groups continue to remain below the prereform situation (row 8). This deterioration occurs mainly because women did not get an actuarial benefit reduction for retiring at age sixty in the old system, as they do in the new system.

When the survivor's benefit is added, this leaves old system ratios largely unchanged, but raises new system female/male ratios dramatically, to the point where they exceed prereform levels for average married women in most

Table 4.13: Simulated Female/Male Ratios of EPV of Lifetime Benefits in New versus Old Systems in Chile

	Incomplete Primary	Incomplete Secondary	Complete Secondary	Up to 4 Years Postsecondary	5+Years Postsecondary
	Education				
Old system (woman/average man) (%)					
1. Average single woman	72	56	88	91	71
2. Average married woman	73	61	88	91	73
3. Full-career single woman	82	72	94	68	70
4. Full-career married woman	82	72	94	68	70
5. Ten-year married woman	73	52	50	54	42
New system (average woman/average man) (%)					
6. Single, own annuity	52	50	59	70	56
7. Single, own annuity + MPG (price indexed)	64	50	59	70	56
8. Single, own annuity + MPG (wage indexed)	121	88	67	70	56
9. Married, own annuity + MPG (price indexed) + joint annuity	87	73	83	94	79
10. Married, own annuity + MPG (wage indexed) + joint annuity	140	110	90	94	79
New system (full-career woman/average man) (%)					
11. Single	88	82	89	88	66
12. Married	112	105	113	111	89
New system (ten-year woman) (%)					
13. Married	55	49	46	49	41

Source: Calculations by the authors.

Note: Present values are measured at age 65 for both genders, including benefits that started for women at 60. Denominator is pension for married man. In old system, single and married men got same pension. In new system, married men get smaller pension than single men, because they must purchase joint pension. Single women are assumed to have same work and wage history as married women, but do not get widow's benefit. Single and married full-career women got same pension in old system, as their own pension outweighed widow's benefit. In new system, married women get joint pension plus own pension.

MPG is assumed to be price indexed, except for rows 8 and 10, where partial wage indexation is assumed (see table 4.10). For average women, same price-indexed MPG is included in new and old systems, although in fact it was not price indexed in old system. Full-career women do not qualify for price-indexed MPG in new or old system. Ten-year women are assumed to get MPG in old system but not new system. Impact of 70% ceiling on replacement rate in old system is not taken into account in this table, because data do not allow us to distinguish between those for whom it did and did not apply. (Workers could evade ceiling by changing sector of job or getting higher wage in final years.) In cases where it applied, old-system ratios of woman/man would have been higher because pension for men would have been lower.

Table 4.14: Simulated Ratios of EPVs of Postreform/Prereform Lifetime Benefits (relative to ratio for married men in top education group) in Chile[a]

	Education				
	Incomplete Primary	Incomplete Secondary	Complete Secondary	Up to 4 Years Postsecondary	5+ Years Postsecondary
	Average Man (%)				
1. Married man	128	118	118	94	100
2. Single man	154	143	143	114	121
	Woman (%)				
3. Average, single	113	106	80	73	79
4. Average, married	152	142	111	97	109
5. Full career, single	138	135	113	122	94
6. Full career, married	175	174	142	154	128
7. Ten year, married	95	112	108	84	98
8. Men + women: average household	138	127	115	95	104

Source: Calculations by the authors.

Note: Includes lifetime benefits from own annuity and price-indexed MPG. Also includes survivor's benefit in old system, joint annuity in new system, for married women. Single women are assumed to have same work and wage history as married women. Each cell i shows $(PVnew/PVold)_i / (PVnew/PVold)_k$, where $(PVnew/PVold)_i$ = ratio of present value of lifetime benefits in new vs. old systems for group i. This is normalized by the ratio for reference group k, where k = married men in highest education category. Groups in rows 3 and 5 do not include widow's benefit in old system or joint annuity in new system. If the number in a cell > 100%, it gained more than top married men.

[a] real rate of return (r) = 5% during accumulation, 3.5% during annuity stage, real wage growth = 2%.

schooling categories (table 4.13, row 2 vs. rows 9 and 10). This effect becomes even more pronounced for married full-career women, where almost all gender ratios exceed 100 percent in the new system (row 4 vs. row 11). This group consistently improves its relative position in the new system because postponed retirement raises their pension amount on an actuarial basis and they no longer have to give up their own annuity to get the widow's annuity. Thus, the new system should induce more women to work full career than the old system. In contrast, ten-year women lose the generous pension and minimum pension guarantee they received for only ten years of work in the old system, so their relative position deteriorates (row 5 vs. row 13).

Ratios of Postreform to Prereform Lifetime Benefits

Finally, to calculate more precisely who gained most in relative position, we present in table 4.14 the ratios of postreform to prereform expected lifetime benefits for each gender-education subgroup. We normalize according to the ratio for the married man in the top education group. That is, we measure the new/old lifetime benefits for each subgroup, which we then divide by the new/old ratio for the highest-income married man.[17] In the following discussion, the term *gain* represents gain in relative position: the group gained more or lost less from the reform than the top-educated married man.

The key observation is that differences among subgroups within each gender are greater than differences between the genders, with education level and marital status mattering the most.

1. Most consistently, men and women in lower schooling groups gain more than others from the reform (table 4.14, columns 1 and 2 vs. columns 3 through 5). This is primarily because they have a flatter age-earnings profile and hence make more of their contributions early on, accumulating interest that produces high annuities in the new system. In contrast, the more educated groups have steeper age-earnings profiles, with high wages at the end of their working lives that produced high benefits under the old system formula.

2. Single men improve their position compared with married men (compare rows 1 and 2). This is because married men must finance a joint annuity in the new system, while single men use their entire fund to finance their own pension. This differs from the old system, in which the widow's benefit was financed by the common pool.

3. In contrast, married women gain more than otherwise identical single women, because they get to keep their own annuity plus the joint annuity, while under the old system they had to choose between the two (compare row 3 with row 4 and compare row 5 with row 6). However, single women tend not to be identical to married women. As we show in chapter 3, they work more. If in fact they work like full-career women, they gain approximately as much as average married women (compare row 4 with row 5).

4. Married men gain less than married women with the same work histories, because the former pay for the joint pension while the latter receive it (compare row 1 with row 6). (This effect would be wiped out if we used the household as the unit of comparison, since it involves transfers from husband to wife.)

5. Relative gains increase with women's attachment to the labor force, because the new system rewards incremental work and postponed retirement more continuously (except in vicinity of the MPG). In the old system most women got very little benefit from their own contributions, as the widow's benefit was greater and crowded it out, while full-career women kept their own benefit but lost the widow's benefit. In contrast, all married women get both benefits under the new system. Full-career married women are the biggest gainers from

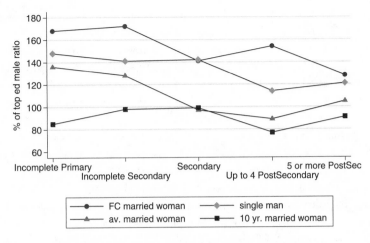

4.11. Postreform/prereform ratios of EPV by group, Chile (normalized by postreform/prereform EPV ratio of top education man). Low-earning full-career married women and single men are the biggest relative gainers from the reform in Chile.

the pension reform, while ten-year women lose relative to other groups and also lose their access to the minimum pension (figure 4.11).

The Main Message from Chile

Women's lower participation rates and wage rates continue to produce a lower pension accumulation and personal annuity after retirement. This lower payout is exacerbated by the lower normal retirement age legislated for women's retirement. Critics of Chile's social security system often point to the smaller personal pensions for women as a reason for their disapproval. But this is only the beginning of the story.

Public transfers from the MPG mitigate this effect for the lowest earners and prevent poverty at a low tax cost. But these transfers do nothing for the gender gap above the bottom schooling group. Low-density women do not even get the MPG because they do not meet the twenty-year eligibility requirement. Moreover, this equalizing impact will become negligible in the future if the MPG is not at least partially wage indexed. If it is wage indexed (as it has been de facto), its effect is larger, broader, and long term, but it will cost the government considerably more money and it may discourage marginal work by low earners.

Mandatory intrahousehold transfers from men to married women through the joint annuity comprise a much larger redistribution toward women. This redistribution is accomplished without placing a large burden on the public treasury and without discouraging women's work. Husbands pay for the joint annuity by taking a lower payment themselves, and widows are not required to give up their own benefit when they receive the joint annuity. For this reason, married working women, especially full-career married women, improve their position relative to men most consistently after the reform. As female labor force participation rises through time for exogenous reasons or as an endogenous response to incentives, the new system will become increasingly favorable toward women.

The following key questions with gender implications remain to be answered by policy makers: How much are they willing to pay to protect future cohorts of low-earning women? (Such protection requires partial- or full-wage linkage of the MPG or other safety net.) What can they do to protect women with fewer than twenty years of contributions while at the same time avoiding the marginal work disincentives faced by those with more than twenty years of contributions? (Having the MPG proportional to years worked or residence based rather than contribution based would help solve both problems.) How can they close the gender gap for middle-earning women? (Equalizing normal retirement ages would help.) What are the special problems faced by divorced women? (Answering this question requires rethinking the MPG, survivors' benefits, and joint pension requirements). What about women who are not covered by the system or have very low density of contributions? (Possible noncontributory benefits are discussed in chapter 8.) Indeed, Chile is now in the process of fine-tuning the public benefit in its system to address these issues.

CHAPTER FIVE

Argentina

The old Argentinean social security system was in serious trouble before its reform. Besides the longterm problem of rising costs due to population aging, a deficit existed even in the short run owing to evasion, early retirement, and haphazardly kept records. The system was in default. The new system was adopted in 1993 and implemented in 1994, with some important modifications since that time.[1] Unlike Chile's new system, which was established during a dictatorial regime, the new Argentine system was developed by a democracy, which required many political compromises in order to gain the support of diverse constituencies. We analyze how women fared in this process. The methodology is the same as that used for Chile, so we suggest that the reader refer back to chapters 3 and 4 for a fuller description.

However, an additional caveat is needed because it is much more difficult to define the new and the old system in Argentina. In the years leading up to the reform, the system changed frequently due to fiscal pressures to cut costs on the one hand and political pressure to maintain benefits on the other hand. Enforcement of the rules was uneven and records sparse. Ambiguities sometimes led to litigation, with the net result undetermined before yet another change took place.

These ambiguities persist in the new system. The government has been continuously modifying the system, particularly the financing source, size, and eligibility requirements for the public benefit—especially after the financial crisis of 2002 and resulting economic turmoil. Thus, it is difficult to ascertain whether women gained or lost due to the reform, because it is difficult to define either the reform or the counterfactual; we are chasing a moving target. We start by describing the stylized version of the old and new system that we analyze in this chapter, while warning the reader that it probably will have changed again before this book is published. Most important, we focus on the issue of which design features matter the most in determining the gender outcome.

The Old and New Systems and Our Data for Comparing Them

The Old System

The old system was a traditional pay-as-you-go defined benefit system. It was highly fragmented, with different schemes for public- and private-sector employees and for particular occupations within each sector. Moreover, it was frequently modified in efforts to make it more generous on the one hand and more fiscally affordable on the other hand. We describe the largest plan for private-sector workers as it existed shortly before the reform. It is not very different from (albeit a bit more generous than) the old Chilean system.

Workers with at least twenty years of contributions received 70 percent of base salary plus an additional 1 percent for every contribution year over thirty, with base salary defined as the best three out of the last ten years. Men could retire at age sixty, women at fifty-five. Workers with ten years of work received 50 percent of base salary plus an additional 1 percent for every contribution year over ten and could retire at age sixty-five. Women were more likely to take the ten-year option. Past salaries were not indexed up for inflation to determine the reference wage, nor was the pension price indexed automatically after retirement. In the context of Argentinean inflation, this policy made the real benefit much less generous than it appeared at first. But a minimum pension that was raised on an ad hoc basis with inflation meant that low earners with ten years of service received a generous (albeit uncertain) pension relative to their contributions.[2]

The New System

Argentina's new multipillar system took Chile's scheme as its model but included important modifications. Like Chile, Argentina included a privately managed retirement saving account and a public benefit that provides a safety net. However, the safety net is larger and much less narrowly targeted than that in Chile, the private account is smaller, and workers are offered a public defined benefit alternative to the private scheme. As of 2001, more than 80 percent of all contributors, including most women, were in the private account option, so in this study we focus on it, as well as the safety net that covers all eligible workers.[3]

Initially workers were required to contribute 11 percent of payroll into their retirement saving accounts and to choose among numerous managers (*administradoras de fondos de jubilacion y pension*, or AFJPs) to invest these funds. This contribution rate was reduced after Argentina's fiscal crisis. Pensions depend on amounts accumulated, as in Chile. Unlike in Chile, where a separate payment is made to cover administrative fees plus survivors' and disability insurance, in Argentina these fees are taken out of the mandatory contribution. The fees fluctuate from year to year in response to changing administrative and insurance costs. Initially they totaled about 3.25 percent of wages, leaving a net of 7.75 percent of wages for investment, and we used this number in our simulations. By 2005 fees were only 2.5 percent of payroll (James et al. 2000; James, Smalhout, and Vittas 2001; AIOS 2005). The reduction in fees will leave a larger amount to be invested and hence will increase annuities. At the same time, the reduction in contribution rate will decrease accumulations and annuities. Neither effect will alter the gender ratios of annuities from the private accounts.

Upon retirement (age sixty-five for men, sixty for women), the accumulated assets are taken out in the form of gradual withdrawals or annuities, with lump sums allowed for amounts in excess of a specified floor. For married men as well as married women, the annuity must be joint with 70 percent to the survivor; however, this requirement implies a cost mainly for men, as women are expected to outlive their husbands.

For the safety net, Argentina provides a basic "flat" benefit, starting at age sixty-five for men and age sixty for women. Unlike Chile's minimum pension guarantee (MPG), the flat benefit is not a top-up—instead, all eligible workers receive it. But eligibility for the full benefit was restricted to workers with at least thirty years of contributions—a provision that excludes most women. As an alternative that applied mainly to women, workers who reached age seventy with ten years of contributions were granted a reduced flat pension that is 70 percent of the full amount. Initially the flat benefit, plus transition costs (in the form of compensatory payments to workers for credits earned under the old system), were financed by a 16 percent payroll tax paid by employers. More recently, the payroll portion has been reduced to less than half of this amount, and the rest is financed out of general revenues and debt.[4]

Argentina's public benefit has been under constant revision. For example, a minimum pension has long existed, but it is strictly ad hoc and therefore impossible to model for the long run. Recently the minimum pension was raised to a level that is more than double that of the flat benefit, so in about half the cases it supplants the flat benefit for both men and women. (Workers with less than thirty years of contributions get a partial minimum.)

Also, a recent law allows retiring workers to report any number of years of self-employment prior to 1993 in order to enable them to qualify for the flat or minimum benefit. Our analysis focuses on the benefit structure that was set up in 1994, but we discuss the potential impact of these changes on women's relative position.

Participation in both parts of Argentina's system is mandatory for the self-employed as well as employees, a much more ambitious requirement than seen in Chile's new system. But data on actual contributions suggest that this ambitious mandate is being enforced much less effectively than that in Chile, with a resulting low density of contributions that has a large impact on the final pension. (See table 5.1 for a comparison of the old and new systems and basic economic and demographic data about Argentina, and see table 5.2 for data on the low density of contributions, especially among the self-employed, during a thirty-six- to ninety-month window.)

Data

As we did for our calculations on the Chile system, we construct synthetic representative individuals based on cross-sectional data and simulate their pension benefits under the old and new systems. Our primary data source is the *Encuesta Nacional de Gastos de los Hogares* (ENGH), a nationally representative household survey carried out by the Instituto Nacional de Estadística y Censos de la República Argentina in 1996–1997. All the regions covered by the survey are considered urban. Nearly 42 percent of the working-age population resides in Metropolitan Buenos Aires. The survey collects detailed information on household expenditures, demographics, educational attainment, occupation, employment, and income.

We use these data to observe the work and earnings history of men and women at different stages of their life cycle and construct our synthetic individuals under the assumption that today's young workers will follow the path indicated by this cross-section. Shortcomings of this approach were discussed in chapters 3 and 4. To handle these shortcomings and to indicate the heterogeneity among women, we construct different employment histories for five education categories and three different degrees of labor force attachment: average women, full-career women (whose labor force participation is the same as that of men) and ten-year women (who work continuously for ten years prior to having children). Most women in the past may have behaved like ten-year women, while in the future, Argentina may have many full-career women due to changing educational composition and social

Table 5.1: Main Features of Old and New Systems in Argentina

	Old System[a]	New System
Structure	Pay-as-you-go defined benefit	Private pillar: funded individual accounts *or* public defined benefit Public pillar: flat or reduced flat benefit
Contribution Rate	27% (lower before 1994)	11% to private pillar[b] 6–16% to public pillar (varies by region and time)
Benefits[c]	JO: 70% of base salary + 1% for every year over 30; JEA: 50% of base salary + 1% for every year over 10	Private pillar: annuity or programmed withdrawals Public pillar: flat benefit after 30 years' work or reduced flat benefit at age 70 after 10 years
Base Salary	Average of 3 highest annual salaries within last 10 years	n.a.
Pensionable Age	JO: Men, age 60; women, age 55 JEA: age 65	For annuity: 65 for men, 60 for women; earlier if meet conditions For flat benefit: 65 for men, 60 for women Reduced flat: age 70
Years for Eligibility[c]	JO: 20 years' contributions (15 before 1991) JEA: 10 years' service	30 years for full flat benefit 10 years for reduced flat benefit No minimum requirement for pension from account
Pension if Worked Less than 10 Years	0	Pension from account
Indexation Provisions	No automatic indexation	Ad hoc for public benefit; not yet determined for annuity
Minimum Pension	Ad hoc minimum after 10 years service, no indexation	Minimum pension fixed on ad hoc basis, no indexation
Widows	75% of husband's pension and/or own pension	70% of husband's annuity + 70% of husband's flat benefit + own pension

[a] Argentina had special provisions for the self-employed and many special regimes. We focus here on the main scheme for employees.

[b] Fees for survivors and disability insurance plus administrative costs are taken out of this contribution rate. Initially these fees totaled 3.25%. Currently they are about 2.5%.

[c] JO = Jubilacion Ordinaria; JEA = Jubilacion por Edad Avanzada. Under the old system, the JO applied to those with 20 years of contributions, while the smaller JEA applied to those with at least 10 years of contributions.

Table 5.2: Contribution Density among Affiliates by Employment Status in Argentina (%)

% of Time Contributing	Employee	Self-Employed	Domestic Service	Voluntary	Total
0–16	28	40	21	56	30
17–50	15	18	15	24	16
51–83	15	12	16	5	15
84–100	41	29	49	15	40
Total	100	100	100	100	100

Source: SAFJP and Instituto Torcuatto di Tella (1999).

norms. Single women today work almost as much as full-career women. The typical woman is assumed to be single initially and to marry at the median marriage age for women in her schooling category.

Years of Work and Contributions

Table 5.3 shows that men work thirty-nine to forty-one years (about 80 percent of the time between age sixteen and their normal retirement age of sixty-five), while women work eighteen to thirty-four years (40 to 75 percent of the time between age sixteen and their normal retirement age of sixty). For women, participation is strongly correlated with education. Thus higher modal education for younger female cohorts is likely to increase their aggregate participation rates. For both genders, but especially for women, participation drops off dramatically after age sixty.

We know that the compliance rate in Argentina is much lower than that in Chile, so contributing years are likely to be far less than working years among affiliates. Two recent studies, following affiliates during a thirty-six-month window and a ninety-month window, respectively, found that the average affiliate contributed 50 to 60 percent of the time (SAFJP and Instituto Torcuatto di Tella 1999; Bertranou and Sanchez 2003). At one extreme, about 40 percent of working affiliates contribute more than 80 percent of the time; at the other end, about 30 percent contribute less than 20 percent of the time; and about one-third of all affiliates contribute varying amounts from 20 percent to 80 percent of the time (table 5.2). These studies did not distinguish between men and women. To capture this heterogeneity in our analysis, we depict two types of affiliates—those who contribute regularly when they work and those who contribute only 60 percent of their working time. This variation does not affect our estimates of the gender ratio of private pensions, but, as we shall see, it may differentially affect the eligibility of men versus women for the flat benefit.

Table 5.3: Estimated Years of Work in Urban Areas by Age, Education, and Gender in Argentina[a]

Age	Education				
	Incomplete Primary	Incomplete Secondary	Complete Secondary	Some Postsecondary	University Degree
Males					
16–20	3.25	2.33	3.85	1.67	0.00
21–25	3.94	4.53	4.53	3.17	4.69
26–30	4.27	4.78	4.85	4.39	4.92
31–35	4.20	4.87	4.93	4.73	4.94
36–40	4.66	4.75	4.89	4.97	4.90
41–45	4.68	4.80	4.87	4.94	4.89
46–50	4.54	4.68	4.86	4.86	4.93
51–55	4.29	4.51	4.42	4.64	4.81
56–60	3.86	3.99	3.96	3.88	4.65
61–65	1.24	1.41	1.66	1.89	2.08
Total 16–65[b]	38.93	40.74	42.82	39.14	40.86
Density of work[c]	78%	81%	86%	78%	82%
Females					
16–20	1.60	1.31	3.27	1.16	0.00
21–25	1.11	2.44	4.32	2.92	4.58
26–30	1.87	1.91	2.22	3.72	4.63
31–35	2.10	2.30	2.62	3.61	4.31
36–40	2.32	2.47	2.65	2.89	4.18
41–45	2.58	2.55	2.93	3.98	4.18
46–50	2.37	2.53	2.93	3.75	4.61
51–55	2.12	1.88	2.29	3.15	3.97
56–60	1.38	1.70	1.63	2.54	3.31
61–65	0.47	0.44	0.40	0.77	1.34
Total 16–65	17.92	19.53	25.26	29.49	34.43
Total 16–60[b]	17.45	19.09	24.86	28.72	33.09
Density of work[c]	39%	42%	55%	64%	74%

Source: Calculations by the authors based on ENGH (INDEC 1996–1997).

[a] Based on labor force experience of a cross-section of adults (affiliates + nonaffiliates) in urban areas covering most of the Argentine population. For details on data sources, see appendix 1.

[b] Total years of work to normal retirement age, 60 for women and 65 for men.

[c] Density of work = total working years to normal retirement age/total possible years from age 16 to normal retirement age. We define low-density worker as one who contributes only 60% of working time.

Earnings

As we did for Chile, we estimate for Argentina an average wage for each sex-age-schooling cell (table 5.4) using five-year age groupings. For men, monthly wage rates rise until age fifty, then level off and decline. For women, wage rates rise less steeply.[5] The female/male ratio of monthly wages varies

Table 5.4: Estimated Average Monthly Wage for Full-Time Plus Part-Time Urban Workers in Argentina (1996 data in 2002 US$)[a]

| Age | Education | | | | |
	Incomplete Primary	Incomplete Secondary	Complete Secondary	Some Postsecondary	University Degree
Males					
16–20	$68	$102	$121	$150	
21–25	$121	$163	$179	$194	$417
26–30	$137	$196	$268	$286	$502
31–35	$177	$230	$328	$370	$629
36–40	$164	$235	$382	$433	$710
41–45	$183	$273	$388	$419	$895
46–50	$194	$269	$425	$566	$809
51–55	$181	$260	$509	$447	$801
56–60	$176	$272	$320	$316	$775
61–65	$142	$223	$335	$342	$843
Females					
16–20	$67	$80	$117	$92	
21–25	$77	$117	$141	$167	$274
26–30	$82	$123	$169	$211	$365
31–35	$121	$134	$238	$225	$371
36–40	$130	$148	$245	$249	$379
41–45	$118	$149	$247	$318	$393
46–50	$108	$134	$256	$271	$519
51–55	$119	$142	$227	$321	$545
56–60	$102	$142	$263	$228	$372
60–65	$96	$138	$428	$378	$627

Source: Calculated by the authors based on data in ENGH (INDEC 1996–1997).

[a] Wage estimates are based on all workers (both full time and part time) in metropolitan areas. For more details on data and methodology, see appendix 1.

between 50 percent and 80 percent. It is generally somewhat lower than in Chile, perhaps because the Argentinean sample includes part-time as well as full-time workers and includes nonaffiliated and irregular workers as well as affiliates.

How Women Fare—Accumulations and Pensions from Their Own Accounts

How Much Do Men and Women Accumulate?

We show the accumulation of funds in the retirements savings accounts of our representative men and women, broken down into five education groups and three degrees of labor force attachment among women—average women, full-career women (who adopt male work propensities), and ten-year women (who work only ten years prior to child-bearing). In addition to the results for individuals who contribute regularly when they work, we also show the results for low-density individuals.

We base our simulations on a net contribution rate of 7.75 percent (11 percent minus 3.25 percent for administrative fees and survivors' and disability insurance fees). Applying this net contribution rate to the average wage and work patterns developed above for each gender-age-schooling cell, we obtain the expected retirement accumulation for each type of worker. In our baseline scenario, we add a secular growth rate of 2 percent per year to real wages; the rate of return is 5 percent during the accumulation stage and 3.5 percent during the payout stage. We also simulate a slow-growth scenario in which real wage growth is 0 and the interest rates during accumulation and payouts are 3 percent and 1.5 percent, respectively; in recent years Argentina has gone through a spell of slow growth. We assume that men retire at the legally allowable age of sixty-five and women retire at sixty, although we also show the consequences when women postpone age of pensioning to sixty-five.

We would expect women to have lower accumulations and benefits relative to men in Argentina than in Chile, because of their relatively lower wages and contribution propensities. Indeed this expectation turns out to be the case (table 5.5). The average woman accumulates only 24 to 40 percent as much as the average man—considerably less than women's accumulation in Chile. This gender ratio is unchanged whether the contribution density is 100 percent or 60 percent (table 5.5, row 9 vs. row 14). As in Chile, the accumulation increases by almost 30 percent if women postpone their age of pensioning to sixty-five (rows 3 and 10), and the gender ratio is hiked to 65 percent if women adopt the work patterns of men (table 5.5, rows 4 and 11; figure 5.1). But a large gap remains, even larger than in Chile for full-career women, due to the larger wage differential in Argentina (compare rows 11 and 12).

Expected Pension Benefits

Upon retirement, workers in Argentina, as in Chile, have a choice between gradual withdrawals and annuities, but our simulations assume the latter. Annuities and programmed withdrawals must be joint for both spouses, with the widow getting 70 percent of the husband's full benefit when he dies. Insurance companies use gender-specific tables to determine annuity payouts, although unisex tables are under discussion. Later, we compare their effects. On average, wives are three years younger than husbands and have a life expectancy that is three to four years greater than men. Men

Table 5.5: Simulated Gender Differences in Fund Accumulation in Argentina: Decomposition of Male/Female Differences[a]

	Education				
	Incomplete Primary	Incomplete Secondary	Secondary	Some Postsecondary	University Degree
Accumulated funds at retirement (in 2002 US$000)					
1. Woman retiring at 60 with 10 years' contributions	$4.5	$6.7	$8.6	$10.5	$17.7
2. Average woman retiring at 60	6.5	9.3	18.4	25.7	50.3
3. Average woman retiring at 65	8.4	12.1	23.8	33.2	64.7
4. Full-career woman retiring at 65	18.2	25.1	40.9	42.8	74.4
5. Man at 65	27.7	42.2	63.2	65.5	126.9
6. Low-density man at 65	16.6	25.3	37.9	39.3	76.1
Fund ratios of women relative to men retiring at 65 (%)					
8. Woman retiring at 60 with 10 years' contributions	16	16	14	16	14
9. Average woman retiring at 60	24	22	29	39	40
10. Average woman retiring at 65	30	29	38	51	51
11. Full-career woman retiring at 65	66	59	65	65	59
12. Full-career woman retiring at 65, male wages	100	100	100	100	100
13. Man at 65	100	100	100	100	100
14. Low-density woman at 60/low-density man at 65	24	22	29	39	40

Source: Calculations by the authors.

Note: This table gives projected fund accumulations at retirement for young workers entering labor force today. Average women retiring at 65 work as average women to 60, then keep money in account until pensioning at 65. Women with 10 years of contributions work 10 years from age 21 to age 30. Full-career women work with same intensity as men but earn the same wages that other women earn. Low-density worker contributes only 60% of the time he or she works.

[a] Based on 1996 data and assumptions of 5% real return and 2% real wage growth.

retiring at age sixty-five survive 14.5 years, while women retiring at sixty are expected to live 22.5 years. Their earlier retirement age and greater life expectancy will obviously reduce the monthly annuity women get from their accumulation.

The resulting annuities for married men retiring at age sixty-five range between US$153 and US$701 (in 2002 US$) depending on schooling (table 5.6, row 1)—much less than in Chile due to the lower contribution rate. Annuities for the average woman retiring at age sixty are 20 to 35 percent of the corresponding male annuity (rows 3 and 8). For those with 60 percent density, the annuity value falls proportionately but the gender ratio is

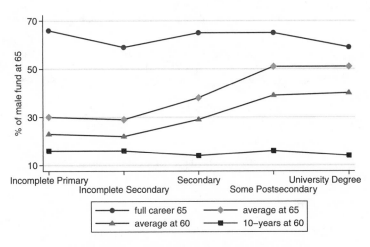

5.1. Female/male ratios of fund accumulation at retirement, Argentina. More work and postponed retirement would increase female/male ratios of accumulations in Argentina.

unchanged (rows 2, 7, and 12). Women in Argentina get lower annuities relative to men than they get in Chile because of their relatively lower years of work and wages. Postponing pensions to age sixty-five will raise the typical woman's annuity by 50 percent (rows 4 and 9). The gender gap falls substantially with more schooling, but this is entirely due to the greater labor force participation of educated women. When we hold participation constant by assuming that women work the same as men (full-career women), we eliminate and even reverse the equalizing impact of education on the gender gap (rows 5 and 10). The female/male ratio of pensions is then about 65 percent, except for the highest university group, where it is 59 percent. (Apparently in Argentina, as in Chile, higher education brings much greater rewards to men than to women.)

Finally worth noting is the very low ratio between the annuities of women with top and bottom education—only 13 percent—compared with 22 percent for men. The gap is much larger for women because the labor force participation of women is positively correlated with education. We return to this gap when we discuss the role of the public benefit.

The Flat Benefit

Until now the story has been very similar, in general outline, to that in Chile. However, the flat benefit is completely different in targeting, cost, and incentives from Chile's MPG.

Table 5.6: Simulated Monthly Annuities from Individual Accounts in Argentina (in 2002 US$)[a]

	Education				
	Incomplete Primary	Incomplete Secondary	Complete Secondary	Some Postsecondary	University Degree
Average married males, monthly annuity (US$)					
1. Annuity at 65	153	233	349	362	701
2. Low-density man at 65	92	140	209	217	421
Females, monthly annuity (US$)					
3. Average woman at 60	32	46	91	127	248
4. Average woman at 65	47	67	132	185	360
5. Full-career woman at 65	101	140	228	238	414
6. Ten-year woman at 60	22	33	42	52	87
7. Low-density woman at 60	19	27	53	74	145
Ratio of female's annuity to average married man's annuity (%)					
8. Average woman at 60	21	20	26	35	35
9. Average woman at 65	31	29	38	51	51
10. Full-career woman at 65	66	60	65	66	59
11. Ten-year woman at 60	14	14	12	14	12
12. Low-density women at 60/low-density man at 65	21	19	25	34	35

Source: Calculations by the authors.

[a] This table gives projected annuities at retirement for young workers entering labor force today. For notes, see appendix 1. Flat benefit is not included in this table. Married men and women in Argentina both must purchase joint annuity, with 70% to survivor. Gender-specific tables are used. Low density means individual contributes 60% of the time he or she works. Based on 1996 data and assumptions of 5% return in accumulation stage, 3.5% in annuity stage, and 2% real wage growth.

The Full Flat Benefit—Mainly for Men

Every eligible retiree gets a monthly benefit of 200 Argentinean pesos from the public treasury. In 1996, when the Argentine peso was pegged to the dollar, its value was equal to US$200. It was 30 percent of the average male wage, 45 percent of the average female wage, and 130 percent of the poverty line. It remains at Argentine $200, but with dollarization gone, at 2002 exchange rates the U.S. dollar value has fallen to $77. As a percentage of average wage, the full flat benefit is very similar to Chile's MPG. However, the full $77 goes to all eligible workers in Argentina, and they receive it in addition to their own annuity, rather than as a partial top-up for a small group, as in Chile. This provides a more diversified pension source in Argentina. Needless to say, Argentina's flat benefit is much more costly than Chile's MPG.

To contain costs, Argentina has set different eligibility conditions from those in Chile. For the full flat benefit, thirty years of contributions are required. This high number of contributory years means that men will be the primary recipients. The typical man in all education groups will meet the thirty-year requirement and get the full $77 starting at age sixty-five, providing he contributes most of the time that he works (in reality this turns out to be a big proviso because many men evade contributing and become low-density men). The flat benefit adds another 10 to 50 percent to male recipients' own annuities (table 5.7, rows 2 and 3). Because it adds a constant absolute amount, and thus a proportionately larger amount to the retirement income of workers with small annuities, it reduces the pension gap between high- and low-earning men.

In contrast, only full-career women and average women in the top education category meet the thirty-year eligibility requirement. As a result, at age sixty pension differentials are increased further between women with high and low education (table 5.7, row 6). And at sixty-five, when men get the full flat benefit but most women do not, the differential is increased between men and women except for the top schooling group (row 14). This is the exact opposite of the targeting of the MPG in Chile, where most men do not get a top-up and women in the bottom schooling group constitute the main recipient group.

The Reduced Flat Benefit for Women

However, the story does not end here—the politics of benefit entitlement in Argentina are never so simple. Most women workers with primary and secondary education are eligible for the reduced flat benefit—US$54—starting at age seventy, which requires only ten years of contributions. Even though this benefit is smaller in absolute value than the full flat benefit that more educated women get, it represents a much larger proportionate addition to the retirement income of these women. It also constitutes a much larger proportionate increment for women than for men. It doubles the monthly pensions of low-earning woman with average work histories and trebles the monthly pension of ten-year women (figure 5.2). Thus, at age sixty-five, women at the lower end of the education spectrum have a retirement income that is only 15 to 20 percent as much as their male counterparts, but at age seventy this proportion doubles (table 5.7, row 14 vs. row 15).

Focusing on age seventy, if we compare Chile's MPG with Argentina's flat benefit we find that the flat benefit narrows the gender ratio across all education groups, not simply the lowest group, because it is paid to all retirees, not simply the lowest earners. It also narrows the pension ratio between workers with top and bottom education more than in Chile, because it is a larger

Table 5.7: Simulated Impact of Public Benefit on Gender Ratios of Monthly Pensions, Argentina (in 2002 US$)[a]

	Education[b]				
	Incomplete Primary	Incomplete Secondary	Complete Secondary	Some Postsecondary	University Degree
Married man					
1. Annuity at 65	$153	$233	$349	$362	$701
2. Annuity + flat at 65	$230	$310	$426	$439	$778
3. % increase, flat	50%	33%	22%	21%	11%
4. Low-density man, annuity + flat at 70	$146	$194	$263	$271	$475
Married woman					
5. Annuity at 60	$32	$46	$91	$127	$248
6. Annuity + flat at 60	$32	$46	$91	$127	$ 325
7. Annuity + flat at 70	$86	$100	$145	$181	$325
8. % increase by flat at 70	169%	118%	60%	43%	31%
9. Full-career, annuity + flat	$178	$217	$305	$315	$491
10. % increase by flat, full-career woman at 65	76%	55%	34%	32%	19%
11. Ten-year woman, annuity + flat at 70	$76	$87	$96	$106	$141
12. % increase by flat, ten-year woman at 70	244%	164%	128%	104%	62%
Female/male ratios (%)					
13. Own annuity	21	20	26	35	35
14. Annuity + flat at 65	14	15	21	29	42
15. Annuity + flat at 70	37	32	34	41	42
16. Annuity + flat, full-career woman at 65	77	70	71	72	63
17. Annuity + flat, ten-year woman at 70	33	28	23	24	18
18. Low-density female/low-density male at 70	50	42	41	47	42

Source: Calculations by the authors.

[a] Based on 1996 data and assumptions of 5% return in accumulation stage, 3.5% in annuity stage, and 2% real wage growth.

[b] This table gives projected pensions at retirement for young workers entering labor force today. Full flat benefit of $77 begins at age 60 for women, 65 for men, after 30 years of contributions. Full-career women retire and begin full flat benefit at 65. Reduced flat of $54 begins at age 70; ten years of contributions are required for eligibility. Flat benefit is treated as if it is price indexed, although it is not. For comparison, the poverty line in Argentina was $60 in 1999, in 2002 US$. Men and women with low density of contributions contribute 60% of the time they work. Both qualify for the reduced flat benefit at 70. For rows 13–17, denominator is average man.

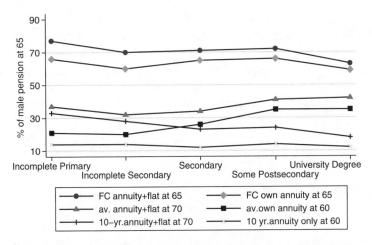

5.2. Female/male ratios of annuities plus flat benefit, Argentina. Large percentage increment to ten-year women and low earners from flat benefit in Argentina.

share of the total pension. It is therefore much more equalizing than Chile's MPG. It diversifies risk for both men and women, because their total pension comes from two very different sources—investment accounts and public treasury. Moreover, the reduced flat benefit provides protection to women with limited labor force attachment, such as ten-year women. Of course, it costs much more than Chile's MPG.[6]

Insurance against Slow Growth

In a slow-growth environment, the flat benefit plays a relatively more important role, and all these disparities in gender ratios are narrowed further, because the accumulations and annuities are smaller but the flat benefit retains its constant value. The flat benefit is now greater than the personal annuity for most women and also for many men (see appendix 4, table A7). It is a major source of insurance against an economic downturn—pensioners are protected much more than workers. Argentina's flat benefit is much more all encompassing and equalizing than Chile's MPG. But it also costs much more.

Work (Dis)Incentives

Argentina's attempt to extend this flat benefit to most old people while also rewarding work leads to a puzzling pattern of work (dis)incentives. Women face a large reward and redistribution for working ten years in the formal labor market but no marginal benefit from the public pillar over years ten to twenty-nine; then in year thirty the public benefit jumps discontinuously to a full flat benefit that starts at a much earlier age. This arrangement is costly for the public treasury, its equity is questionable, and it does not seem consistent with positive work incentives over the range of years in which most women now work (see discussion of marginal money's worth ratios below). This discussion underscores the extreme sensitivity of gender outcomes to detailed eligibility rules.

The Widow's Flat Benefit

In addition to the flat benefit that is paid to workers, the public system pays all widows a flat benefit that is 70 percent of the husband's flat benefit when the husband dies. In effect, this doubles women's own flat benefit for very old women, providing they have been married. Unlike Chile and Mexico, Argentina continues to subsidize married women over single women.

Low Density of Contributions, (Lack of) Indexation, and Recent Reforms

So far we have assumed that workers contribute as required. But in countries with a large informal sector and substantial self-employment, it is very difficult for governments to enforce this mandate. As a result, a high proportion of workers contribute for only part of their working lives and will accumulate smaller retirement savings than estimated above. We encountered this problem before, in Chile—it has become a major social issue in Latin America and other low- and middle-income countries.

Annuities of low-density men will be, on average, only 60 percent as great as those for men who contribute regularly. Moreover, these men will be eligible only for the reduced flat benefit rather than the full flat benefit. In this sense, they become more like women. Ironically, this narrows the gender differential, albeit at low absolute pension levels. But some women will not even be eligible for the reduced flat benefit because they have contributed for less than ten years.

An additional problem stems from the fact that Argentina's flat benefit is neither price nor wage indexed—unlike Chile's MPG. When Argentina devalued its currency relative to the dollar, the flat benefit remained fixed in nominal pesos, which meant that it fell dramatically in dollar terms and in purchasing power as well.

To solve the problem of low density of contribution and falling value of the flat benefit, Argentina, like Chile, is in the process of modifying the system. The government recently added a new higher minimum pension; it is about double the value of the flat benefit and applies against the combined total of the personal annuity plus the flat benefit. Table 5.7 demonstrates that, if this situation continues, average women in the bottom two education categories and most ten-year women will get the minimum. In effect, both the flat benefit and their own annuity will become irrelevant to them.[7]

Workers with thirty years of contributions will get the full minimum, and those with ten years will get a reduced minimum. Moreover, retirees are now allowed to claim additional years of self-employment upon retirement to become eligible for the flat benefit. Their belated "contributions" are financed by taking a reduction in the public benefit. In effect, this arrangement makes the minimum benefit noncontributory and universal for anyone who knows how to manipulate the system.

The new minimum pension avoids the problem that very low-density individuals will fail to have a living income in old age. It particularly helps women, who are most likely to find themselves in this situation. On the one hand, it tends to equalize pensions of men and women and of high versus low earners. But on the other hand, it completely undercuts the linkage between benefits and contributions, encourages further evasion, and raises the fiscal cost to the government. It adds another disincentive to formal-sector work, thereby perpetuating the low-density problem that it was designed to solve and deterring financial independence for women. This illustrates the tension that pension systems face between equality and efficiency. We return to this difficult trade-off in chapter 8.

Replacement Rates

Because pensions are designed to replace wages at a point when the individual is too old to work, they are often compared with the wage rate that the individual earned as an indicator of adequacy. This tells us whether the individual will be able to maintain his or her previous standard of living. Replacement rates of 40 to 60 percent are often considered a target for mandatory pension systems. Gender ratios of replacement rates tell us whether women's relative position rises or falls during the retirement stage as compared with the working stage. It is commonly believed that women must have lower replacement rates than men because they have worked fewer years and have an earlier normal retirement age, hence the annuity must cover more years, implying smaller annual payouts. Actually, the situation is much more complicated, with alternative definitions yielding very different results, and under reasonable scenarios women have higher replacement rates than men.

A key factor in the definition is the choice of reference wage with which the pension is compared. As in the case of Chile, we start by using wage rates and earnings for workers at ages fifty-one to fifty-five, which was close to the peak period for men and women. We measure replacement rates as of age seventy, by which time women as well as men receive the flat benefit. Since the replacement rate implicitly normalizes the benefit by the reference wage, we expect it to be more similar for men and women than absolute benefits are, and indeed this is the case. Still, women's own annuities replace only a small percentage of their wage—14 to 24 percent, much lower than for men (table 5.8, rows 5 and 9). When the flat benefit is added, replacement rates jump ahead for both genders, especially for low earners. Women now replace more than one-third of their wages, men replace more than one-half of their wages, and gender ratios narrow (rows 6 and 10). But female/male ratios of replacement rates remain far less than 100 percent, indicating that women's relative position during the retirement stage is much worse than that during the working stage.

This situation changes completely, however, for full-career women, who work as much as men. Their replacement rates reach 50 to 80 percent, higher than those of men (table 5.8, rows 7 and 11; figure 5.3). As in the case of Chile, this outcome is a consequence of the later retirement age, hence larger annuity for full-career women, their qualification for the full flat benefit, and the fact that they have a flatter age-earnings profile than that of men.

Actually, very few women earn the wage rate that we are using as the reference wage. In any given period the average woman works less than half the time of that period, and therefore her annual earnings are only a fraction of the full-time wage rate. When thinking of pensions as a replacement of wage income, it would seem that the reasonable wage income to use is one that women actually earn, rather than a theoretical full-time rate. We therefore change our reference wage to reflect actual earnings by adjusting for proportion of time worked between ages fifty-one and fifty-five. We then find that the pension (annuity plus flat benefit) of the average woman with primary or secondary education replaces 72 to 97 percent of her earnings, much more than that of her counterpart male colleagues (table 5.8, rows 8 and 12). Women with higher education continue to have lower replacement rates than men, unless they postpone their retirement to age sixty-five, like men.

In summary, women get lower replacement rates from their own

Table 5.8: Simulated Replacement Rates at 70 in Argentina (pension/reference wage)

	Education				
	Incomplete Primary	Incomplete Secondary	Complete Secondary	Some Postsecondary	University Degree
Replacement rates for average married male, retirement age = 65 (%)					
1. Annuity only	44	47	36	42	46
2. Annuity + flat benefit	66	62	44	51	51
3. Annuity + flat benefit/adjusted reference wage	77	69	49	55	53
4. Annuity + flat benefit, low-density man	42	39	27	32	31
Replacement rates for married females (%)					
5. Annuity only	14	17	21	21	24
6. Annuity + flat benefit	38	37	33	29	29
7. Annuity + flat benefit, full-career woman	78	79	70	51	47
8. Annuity + flat benefit/adjusted reference wage	89	97	72	46	36
Female/male replacement rates (%)					
9. Annuity only	32	36	58	49	52
10. Annuity + flat benefit	57	59	76	57	57
11. Full-career woman, annuity + flat benefit	118	128	160	100	93
12. Annuity + flat benefit/adjusted reference wage	115	141	147	84	69
13. Annuity + flat benefit, low-density man and woman	76	76	91	66	62

Source: Calculations by the authors.

Note: Replacement rates are defined as pension/reference wage. Reference wage is defined as average wage at ages 51–55. Wage is from table 5.4, indexed up by 2% wage growth to get wage that young worker entering labor force today will receive when he or she is 51–55. Annuity is from table 5.6, and flat benefit is from table 5.7. Men are assumed to retire at 65. Replacement rates are given for "average women" who retire at 60, except for rows with full-career women who retire at 65. But replacement rates are measured as of age 70, when the reduced flat benefit begins. Low-density means worker contributes only 60% of time he or she works. This affects size of annuity and eligibility for full flat benefit. For rows 3, 8, and 12, with adjusted reference wage: wage rate from table 5.4 is adjusted by percentage of time individual worked at ages 51–55, to obtain a measure of actual earnings (monthly wage rate * % time worked).

annuities, but this is only the beginning of the story. The gender gap is narrowed substantially by the flat benefit, especially for low earners. In fact, when we use actual amount earned per year by the individual as the reference wage and include the public benefit as well as the private benefit, replacement rates for women with primary and secondary education exceed those of men. However, their lower retirement age continues to penalize women at the high end.

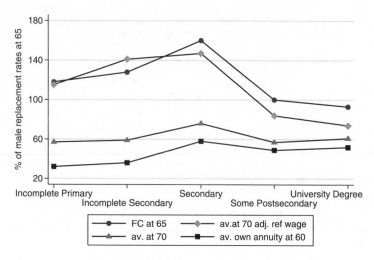

5.3. Female/male ratios of replacement rates, Argentina. Full-career women and average women with adjusted reference wage have higher replacement rates than men in Argentina.

Joint Annuities

The Impact of Joint Annuities on Men and Women

Married men are required to purchase joint annuities or joint programmed withdrawals when they retire—as in Chile, but with a more generous percentage of 70 percent to the surviving widow. In Argentina, as in Chile, insurance companies use gender-differentiated survival tables, although a law to require unisex tables has been under discussion since 2000. We estimate how much men's benefits are reduced and widows' benefits are increased by the joint annuity, and how this situation would change if unisex mortality tables were required. Table 5.9 reports these results for men retiring at age sixty-five and women retiring at sixty.

Male payouts fall by 21 percent when a joint annuity is purchased (row 3 versus row 1)—a larger drop than in Chile because of the larger survivor's percentage as well as the greater gender difference in life expectancy. Women are also required to purchase joint pensions, but when they do so their own annuities fall by only 5 percent because they are likely to outlive their husbands, hence the survivors' benefit costs women relatively little.

One of the controversial issues is whether to use unisex or gender-specific mortality tables when calculating annuity payouts. For single men and women purchasing individual annuities, gender-specific tables exacerbate

Table 5.9: The Impact of Joint Annuities and Unisex Tables in Argentina (in 2002 US$)[a]

	Education				
	Incomplete Primary	Incomplete Secondary	Complete Secondary	Some Postsecondary	University Degree
Males retiring at 65					
1. Individual, gender specific	$194	$296	$443	$459	$889
2. Individual, unisex	177	269	404	418	810
3. Joint, gender specific[b]	153	233	349	362	701
4. Joint, unisex	151	230	344	357	692
Females retiring at 60					
5. Individual, gender specific	$34	$48	$96	$134	$261
6. Individual, unisex	36	52	102	143	280
7. Joint, gender specific[b]	32	46	91	127	248
8. Joint, unisex	33	47	93	131	256
9. Widow's joint annuity	107	163	244	253	491
10. Total widow's pensions	247	317	443	488	869
11. Total widow's pensions as % of total husband's + wife's pensions[c]	78%	77%	78%	79%	79%

Source: Calculations by the authors.

[a] The flat benefit is not included in annuity calculations, rows 1–9. It is included in rows 10 and 11. Joint annuity assumes 70% to survivor. Based on 1996 data and assumptions of 5% return during accumulation stage, 3.5% during annuity stage, real wage growth = 2%.

[b] Corresponds to own pensions in table 5.6.

[c] Numerator includes (own annuity + flat benefit of wife) + widow's flat benefit (i.e., 70% of husband's flat benefit) + widow's joint annuity. Denominator includes (own annuity + flat benefit) of husband + (own annuity + flat benefit) of wife while husband was alive. (Wife's flat benefit begins at age 70, except for those in top education category, where women receive full flat benefit at 60).

the differences stemming from differential accumulations and produce much larger annuities for men. When unisex mortality tables are applied, this disparity is narrowed: the payout falls by 9 percent on individual male annuities and rises by 7 percent on individual female annuities (table 5.9, row 2 vs. row 1 and row 6 vs. row 5). But as in Chile, the switch to unisex tables produces practically no impact on payouts from joint annuities (row 3 vs. row 4 and row 7 vs. row 8): payouts fall by only 1 percent for men and rise by 3 percent for women (see figure 4.4). The controversial unisex issue largely disappears for countries that mandate joint annuities.

Women receive the joint annuity after their husband's death. On a monthly basis, it is greater than their own annuity plus their flat benefit plus the widow's flat benefit; that is, it outweighs all other pension sources for most schooling groups. It also provides an income for widows who have not worked in the market and therefore have little or no pension of their own. It is a partial response to the problem of women with low contributory histories—and it does not cost the public treasury any money. But there is no provision for divorced women. Although lawyers may negotiate some benefits for them, divorced women have no property rights in their husband's accumulation and do not get the joint annuity upon which they may have been counting.

For women who remain married, the combined household income after the husband's death is 78 percent of the previous income, which allows widows to raise their standard of living, given the usual assumptions about scale economies (table 5.9, row 11). Is this the best allocation of these public and private resources? The money spent on the widow's flat benefit, for example, could alternatively be spent on benefits while both spouses were alive, redistributed across income classes, or used to reduce the required contribution rate. This is an example of the difficult decisions about priorities that need to be made.

Lifetime Benefits and Imputed Taxes

In Argentina women can retire and start collecting their own annuities at sixty, and highly educated women who have worked and contributed for thirty years also start receiving the full flat benefit at that age. Women with ten to thirty years of contributions are not eligible for the full flat benefit but are eligible for the reduced flat benefit beginning at age seventy. Men retire with the full flat benefit at sixty-five. Their widows start the joint annuity and the widow's flat benefit sixteen years later, on average. To compare benefits in light of all these differences in starting and ending ages, it is necessary to shift to a lifetime basis. Lifetime analyses are more favorable toward women than are monthly analyses because women live longer, retire earlier, and therefore collect the benefits for more years. We examine lifetime benefits and also lifetime costs to see who is receiving redistributions and who is paying, on balance.

Gross Benefits

Table 5.10 presents the expected present value (EPV) of the lifetime personal annuity, flat benefit, joint annuity, and widow's flat benefit—whose monthly values were reported in previous tables—as evaluated by the worker at age sixty-five. We use the same 3.5 percent rate to discount the stream of retirement benefits that we used for the annuity calculation during the payout stage.

For men, the lifetime present value of the flat benefit is smaller than the value of the annuity, but it is still substantial, and relatively large for

Table 5.10: EPV of Gross Lifetime Benefits from Personal Annuities, Joint Annuities, and Public Benefits in Argentina[a] (1996 data in 2002 US$000)

	Education				
	Incomplete Primary	Incomplete Secondary	Complete Secondary	Some Postsecondary	University Degree
Average married man					
1. Individual annuity	$27.7	$42.2	$63.2	$65.5	$126.9
2. Flat benefit	11.0	11.0	11.0	11.0	11.0
3. Widow's flat benefit	0.6	0.6	0.6	0.6	0.6
4. Joint paid for wife	−5.8	−8.9	−13.3	−13.8	−26.7
5. Joint annuity received	0.4	0.5	1.0	1.4	2.8
6. Total, married man	$33.8	$45.4	$62.5	$64.8	$114.6
7. *% increase from flat benefit*	*40*	*26*	*17*	*17*	*9*
8. *% decrease from joint paid*	*−21*	*−21*	*−21*	*−21*	*−21*
Low-density man					
9. Individual annuity	16.6	25.3	37.9	39.3	76.1
10. Reduced flat benefit	4.7	4.7	4.7	4.7	4.7
11. Joint paid for wife	−3.5	−5.3	−8.0	−8.3	−16.0
12. Total, married man[b]	18.8	25.8	36.2	37.7	68.2
13. *% increase from flat benefit*	*25*	*19*	*13*	*13*	*7*
Average married woman					
14. Own annuity	$7.7	$11.0	$21.9	$30.5	$59.7
15. Flat benefit	6.1	6.1	6.1	6.1	17.6
16. Widow's flat benefit	3.3	3.3	3.3	3.3	3.3
17. Joint paid for husband	−0.4	−0.6	−1.1	−1.6	−3.1
18. Joint annuity received	6.5	9.9	14.8	15.3	29.6
19. Total, average married woman	$23.1	$29.7	$44.8	$53.6	$107.1
20. *% increase from flat benefit*	*79*	*55*	*28*	*20*	*29*
21. *% increase from widow's flat benefit*	*42*	*29*	*15*	*11*	*5*
22. *% increase from joint received*	*84*	*89*	*68*	*50*	*50*
23. *% decrease from joint paid*	*−5*	*−5*	*−5*	*−5*	*−5*
Full-career married woman					
24. Own annuity	$18.2	$25.1	$40.9	$42.8	$74.4
25. Joint paid for husband	−1.1	−1.5	−2.5	−2.6	−4.6
26. Flat benefit	13.0	13.0	13.0	13.0	13.0
27. Total, full-career married woman	$39.8	$49.7	$69.4	$71.7	$115.7
28. *% increase from flat benefit*	*71*	*52*	*32*	*30*	*17*
29. *% increase from widow's flat benefit*	*18*	*13*	*8*	*8*	*4*
30. *% increase from joint received*	*36*	*39*	*36*	*36*	*40*

(continued)

Table 5.10: *continued*

	Education				
	Incomplete Primary	Incomplete Secondary	Complete Secondary	Some Postsecondary	University Degree
Ten-year married woman					
31. Own annuity	$5.3	$8.0	$10.2	$12.5	$21.0
32. Joint paid for husband	–0.3	–0.4	–0.5	–0.7	–1.1
33. Flat benefit	6.1	6.1	6.1	6.1	6.1
34. Total, ten-year married woman	$20.9	$26.7	$33.8	$36.5	$58.9
35. *% increase from flat benefit*	*120*	*81*	*63*	*51*	*31*
36. *% increase from widow's flat benefit*	*64*	*43*	*34*	*28*	*16*
37. *% increase from joint annuity*	*128*	*131*	*153*	*130*	*149*
Married women/married men (%)					
38. Average woman/married man	68	65	72	83	93
39. Full-career woman/married man	118	109	111	111	101
40. Ten-year woman/married man	62	59	54	56	51

Source: Calculations by the authors. See notes to table 4.11.

[a] EPV is given for men and women at age 65. 3.5% rate is used to discount or compound all benefits to age 65. Husbands and wives are assumed to belong to the same education group. Absolute amount of joint annuity benefit and widow's flat benefit are same for average, full-career, and ten-year woman. Joint benefit for husband assumes he is married to average woman. Percentage increase is based on individual annuity without flat benefit, in denominator. Return during accumulation is 5%, 3.5% during annuity stage, real wage growth = 2%.

[b] Includes joint annuity received and widow's flat benefit, which is the same as for the average man.

low earners (table 5.10, row 1 vs. row 2, also row 7). It is smaller for low-density men, who only qualify for the reduced flat benefit that starts at age seventy (rows 9, 10, and 13). This contrasts with Chile, where the average man is above the MPG level and therefore gets no public benefit, while some low-density men do get it (if the MPG is waged-indexed). Unlike Chilean men, Argentine men get a widow's benefit (70 percent of their wife's joint annuity and 70 percent of her flat benefit), but their expected present values are tiny, given their small amounts multiplied by the small probability that men will outlive their wives. The opportunity cost of the joint annuities that married men must purchase is much greater than the widows' benefits they receive—a 21 percent reduction in payouts from the individual annuity. Although the proportionate reduction is the same for all schooling groups, this reduction produces a greater absolute cost for highly educated men, whose widows in turn receive a higher benefit (table 5.10, rows 4 and 8).

This represents a larger cost than in Chile because of the higher survivors' benefit rate and greater female longevity advantage in Argentina. As in the case of Chile, for some households this mandatory insurance simply replaces life insurance that the husband would have provided for his wife on a voluntary basis. But for husbands who would have acquired less insurance voluntarily, the joint annuity requirement represents a real cost of forgone income.

Turning to the average woman, the lifetime value of her own annuity is larger than her fund accumulation at retirement age of sixty, because we are now viewing the present value of benefits from the vantage point of age sixty-five. The lifetime value of the public benefit is smaller than that of men in absolute terms but is much larger for women relative to their own annuities. Women in the top education category, of course, get a larger lifetime personal annuity, and they also get a larger lifetime flat benefit than women with less education, because they work more, contribute more, and are eligible for the full flat benefit starting at age sixty (table 5.10, rows 14 and 15). This scenario is once again a sharp contrast to the benefit structure in Chile, where women in the top education categories get no public benefit. But the reduced flat benefit that less educated women get at age seventy represents a much larger proportional lifetime increment to their own annuities (table 5.10, row 20; see also figure 4.5).

The lifetime value of the joint annuity, in turn, exceeds the flat benefit, even though it starts much later, for most education and labor force attachment groups (table 5.10, rows 15, 26, and 33 vs. 18; see also figure 4.6). The joint annuity plays an even larger role than it did in Chile, because it is a larger percentage of the husband's pension and the widow gets it for more years, on average.

Taking all transfer payments as a group—the flat benefit, widow's flat benefit, and joint annuity—they roughly double the total retirement income of women in the top education groups and treble retirement income in the bottom groups. For full-career women the percentage increase is somewhat smaller, and for ten-year women it is larger. The lifetime retirement income of average women is two-thirds that of men, and for full-career women it exceeds that of men (figure 5.4). The joint annuity plays a major role in raising and equalizing the benefits of elderly women.

Imputed Net Benefits and Money's Worth Ratios

The expected present value of the personal annuity is exactly equal to its cost—the accumulation in the accounts. In that sense, there is no net benefit

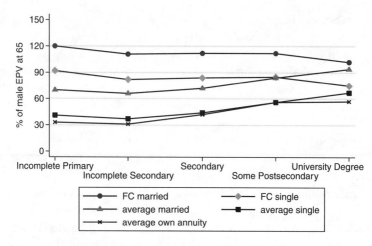

5.4. Female/male ratios of EPV of lifetime benefits, Argentina. EPV of full-career married women exceeds that of men in Argentina.

or redistribution to the individual from the defined contribution plan, except for the joint pension requirement, which generates an intrafamily transfer from husbands to their wives.

The flat benefit and widow's flat benefit, however, are financed out of the government's general budget, so benefits may diverge from costs for each family or subgroup. To measure the implied redistributions, we need to estimate the total tax bill and its allocation among subgroups. As in the case of Chile, we assume that each cohort pays its own full cost, and within each cohort taxes are distributed proportional to lifetime earnings (see appendix 3). Also, as for Chile, we use three measures of redistribution: (1) net public benefit (= gross public benefit – imputed taxes used to finance it); (2) money's worth ratio from the public benefit (MWR_{pub} = (EPV of flat + widow's flat benefits)/EPV of imputed tax cost); and (3) money's worth ratio from the public plus private benefits ($\text{MWR}_{\text{pub+pvt}}$ = (EPV of flat + widow's flat + own annuity)/(EPV of imputed tax cost + contributions)). For women we use a fourth measure, $\text{MWR}_{\text{pub+pvt+jt}}$, which adds the joint annuity into the numerator.

Unlike Chile, all subgroups receive a substantial public benefit in Argentina (table 5.11). This, of course, costs much more than Chile's MPG—our imputed tax rate for Argentina is almost 6 percent of wages, compared with 1 percent in Chile. Given this high tax cost, net public benefits turn out to be very negative for most men (except for those in the bottom schooling groups), while they are strongly positive for most women (except for full-career women at the top end). Similarly, MWR_{pub} is far less than 100 percent

Table 5.11: Expected Lifetime Public Benefits, Imputed Tax Cost, and Imputed Public and Private MWR in Argentina (US$000 and %)

	Education				
	Incomplete Primary	Incomplete Secondary	Complete Secondary	Some Postsecondary	University Degree
Average man					
1. Flat + widow's flat benefit	11.6	11.6	11.6	11.6	11.6
2. Imputed tax cost	6.7	10.3	15.7	16.7	33.1
3. Net public benefit	4.9	1.3	−4.1	−5.1	−21.5
4. MWR_{pub}	173%	113%	74%	70%	35%
5. $MWR_{pub+pvt}$, married man	97%	86%	78%	77%	70%
6. $MWR_{pub+pvt}$, single man	114%	103%	95%	94%	87%
Low-density man					
7. Flat + widow's flat	5.3	5.3	5.3	5.3	5.3
8. Imputed tax cost	4.0	6.2	9.4	10.0	19.8
9. Net public benefit	1.3	−0.9	−4.1	−4.7	−14.5
10. MWR_{pub}	132%	86%	56%	53%	27%
11. $MWR_{pub+pvt}$, married man	89%	80%	74%	74%	68%
Average woman					
12. Flat + widow's flat	9.4	9.4	9.4	9.4	20.9
13. Imputed tax cost	1.9	2.6	5.1	7.6	14.9
14. Net public benefit	7.5	6.8	4.3	1.8	6.0
15. MWR_{pub}	484%	358%	184%	123%	140%
16. $MWR_{pub+pvt}$	173%	145%	112%	100%	104%
17. $MWR_{pub+pvt+jt}$	240%	218%	166%	141%	144%
Full-career woman					
18. Flat + widow's flat	16.3	16.3	16.3	16.3	16.3
19. Imputed tax cost	4.3	5.8	10.0	10.8	18.6
20. Net public benefit	12.0	10.5	6.3	5.5	−2.3
21. MWR_{pub}	378%	280%	163%	151%	87%
22. $MWR_{pub+pvt}$	148%	129%	107%	105%	93%
23. $MWR_{pub+pvt+jt}$	177%	161%	136%	134%	124%
Ten-year woman					
24. Flat + widow's flat benefit	9.4	9.4	9.4	9.4	9.4
25. Imputed tax cost	0.6	0.9	1.2	1.5	2.5
26. Net public benefit	8.8	8.5	8.2	7.9	6.9
27. MWR_{pub}	1501%	997%	769%	631%	373%
28. $MWR_{pub+pvt}$	243%	190%	167%	152%	125%
29. $MWR_{pub+pvt+jt}$	353%	299%	296%	261%	250%
Female/married male ratios for $MWR_{pub+pvt}$					
30. Average woman	178%	170%	143%	130%	149%
31. Full-career woman	152%	151%	138%	137%	132%
32. Ten-year woman	249%	222%	214%	197%	178%

Source: Calculations by the authors based on data in table 5.10 and assumptions described in text and appendix 3. Imputed MWR_{pub} = (flat + widow's flat)/imputed tax cost. Imputed $MWR_{pub+pvt}$ = (annuity + flat + widow's flat)/(imputed tax cost + contribution). All values are lifetime values discounted to age 65. Imputed tax rate = 5.9%. Imputed $MWR_{pub+pvt+jt}$ adds joint annuity received to numerator.

for most men (except those in the lowest education categories), while it is much greater than 100 percent (sometimes even greater than 200 percent) for most women (rows 3, 4, 9, 10, 14, 15, 20, 21, 26, and 27).

This remains true for $\text{MWR}_{\text{pub+pvt}}$; women's MWRs are 50 to 100 percent greater than those of men—in part because married men get a smaller personal pension because they must pay for the joint pension (rows 5, 11, 16, 22, 28, 30, 31, and 32). Gender differentials widen still further in favor of married women if we add the joint pension they receive (rows 17, 23, and 29). The clear implication is that the flat and widow's flat benefits redistribute very broadly from men to women, especially low-earning women, and the joint pension requirement redistributes from husbands to wives.

Perhaps most interesting is the large net benefit and high money's worth ratio that goes to women who work only ten years. This contrasts with Chile, where this group is not eligible for the MPG. In Argentina they receive the same flat and widow's flat benefits as average women, but their earnings and taxes paid are smaller, because they work less. As a result, they get, by far, the highest money's worth ratios of all our subgroups (figure 5.5). Their limited labor market attachment is rewarded. Ironically, women who work slightly less than ten years get no public benefit.

Should eligibility requirements be tightened to economize on costs or eased to expand coverage? Both these measures are problematic. On the one hand, without access to some public benefit, many women would find themselves in dire financial straits when they grow very old. This would hold

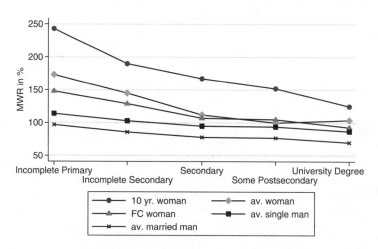

5.5. Money's worth ratios, public plus private benefits, Argentina [MWR calculated as (public + private benefit)/(tax + contribution)]. Ten-year woman gets highest money's worth ratio in Argentina.

particularly for those who are divorced or whose husbands are not covered by the system and do not have other savings. On the other hand, many ten-year women come from middle- or upper-class households and are living far from the poverty line. The rationale for giving them a large subsidy is not clear. Besides the equity considerations, this pattern of redistributions and the high tax rate it requires may discourage work and keep women dependent on transfers.

Marginal Money's Worth Ratios and Work (Dis)Incentives

To investigate the behavioral incentives that may be created by these returns, we calculate the marginal net benefits and marginal MWRs that several types of individuals face when thinking of changing their labor market attachment: (1) ten-year women who are considering taking on average work amounts (about twenty years), (2) average women who are considering working full career, and (3) low-density men who are considering more regular work and contributions. Marginal net public benefits are their increased flat benefits, if any, minus their increased tax cost. Marginal MWRs are their increased flat benefits plus annuity payments divided by their increased tax cost plus contributions for their incremental work.

In table 5.12 we see that these incentives are exactly the mirror image of those in Chile. Women in all education categories get a negative marginal net benefit and a marginal MWR of only 60 to 70 percent if they move from

Table 5.12: Marginal Net Benefits and MWR for Incremental Work in Argentina (in US$000 and %)

	Education				
	Incomplete Primary	Incomplete Secondary	Complete Secondary	Some Postsecondary	University Degree +
Marginal net public benefit for incremental work (in 2002 US$000)					
1. Ten-year to average woman	−1.3	−1.7	−3.9	−6.1	−0.9
2. Average to full-career woman	4.5	3.7	2.0	3.7	−8.4
3. Low-density to average married man	3.6	2.2	0.0	−0.4	−6.9
Marginal MWR$_{pub+pvt}$ for incremental work (%)					
4. Ten-year to average woman	62	60	71	71	94
5. Average to full-career woman	130	116	103	118	47
6. Low-density to average married man	109	93	83	82	72

Note: Marginal net public benefit from level i to j = (flat$_j$ − flat$_i$) − (T$_j$ − T$_i$).

Marginal MWR from level i to j = ((flat$_j$ − flat$_i$) + (annuity$_j$ − annuity$_i$))/((T$_j$ − T$_i$) + (contrib$_j$ − contrib$_i$)).

ten-year to average status because, in most cases, they get no additional flat benefit but must pay additional taxes for their incremental wages (rows 1 and 4). Thus, unlike in Chile, ten-year women in Argentina face a strong incentive to remain at the ten-year point (see figure 4.9).

However, women who start out working an average amount face a strong incentive to move toward full-career status—again in contrast to Chile. In most cases their marginal net public benefit from incremental work is positive because it enables them to qualify for the full flat benefit rather than the reduced flat benefit. This extra benefit exceeds their extra tax cost so their marginal MWR is 103 to 130 percent—a high return (table 5.12, rows 2 and 5; see also figure 4.10).

The one exception is for women with university education (last column in table 5.12). Their marginal net benefit from switching from average to full-career work behavior is negative, and their marginal MWR is only 47 percent—they get back, in retirement income, barely half of their extra cost (rows 2 and 5). This is because they work enough as average women to qualify for the full flat benefit. Switching to full-career status means postponing their pension to age sixty-five, paying additional taxes, but getting no incremental flat benefits. This discourages them from working full career, despite the loss of wage and annuity income for them and productive capacity for the economy. In contrast, highly educated women in Chile face more positive work incentives because of Chile's lower tax rate and greater emphasis on the personal annuity.[8] Argentina needs to determine whether this is its desired pattern of redistribution and incentives and whether it has the capacity to collect the taxes needed to finance it.

Who Gained (or Lost) the Most from the Reform?

Did women benefit or lose from the pension reform? Since on a priori grounds we could argue in both directions, we use empirical evidence and simulations to investigate this question. We apply the lifetime benefits estimated above for the new system, compare them with simulated lifetime benefits based on the old system formula, and ask the following questions: (1) Did gender ratios get larger or smaller in the process of the reform? (2) Who gained or lost the most from the reform?

Methodological Problems

As discussed above, the old system was nonsustainable and unable to provide the promised benefits. In fact, the Argentine government was already defaulting on its payments to pensioners, one of the factors that discredited the old system and built political support for change. We do not know how solvency would have been achieved if the old structure had been maintained. For that reason, we do not compare absolute benefits under the new and old systems, but instead we compare relative positions of various gender-education groups ex ante and ex post. Implicitly, we are assuming that fiscal adjustments to the old system to keep it afloat would have maintained relative positions intact, and we are using this as our counterfactual.

Additionally, in Argentina it is difficult to define the old system because several different subsystems coexisted, fragmented along occupational and industrial lines; the rules as written down sometimes differed from the rules as implemented, and interpretations changed frequently (cuts due to fiscal exigencies, increases due to political pressures and lawsuits). The new system is also in flux, as we indicate above. Therefore, it is impossible to make actual pre- and postreform comparisons in Argentina.

Instead, in tables 5.13 and 5.14 we present a stylized picture of an Argentine-type system pre- and postreform that captures the most important design features we wish to explore: (1) in the old system women had to give up their own pension to get the widow's pension;[9] (2) in the new system they get both their own annuity and the joint annuity; (3) in the new system they also get the full flat benefit with thirty years of contributions or the reduced flat benefit with ten years of contributions; and (4) in the old system they got a minimum pension, backing up the earnings-related defined benefit.

How Gender Ratios Changed due to the Reform

In table 5.13 we present gender ratios in the new and old systems to see how they changed under the reform. If ratios were 100 percent in the top panel of table 5.13, the lifetime benefits promised to men and women were equal in the old system; the bottom panel shows the same relationship for the new system. When we compare gender ratios for single women with average work histories before and after the reform, we find they have risen—substantially for low earners, marginally for high earners (row 1 vs. rows 6 and 7). Even more striking, for married women, gender ratios in the new system jump way ahead in all education and labor force attachment groups, more uniformly and broadly than in Chile, because of the widow's flat benefit and generous joint annuity provisions (rows 2 and 4 vs. row 8 and 10). For full-career married women, lifetime retirement income exceeds that of men in the new system, but not in the old system (row 10 vs. row 4). But the biggest

Table 5.13: Simulated Female/Male Ratios of EPV of Lifetime Benefits in New versus Old Systems in Argentina (%)

	Education				
	Incomplete Primary	Incomplete Secondary	Complete Secondary	Some Postsecondary	University Degree
Old system					
1. Average single woman	21	13	33	55	60
2. Average married woman	40	30	47	64	68
3. Full-career single woman	76	50	48	68	62
4. Full-career married woman	80	57	55	69	65
5. Ten-year married woman	40	30	27	31	30
New system (average woman/average man)					
6. Single woman, own annuity	33	31	42	56	57
7. Single, own annuity + flat benefit	41	37	44	56	67
8. Married	68	65	72	83	93
New system (full-career woman/average man)					
9. Single, own annuity + flat benefit	92	82	84	85	75
10. Married	118	109	111	111	101
New system (ten-year woman/average man)					
11. Married	62	59	54	56	51

Source: Calculations by the authors.

Note: Denominator is married man with or without flat benefit, as indicated. In old system single and married men got same pension. In new system married men get smaller pension than single men because married men must purchase joint pension. Present values are measured at age 65 for both genders, compounded up to 65 for widows' benefits that potentially start for women at 62. Single woman is assumed to have same work and wage history as married woman but does not get survivors' benefit in old system, joint annuity or widow's flat benefit in new system. She also does not have to pay for joint annuity for her husband.

improvement is experienced by ten-year married women, whose gender ratios almost doubled (row 11 vs. row 5).

Ratios of Postreform to Prereform Lifetime Benefits, Normalized

To pin down the impact of the reform on various subgroups more precisely, table 5.14 compares the female/male ratios of expected present value postreform to expected present value prereform for each of the subgroups considered. As in the case of Chile, we normalize according to the ratio for married men in the top education group. Thus a value greater than 100 percent indicates that the relevant subgroup has gained proportionately more than highly educated married men, while a value less than 100 percent indicates

Table 5.14: Simulated Ratios of EPVs of Postreform/Prereform Lifetime Benefits (relative to ratio for married men in top education group) in Argentina (%)[a]

	Education				
	Incomplete Primary	Incomplete Secondary	Complete Secondary	Some Postsecondary	University Degree +
	Average man				
1. Married	188	130	94	111	100
2. Single	219	154	112	132	121
	Woman				
3. Average single	373	366	128	114	112
4. Average married	325	281	144	143	137
5. Full-career single	228	216	167	140	123
6. Full-career married	278	251	188	178	155
7. Ten-year married	294	252	186	204	173
8. Men + women: average household	227	167	110	123	115

Source: Calculations by the authors.

[a] r = 5% during accumulation, 3.5% during annuity stage, real wage growth = 2%.

Includes lifetime benefits from own annuity and own flat benefit. Also includes survivors' benefits in old system, joint annuity and widow's flat in new system, for married individuals. Each cell i shows $(PVnew/PVold)_i/(PVnew/PVold)_k$, where $(PVnew/PVold)_i$ = ratio of present value of lifetime benefits in new vs. old systems for group i. This is normalized by the ratio for reference group k, where k = married men in highest education category. If the number in a cell > 100%, it gained more than top married men.

that the subgroup has lost in relative position. This normalization allows us to compare relative gains or losses from the new system for different groups without fixing their absolute gains or losses (see table 5.14 and chapter 4 for the formal definition of this normalized ratio).

The first thing we notice is that virtually all subgroups improved their position relative to high-income men, that is, practically no ratios are less than 100 percent. Second, for every education category, women gained more than men. Third, for both genders, those with the least education (lowest earnings) gained the most (figure 5.6). This is due to the influence of the flat benefit, as well as the shift to an investment-based system in which workers with flat age-earnings profiles are not penalized. We found this picture in Chile, too. However, in Argentina relative gains by the bottom education groups are larger and broader, because the flat benefit is so much larger and reaches far more workers than Chile's MPG. Notably, ten-year women and average women improved their positions relative to full-career women, a sharp contrast to Chile and Mexico, where full-career women were the biggest gainers. This is due to the smaller individual account and flat benefit

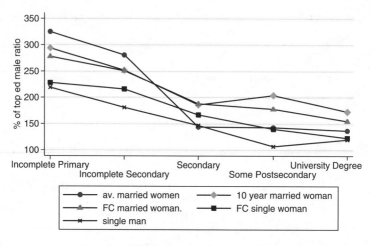

5.6. Postreform/prereform ratios of EPV by group, Argentina (normalized by postreform/prereform EPV ratio of top education man). All groups gained relative to top-earning men, but low-earning and ten-year married women gained most of all in Argentina.

that is not linked to work in Argentina. Finally, as in Chile and Mexico, single men gained more than married men due to the financing rules for the joint annuity.

The Main Message from Argentina

Despite many features in the old system that seemed to favor women—a high replacement rate for only ten years of work and early retirement age without an actuarial penalty, for example—women have gained relative to men due to the reform. This stems mainly from the equalizing impact of the generous flat benefit and widow's flat benefit, the intrahousehold transfer from the joint annuity, and the fact that women do not have to give up their own benefit to receive the annuity. Also playing a role is the heavier weight placed on early contributions due to compound interest in the new system and the removal of advantages for men for their steeply rising wage profiles in the old system.

The Argentine case, in which ten-year women are heavily subsidized, forces us to confront difficult policy issues about priorities. How closely connected should the public benefit be to contributions? What kinds of work incentives should they embody? Should public benefits be available equally to all and be financed out of general revenues? Should they be targeted toward retirees with low pensions because they have not worked, or to those who have worked but earned low rates of pay and contributions? Should family income and other sources of individual income be taken into account in targeting redistributions (as many women who chose not to work in the market did so because other family members supplied financial support)? If low density of contributions, which implies low capacity to collect taxes, is a root problem that leads to noncontributory benefits, how will the government get the money to pay these benefits in addition to financing other public services? Or will its efforts to collect higher taxes simply exacerbate the incentive to evade? How should the government treat women, who may have low contribution histories not because of an intention to evade but rather because they have preferred to take on household responsibilities? The Argentine government is now grappling with these policy questions, and we return to them in chapter 8.

CHAPTER SIX

Mexico

Mexico, like Chile and Argentina, decided to reform its pension system as part of a broader set of market-oriented reforms designed to spur economic growth. In 1997 Mexico replaced its old, traditional, pay-as-you-go defined benefit system with a multipillar system that included a funded defined contribution component. Mexico's population is younger than those in Chile and Argentina, so the contribution rate in the old system was still very low, the benefit rate high, and fiscal pressures less pressing. However, projections showed that the contribution rate would have to be raised and benefits cut substantially in the medium term. Structural change was seen as the best way to plan for future demographic changes and prevent a mounting fiscal obligation (Cruz-Saco and Mesa-Lago 1998).

Although less than half of all workers contribute to, and an even smaller proportion of older people get, benefits from the formal system in Mexico, for these individuals the social security benefit is the mainstay of income in old age. Moreover, given the strength of the family system in Mexico, the pension given to an old person reaches many other family members as well. Among those households where a pension is received, it often constitutes half of the total household income, and this segment includes many multi-generational extended families (Parker and Wong 2001; Gómez de León and Parker 1998). In such cases, it may facilitate school attendance for children and help buffer periods of unemployment for prime-age adults. Additionally, affiliation with the social security system brings with it health care coverage, including coverage for spouses and parents.

The probability of affiliation is twice as high for men as for women (AIOS 2005). Among people receiving pensions, three-quarters of the men receive their own pension, while more than two-thirds of the women receive pensions by virtue of being widows or surviving parents (see table 2.2). Thus, these formal social security arrangements ultimately reach more than half of the Mexican population, but they reach men and women in different ways. When the structure of the system is changed, it is important to figure out how the costs and benefits are distributed and how the new system may affect the behavior of workers and their family members, including their incentive to participate in formal market work.

The Old and New Systems and Our Data for Comparing Them

The Old System

The main social security institutions in Mexico are the Mexican Institute of Social Security (IMSS), for private-sector workers, and its counterpart, the Institute for Social Security and Services of the State Workers (ISSSTE), for public-sector workers. Affiliation in IMSS is mandatory for all salaried employees, although a large noncovered informal sector exists. We focus on the scheme for private-sector workers, which was the first to reform.

Prior to 1997, IMSS provided a defined benefit pension plan with a complex formula that was designed to protect short-term and low-earning workers in addition to higher-income, long-term workers. Eligibility for benefits required ten years of contributions, as in Chile and Argentina. The formula paid a proportion of the base salary for the first ten years plus an increment for every year over ten. The proportion of the base paid out varied negatively with wages, ranging from 13 percent for high earners to 80 percent for low earners. The accrual rate for additional years varied positively with wages, ranging from .56 percent to 2.45 percent per year. Moreover, the monthly pension was paid for thirteen months instead of twelve. Thus, a low earner would get 88 percent of his base salary after contributing for only ten years and relatively little for additional years thereafter. In contrast, a high earner got only 14 percent of base for ten years but almost 70 percent after working for thirty years. Given this formula, low earners had a high incentive to work in the formal sector for ten years, just long enough to qualify for benefits, and then move to the informal sector to avoid contributing.

Besides benefiting from a high replacement rate, low earners were also protected by a minimum pension that equaled the minimum wage, neither of which was automatically indexed to the price level. The value of this protection therefore varied widely depending on the rate of inflation and the lag before the minimum pension caught up with rising prices. In 1997 it was about 40 percent of the average wage.

The base salary was the average of earnings during the last 250 working weeks. High earners benefited from this base because they were likely to have steep age-earnings profiles and therefore got a large pension relative to their lifetime wages and contributions, while the opposite was true for low earners. Neither the base salary nor the pension was adjusted for inflation, a major problem in Mexico's inflationary environment. Women were especially disadvantaged by the failure to revalue the wage base and the requirement that it should depend on earnings during the five years immediately prior to retirement, because their work may have been done much earlier.[1] But women received the advantage of a very generous survivors' benefit— widows got 90 percent of their husband's pension in addition to their own pension. Unlike in Chile and Argentina, retirement age was sixty-five for both genders in Mexico.

These benefits were financed by an 8.5 percent contribution rate—lower than in Chile or Argentina, given the young population and the small number of retirees. To prepare for projected increases in pensioners and costs, a 2 percent contribution to a mandatory saving plan, the Sistema de Ahorro para el Retiro (SAR) was instituted in 1992. However, SAR was never effectively implemented. [For further details, see tables 6.1 and 6.2. On problems of the old system, see Grandolini and Cerda (1998)].

The New System

Mexico's new system, like Chile's and Argentina's, includes a privately managed pillar (an expanded and modified version of SAR) and a public safety net. The private pillar, like that in Chile and Argentina, is a defined contribution mandatory saving plan. The public benefit, like Chile's and Argentina's, is targeted toward low earners but, unlike those in the other countries, is structured to reward formal-sector work and therefore provide work incentives to this group. This structure has major implications for women—it encourages them to enter the formal labor market, thereby becoming more financially independent, but it provides little protection for those who do not work regularly. Thus, Mexico's public benefit presents a sharp contrast to that in Argentina and brings to the fore the question, how should policy ensure a reasonable standard of living for today's older women who have not fully participated in the labor market, while also encouraging today's young women to work and save for their own old age?

Under the new system rules, 6.5 percent of the workers' wage is deposited into his or her personal account (5.15 percent paid by the employer, 1.125 percent by the worker, and .225 percent by the state). Workers have a choice among investment managers, or retirement funds administrators (AFORES),

Table 6.1: Main Features of Old and New Systems in Mexico

	Old System	New System
Structure	Pay-as-You-Go Defined Benefit	Private pillar: Funded individual accounts Public pillar: SQ + MPG
Contribution Rate	8.5% (incl. .425% from government) + 2% (SAR, since 1992)	6.5% (including .225% from government) + 5.5% of minimum wage from government (SQ); SQ + MPG financed from general revenues[a]
Benefits	Defined benefit: 80–100% of base salary (formula in table 6.2)	Private pillar: pension from account Public pillar: pension from SQ; also MPG
Base Salary	Average of last 250 working weeks	Not relevant
Pensionable Age	65	65 for men and women
Years for Eligibility	500 weeks	24 years for MPG; no minimum for pension from account
Pension if Worked Fewer Years	0	Pension from account
Indexation Provisions	No automatic indexation	Annuity, SQ, and MPG are price indexed[b]
Minimum Pension	1 minimum wage after 10 years of contributions[b]	1 minimum wage after 24 years of contributions[b]
Widows	90% of husband's pension + own pension	60% of husband's pension (joint annuity) + own annuity

Note: SQ = social quota; MPG = minimum pension guarantee; SAR = Sistema de Ahorro para el Retiro.

[a] The social quota started at 2.2% of the average wage. It is indexed to prices so will fall as % of average wage as productivity grows. Contribution rate given includes an administrative charge that was about 1.9% of wage initially and now is 1.5% of wage. Separately, about 2.5% of payroll is charged for disability and survivors' insurance.

[b] Under the old system the minimum pension = minimum wage. Linkage of minimum wage to price or wage growth was ad hoc. Under new system, SQ and MPG are formally linked to consumer price index. Mexico also plans for private annuity to be price indexed, but feasibility and cost remain to be determined.

with whom they place their accounts. As in Chile and Argentina, investment options are severely restricted to limit risk and disparities among workers. Workers—both men and women—can retire at age sixty-five, at which point they choose between a gradual withdrawal and an annuity. In this analysis, for expositional simplification, we assume retirees choose annuitization and

Table 6.2: Old System Formula in Mexico

The annual retirement pension is based on:
a. base amount given by a percentage of the income earned during the last 5 years of contribution,
b. an increase for each additional year contributed, and
c. the number of years of contribution in excess of the minimum 10-year requirement.

The value of the annual pension is calculated according to the following expression:

Annual pension = $S * [(Base\%) + (Y) * (AI)]$

where
S = base salary used for the last 5 years of contribution
$Base\%$ = percentage of base salary in base amount
Y = additional years contributed beyond 10 years
AI = annual increment as % of S, for each additional year beyond 10 years.

In addition, the IMSS provides retirees with a yearly bonus equivalent to one month of the pension payment they were receiving. Thus the total annual amount received would be 13/12 of the value obtained by the above expression.

$Base\%$ and AI are rates determined in a table (IMSS 1993), which vary according to the amount S expressed in number of minimum wages. The $Base\%$ is inversely related to S and ranges from 80% to 13%. The annual increment, AI, is directly related to S and ranges from 0.563% to 2.45%.

Below we provide an example of the calculation for levels S of 1 and 6 minimum wages, assuming a total of 30 years of contribution to IMSS.

S	Base%	AI	Y	Estimated annual pension
1 minimum wage	80%	0.56%	20	13/12 * S * (91%) = 99% * S
6 minimum wages	13%	2.45%	20	13/12 * S * (62%) = 67% * S

Thus, replacement rates of base salary range between 67% and 99% for high- and low-wage workers, respectively, who have worked for 30 years. For 10 years of work these replacement rates would be 14% and 87%, respectively.

get back their entire accumulation, plus the risk-free interest rate, over their expected lifetimes. Workers are allowed to take 10 percent out of their accounts every five years if unemployed. Thus, the accounts serve the dual purpose of unemployment insurance and retirement pensions. Survivors' and disability insurance are also provided out of a separate contribution. We focus on the old age insurance in this chapter, and we assume that nothing has been taken out for unemployment.

The accounts in Mexico are smaller than those in Chile and Argentina, and small accounts pose particular problems because of fixed administrative costs per account. These fees have been declining through time. Initially they totaled about 1.9 percent of wages, leaving a net of 4.6 percent for investment (compared with 10 percent in Chile and 7.75 percent in Argentina); we use this number in our simulations. By 2005 fees were only 1.4 percent of payroll (James et al. 2000; James, Smalhout, and Vittas 2001; AIOS 2005). The reduction in fees will leave a larger amount to be invested, hence it will increase accumulations and annuities but will not alter the gender ratios on which we focus. The small contribution rate will have a negative effect on pension amounts in Mexico. However, for women this effect is offset by their later retirement age, compared with Chile and Argentina; in Mexico, it is equal to that of men, at age sixty-five. As we saw earlier, these additional five years effectively raise women's pensions by 50 percent.

Additionally, employers are required to contribute 5 percent of payroll to a housing fund, the Instituto del Fondo Nacional de la Vivienda para los Trabajadores (INFONAVIT), from which workers can borrow to purchase a home. According to the initial reform plan, the balance in these accounts would be added to their retirement accounts at age sixty-five. INFONAVIT is managed publicly and has earned low rates of interest, below the inflation rate, and most people do better by using the money for housing, so the balance left is unlikely to be large.

The public benefit in Mexico takes two forms. First, the federal government contributes a uniform amount per day worked into each worker's account—the "social quota" (SQ). The SQ goes into the accounts of workers, is invested by their AFORES, and eventually becomes part of their annuity. The SQ was set at 5.5 percent of one minimum salary, or about 2.2 percent of the average wage. For the average wage worker, this initially increased the net annual contribution to the account by 50 percent. However, the SQ is indexed to the consumer price index so will fall through time as a percentage of the average wage as productivity and wages grow. It is a variation of the flat benefit concept in Argentina—but flat per day worked rather than per worker regardless of days worked. Unlike the on-off switches for eligibility used by Chile and Argentina, Mexico's SQ is proportional to work—workers who work more, get more. This structure was designed to increase the pension levels of low-income workers while also increasing the incentive for informal-sector workers to formalize their work. At this point it is not clear whether it is having that effect.

Second, the government guarantees a minimum pension (the MPG) from the accounts. Initially this was set at one minimum wage (33 percent of the male and 46 percent of the female average wage), which is a generous guarantee compared with the MPG in Chile. However, this will fall through time as a percentage of the average wage since Mexico's MPG, like the SQ, is indexed to prices. To be eligible for the MPG, twenty-four years of contributions are required, in contrast to the ten years that were required for eligibility under the old system. As we shall see shortly, this high eligibility requirement effectively excludes most women. Both parts of the public benefit are financed out of general revenues.

Securing approval for a pension reform is always a politically difficult task. To pass the Mexican reform the government had to guarantee that no worker would be adversely affected by the change in system. The government also wanted to economize on its transition costs—the payment to current workers for service under the old system. To accomplish these goals, the government required that all workers join the new system without compensation for past service, but it gave them the right to switch back to the old system rules when they retire if they would have fared better under these old rules. Older workers are likely to revert to the old system option because their accounts will still be small when they reach retirement age.[2] Younger workers will stay in the new system, provided that the rate of return they earn is high enough to give them a superior pension. New entrants to the labor force do not have the option to switch back and enter the old system—their fate rests with the new system. We avoid this switch-back option, whose value depends largely on the inflation rate during the retirement period, by projecting future pension benefits for young workers today who never belonged to the old system. Our calculations and measured comparisons assume zero inflation.[3]

Data

As in the previous chapters, we start with household surveys that provide data on the gender, education, and current wage of each household member. Our data come from the 1997 Mexican National Employment Survey completed by the Instituto Nacional de Estadística, Geografía e Informática (1998), the Mexican statistical bureau (hereafter referred to as ENE97). We use the subsample corresponding to more-urban areas (communities of 100,000 people or more), which constitutes about 78 percent of the total sample. This survey contains the standard employment survey questions and a module with employment history and job training questions. The ENE97 yields information on age and sex of the employed and unemployed population, position at work, main occupation, hours worked, labor income, form of payment, and benefits received. It does not allow for the identification of social security affiliates and/or contributions made to retirement plans.

We use these data to construct the work histories of men and women with differing educational attainments and labor market attachments. For each age-gender-education cell we calculate the probable number of years worked and the average wage earned. Wages reflect pay for full time plus part time work in each cell. We use five different education categories, although these are more concentrated at the lower end than was the case for Chile and Argentina. More than half of the sample has nine years of education or less. For women we use three different degrees of labor force attachment: the average woman, who moves through life working like the average woman in each age-education cell; the full-career woman, who earns women's wages but works as much as men; and the ten-year woman, who works full time for ten years from age twenty-one to thirty before having children and then permanently withdraws from the labor market.

We assume that these age-specific work and wage propensities remain constant through time for each education category (except for economywide wage growth). However, as women acquire more education, they will be moving into higher work and wage categories. Therefore, in the aggregate, their earnings and pensions will improve more than those of men, whose labor force participation varies less with education. Moreover, as women are induced to work more within each education category as a result of exogenous social change and endogenous incentives from the new pension system, they will move closer to the full-career category. Therefore, the typical older female today may be personified by the ten-year woman with nine years of education, but the typical female tomorrow may be more like the full-career woman with some postsecondary education. Full-career women may also be indicative of single (never married) women today. Ten-year women are particularly interesting for Mexico, because the old social security system had a requirement of ten years of contributions to qualify for the minimum pension and many women worked only ten years.

Years of Work and Contributions

We estimate work experience based on current employment of the more-urban population in relevant age-education cells. However, we know that density of contributions is very low in Mexico, where the informal sector is large. Many individuals never affiliate with the system and, among affiliates, fewer than 40 percent contribute in any given year (AIOS 2005; Sinha and Yanez 2007). When they retire they will have small accumulations. Years of work may approximate fund accumulations for affiliates who contribute regularly when working but overstate accumulations for low-density affiliates. Therefore, as with Argentina and Chile, we present our main calculations for pensions based on the assumption that individuals contribute regularly when they work. But we also present calculations for low-density affiliates who contribute only 60 percent of the time that they work. Or course, this reduces their pension substantially, as well as their eligibility for the MPG, but it does not change gender ratios of accumulations, annuities, or access to the SQ.

Men in Mexico report greater labor force participation than in Chile or Argentina, working forty-three to forty-five years by the time they reach retirement age. Women, however, work less than twenty-four years, except at the postsecondary level, where this number rises to thirty-two (table 6.3). This immediately tells us that most women will not be eligible for the minimum pension guarantee under the new rules, while they would have been eligible under the old rules. It also tells us that low-earning women will have an incentive to work an extra few years to qualify. The gender gap in years worked is largest at the low education end, but even at the high end it does not completely disappear. In general, women work half as much as men. Even though retirement age is sixty-five for both genders, participation rates drop off after age sixty, especially for women.

Earnings

We estimate an average wage for each sex-schooling cell using five-year age grouping. Male wages rise with age until age fifty to sixty for the lower-educated groups, sixty-five for the top education categories. Women's wages follow a similar pattern but with a less steep trajectory (table 6.4). It is also notable that wages grow much more rapidly for the top education group than for the bottom—for men about 1 percent per year at the bottom and more than 3 percent at the top end. In middle age and later the wage gap between the top and bottom education categories is much larger than the gender wage gap and will probably lead to a large pension gap between high and low earners. While reducing the gender and education pension gaps are not contradictory goals (in fact, they overlap to some extent), policy makers may need to make trade-offs about which is most important, that is, which is a priority need for public resources.

How Women Fare—Accumulations and Pensions from Their Own Accounts

Fund Accumulations

As discussed above, we assume that a contribution rate of 6.5 percent of wages is put into the account of each worker, and of this, 1.9 percent is spent

Table 6.3: Estimated Years of Work in More-Urban Areas by Age, Education, and Gender in Mexico[a]

Age	Education				
	0–5	6–8	9	10–12	13+
Men					
16–20	4.38	4.29	4.17	3.51	2.96
21–25	4.62	4.78	4.78	4.47	3.80
26–30	4.85	4.95	4.90	4.95	4.72
31–35	4.89	4.88	4.93	4.90	4.95
36–40	4.89	4.87	4.93	4.88	4.87
41–45	4.82	4.88	4.86	4.85	4.91
46–50	4.71	4.63	4.68	4.78	4.80
51–55	4.48	4.41	4.39	4.46	4.49
56–60	4.10	3.84	3.85	4.04	4.24
61–65	3.26	2.79	3.06	3.04	3.06
Total 16–65	45.00	44.33	44.55	43.89	42.83
Density of work[b]	90%	89%	89%	88%	86%
Women					
16–20	3.44	3.99	3.89	3.64	3.23
21–25	1.55	1.50	2.55	3.72	3.85
26–30	1.90	1.70	1.90	2.30	3.65
31–35	2.57	2.02	2.10	2.42	3.40
36–40	2.30	2.23	2.42	2.73	3.26
41–45	2.34	2.24	2.60	2.59	3.49
46–50	2.07	2.05	2.05	2.54	3.41
51–55	2.11	1.65	1.81	1.75	2.81
56–60	1.57	1.39	1.74	1.65	2.32
61–65	1.08	1.17	0.79	1.00	2.29
Total 16–65:	20.93	19.92	21.90	24.36	31.71
Density of work[b]	42%	40%	44%	49%	63%

Source: Calculations by the authors based on data from ENE97.

[a] Based on data from more-urban areas, defined as communities with 100,000 people or more. For data sources and methodology, see appendix 1.

[b] Density of work = total working years to normal retirement age/total possible contributing years from age 16 to normal retirement age of 65. We define low-density worker as one who contributes 60% of time that he works.

for administrative expenses, leaving a net amount of 4.6 percent for investment. On the one hand, because administrative costs will probably be lower in the future, this assumption understates the absolute amount of the accumulation. On the other hand, we assume that the full 5 percent contribution to INFONAVIT, with 0 percent interest, is put into the worker's account upon retirement, thereby increasing the total. Since much of the INFONAVIT fund will, in fact, be spent on housing, this assumption overstates the retirement accumulation. To a large extent, the overstatement and understatement will

Table 6.4: Estimated Average Monthly Wage for Full-Time and Part-Time Workers in More-Urban Areas by Age, Education, and Gender in Mexico (1997 data in 2002 US$)[a]

Age	Education				
	0–5	6–8	9	10–12	13+
Males					
16–20	168	175	185	190	217
21–30	230	249	284	351	526
31–40	262	301	344	452	861
41–50	282	326	438	517	1035
51–60	259	366	449	586	1091
61–65	234	328	554	967	1281
Females					
16–20	132	156	163	194	199
21–30	154	168	200	287	413
31–40	152	179	234	357	562
41–50	144	230	281	392	640
51–60	157	209	246	468	688
61–65	124	146	259[b]	418[b]	1049

Source: Calculations by the authors based on data in ENE97.

[a] Estimates are for average monthly wages received by persons employed for pay full time plus part time in more urban areas in 1997. For more details on data and methodology see appendix 1.

[b] Average in the cell obtained from fewer than 30 observations; numbers should be used with caution.

cancel each other out. In any event, they affect the balances of men and women by similar proportions so should not bias the gender ratios. Initially we do not take into account the government's contribution in the form of the SQ; we focus only on the contribution that is tied to the worker's own wage.

By applying these net contribution rates to the average wage and work patterns in tables 6.3 and 6.4, we calculate the expected retirement accumulation for each type of worker (five education types and three degrees of labor force attachment for women). In our baseline scenario we assume that the real rate of return on investments is 5 percent (3.5 percent during the annuitization stage) and economywide wages grow at 2 percent per year, in addition to the age-earnings growth described above. Given the portfolio restrictions that exist throughout Latin America, men and women can be assumed to earn similar rates of return.

It is easily predicted that women will accumulate less than men, and indeed that is the case. The pattern is very similar to that in Chile. Average women accumulate 30 to 50 percent as much as men with the same education (table 6.5, row 7). We do not need to model the average woman

Table 6.5: Simulated Gender Differences in Fund Accumulation in Mexico: Decomposition of Male/Female Differences[a]

	Education				
	0–5	6–8	9	10–12	13+

A. From Personal Contributions; Does Not Include Annuity from SQ

Accumulated funds at retirement (age 65 for men and women) (in 2002 US$000)

	0–5	6–8	9	10–12	13+
1. Woman with 10 years' contributions	$8.2	$9.0	$10.7	$15.1	$21.8
2. Average woman	13.6	16.2	21.5	34.8	71.1
3. Full-career woman	28.3	35.2	43.1	63.3	97.5
4. Average man	46.2	53.7	66.1	83.3	142.5
5. Low-density man	27.7	32.2	39.7	50.0	85.5

Fund ratios of women relative to men (%)

	0–5	6–8	9	10–12	13+
6. Woman with 10 years' contributions	18	17	16	18	15
7. Average woman	30	31	33	43	51
8. Full-career woman	61	65	65	76	68
9. Average man	100	100	100	100	100
10. Low-density woman/low-density man	30	31	33	43	51

B. From Personal Contributions Plus SQ

Accumulated funds at retirement (age 65 for men and women) (in 2002 US$000)

	0–5	6–8	9	10–12	13+
1. Woman with 10 years' contributions	$14.3	$15.0	$16.7	$21.2	$27.9
2. Average woman	22.1	24.7	31.0	45.4	83.4
3. Full-career woman	45.0	51.9	59.8	79.3	112.4
4. Average man	63.0	70.5	82.8	99.2	157.5
5. Low-density man	37.8	42.3	49.7	59.5	94.5

Fund ratios of women relative to men (%)

	0–5	6–8	9	10–12	13+
6. Woman with 10 years' contributions	23	21	20	21	18
7. Average woman	35	35	37	46	53
8. Full-career woman	71	74	72	80	71
9. Average man	100	100	100	100	100
10. Low-density woman/low-density man	35	35	37	46	53

Source: Calculations by the authors.

Note: This table gives projected fund accumulations at retirement for young worker entering labor force today. It is assumed that women with 10 years of contributions work from age 21 to age 30 and full-career women work with the same intensity as men but earn the same wages as other women. Low-density means workers contribute 60% of working time.

[a] Based on 5% real rate of return, 2% real wage growth.

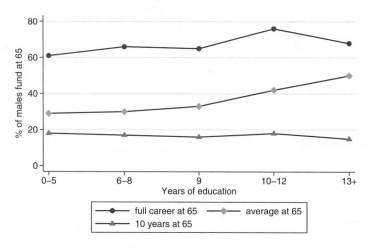

6.1. Female/male ratios of fund accumulation at retirement, Mexico (without SQ). More work would increase female/male ratios of accumulations in Mexico.

who raises her retirement age to equality with that for men, since both genders already have the same normal retirement age of sixty-five in Mexico.

As in Chile and Argentina, the gender ratio of accumulations would be greatly raised—to 60 to 80 percent—if women worked as much as men (table 6.5, row 8; figure 6.1). For women in the lowest education categories, who worked the least, accumulations are doubled when they work full career. Thus, incentives that encourage this behavior could go far toward reducing the gender pension gap, especially at the bottom end. When women work full career they are also likely to get higher wages than those with interrupted careers. Higher wages are, in part, a return to greater experience and anticipated future tenure. We do not have the longitudinal data that would be needed to measure this wage effect. Instead, we use the same monthly wage for women regardless of their labor force attachment. Wage differences between the genders account for the remaining fund gap of 24 to 40 percent between full-career women and men (table 6.5, row 8 vs. row 9).

Expected Pension Benefits ·

Upon retirement, workers in Mexico have a choice between gradual withdrawals and annuities, but we assume the latter in order to depict a stable annual flow. Payouts on annuities depend on survival probabilities, and in Mexico insurance companies are allowed to differentiate between life expectancies of men and women. Male and female life expectancies at sixty-five are projected to be 15.9 and 19.8 years, respectively. Since we have no data on differential life expectancy by years of education, we adopt the same life expectancy for all education groups. Men and women are required to purchase a joint pension with 60 percent of their monthly benefit going to the surviving spouse; later we compare this joint annuity with the higher payout that would have been obtained from an individual annuity. We assume that on average, women marry men who are three years older, thus wives survive their husbands by about 6.5 years.

In our baseline case, projected monthly annuities for men based on their own contributions (no SQ) vary from $267 to $822 in 2002 US$. For those with a 60 percent density the annuity amounts fall proportionately. For average women, projected annuities are 30 to 50 percent as much as their counterpart males (table 6.6, rows 1, 3, and 6). This is approximately the same gender gap that we found in Chile, and much smaller than that in Argentina, despite the fact that the gender gap in employment is larger in Mexico.

Table 6.6: Simulated Monthly Annuities from Individual Accounts in Mexico[a, b]

	Education				
	0–5	6–8	9	10–12	13+
Average married males, monthly annuity (in 2002 US$)					
1. Average man	267	310	381	481	822
2. Low-density man	160	186	229	289	493
Females, monthly annuity (in 2002 US$)					
3. Average woman	78	93	123	199	407
4. Full-career woman	162	201	247	362	558
5. Ten-year woman	47	51	61	86	125
Female/male ratios (%)					
6. Average woman	29	30	32	41	49
7. Full-career woman	61	65	65	75	68
8. Ten-year woman	18	17	16	18	15
9. Low-density woman/low-density man	29	30	32	41	49

Source: Calculations by the authors.

[a] This table gives projected annuity at retirement for young worker entering labor force today. For notes, see appendix 1. Annuity is based on personal contribution; portion from SQ is not included in this table. Men and women are assumed to purchase joint annuity with 60% to survivor, as required for married couples. Gender-specific tables are used. Low-density worker is a worker who contributes 60% of working time he or she works.

[b] Based on 5% real return in accumulation stage, 3.5% in annuity stage, 2% real wage growth, 1997 data, retirement age = 65 for men and women.

Mexico's equal retirement age offsets its greater difference in work histories and narrows the gender gap in pensions. The gender gap is narrower for full-career women and broader for ten-year women (rows 7 and 8). Since low-density men and women are both assumed to get 60 percent of the full amounts, gender ratios are unchanged (compare rows 6 and 9).

Notice that the annuity differential is almost exactly the same as the accumulation differential, suggesting that longevity distinctions between men and women add practically nothing to this gap. This is because we have used joint annuities, and both genders have the same retirement age. We will return to this point below. As we suspected earlier, the pension gap between the bottom and top education categories is also large, and it is especially large for women because of the positive correlations between education, wages, and years of work—women with the least schooling get only 19 percent as much as women with the most schooling.

The Social Quota and Minimum Pension

The Social Quota—Proportional to Work

In reality, payouts are expected to be much larger than those we have just described, and the reason is the social quota. In 1997 the SQ was set up to add 5.5 percent of the minimum wage, or 2.2 percent of the average wage, to each worker's account—a flat government contribution per day worked. It was price indexed and so it maintains its real value. It is similar to Argentina's flat benefit in the sense that it redistributes to low-wage workers, equalizes pensions across gender and education groups, and diversifies risk much more broadly than does Chile's MPG. But it was designed to overcome two disadvantages of Argentina's flat benefit. First, it is prefunded and thus does not build up a large future government obligation. Each year, the SQ is put into the worker's account, where the funds are privately managed. Second, it increases with years worked, so it continuously encourages incremental work, rather than plateauing and then jumping discontinuously, as in Argentina.

The greatest proportional increase in monthly pension goes to the low-education categories and to women, who are the lowest earners in any category (table 6.7 and figure 6.2). An average woman in the lowest schooling group gets a 62 percent increment from the SQ, while her counterpart male gets a 36 percent increment and highly educated men and women get only an 11 percent and 17 percent increase, respectively (table 6.7, rows 3 and 7). As a result, the SQ raises the gender ratio for all schooling levels, and it

Table 6.7: Simulated Impact of Public Benefit on Gender Ratios of Monthly Pensions in Mexico (in 2002 US$)[a]

	Education				
	0–5	6–8	9	10–12	13+
Married man					
1. Own annuity, no SQ	$267	$310	$381	$481	$822
2. Annuity including SQ	$364	$407	$478	$573	$909
3. % increase by SQ	36	31	25	19	11
4. Low-density man including SQ	$218	$244	$287	$344	$545
Woman					
5. Own annuity, no SQ	$78	$93	$123	$199	$407
6. Annuity including SQ	$126	$141	$177	$260	$477
7. % increase by SQ	62	52	44	30	17
8. Full-career woman, annuity including SQ	$258	$297	$342	$454	$643
9. % increase by SQ, full-career woman	59	48	39	25	15
10. Ten-year woman, annuity including SQ	$82	$86	$96	$121	$160
11. % increase by SQ, ten-year woman	74	67	56	41	28
Female/male ratios (%)					
12. Average annuity, no SQ	29	30	32	41	49
13. Average annuity including SQ	35	35	37	45	53
14. Full-career annuity including SQ	71	73	72	79	71
15. Ten-year annuity including SQ	22	21	20	21	18
16. Low-density woman/low-density man, including SQ	35	35	37	45	53

Source: Calculations by the authors.

Note: This table gives projected pensions at retirement for young worker entering labor force today. The public benefit takes the form of the SQ, a uniform payment per day worked, into the account of each worker. The SQ was set equal to 5.5% of the minimum wage initially, and thereafter was indexed to prices. Mexico also has an MPG = $133 in 2002 US$, but this is exceeded in practically every education category after the SQ is added, except for ten-year women and low-density women, who are not eligible for the MPG. For rows 12–15 denominator is average man.

[a] Based on 5% real return in accumulation stage, 3.5% in annuity stage, 2% real wage growth; 1997 data, retirement age = 65 for men and women.

also increases the ratio between pensions of the bottom and top schooling groups for both genders (compare row 1 with row 2, row 5 with row 6, row 12 with row 13).

Unlike the public benefit in Chile, ten-year women and low-density men and women get something from the SQ, proportional to their time worked. However, the largest amount goes to full-career women and men, who get more because they work longer. (This situation is in sharp contrast to that in Chile, where they get little or nothing from the public benefit because they have less "need.") Although men and full-career women get the same

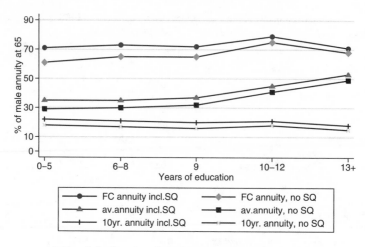

6.2. Female/male ratios of annuities with and without SQ, Mexico.
Larger impact of SQ for low earners who work more in Mexico.

absolute amount, this amount represents a much larger proportional increment for the latter because of their lower wage and contribution base. Consequently, the SQ pushes up the pension of full-career women relative to
that of men (compare tables 6.6 and 6.7). The more women work, the more
they get and the narrower is the gender differential.[4]

Indexation and the Future SQ

Since the SQ is price indexed, it provides valuable inflation insurance, but it
will fall in value relative to wages as time passes and wages grow. Thus, it will
add a smaller and smaller percentage increment over time and will become
less effective as a redistributive device, as observed in the other countries.
Ad hoc increases may alter the outcome, but these are uncertain. If we had
carried these simulations ten years further into the future, all the percentage
increments that we have given here would be reduced. In the short run price
indexation is reasonable given the relatively large size of the SQ initially, but
future cohorts of women will get less protection if the SQ remains constant
in real value in the long run. In addition, it will provide less incentive to formalize employment and contribute, which was one of its objectives.

The Minimum Pension Guarantee

Mexico also offers a minimum pension guarantee equal to the minimum
wage. This was about 33 percent of the average male wage and 46 percent of

the female average wage in 1997—$133 monthly in 2002 US$. It is indexed to prices. Twenty-four years of work are needed for eligibility. Average men in all education categories are eligible, but their own annuity is projected to be well above the MPG level, even with a low density of contributions. The average woman in all education categories except the bottom one will also be above the MPG level, but by a smaller margin. Women with a low density of contributions and ten-year women will fall below the MPG. However, most women who qualify on grounds of pension size will fail to meet the eligibility requirements: they will have small pensions precisely because they work fewer than twenty-four years.

In view of the low contribution rate in Mexico, it may at first seem surprising that personal annuities are projected to be above the pension floor. The main reason is that the MPG is price indexed rather than wage indexed. By the time today's young worker retires, the MPG will be only 16 percent of the average male wage, given our assumed 2 percent economy-wide wage growth. If the MPG were wage indexed, it would maintain a constant proportion (33 percent) of the average wage, and average women in most education categories would find themselves below the pension floor. However, the twenty-four-year eligibility rule would exclude them from coverage.

The SQ and Minimum Pension under the Slow-Growth Scenario

We tested the sensitivity to our assumptions about interest rate and rate of wage growth by simulating a slow-growth scenario in which the rate of return is 3 percent during the accumulation stage, 1.5 percent during the payout stage, and the rate of real wage growth is 0. Of course, this slows down the growth in accumulations and annuities from the workers' own contributions. It increases the stabilizing role of the SQ, which remains fixed in real value as the personal contribution falls. In this sense, the SQ provides insurance against slow wage growth. But since it goes into the worker's account and is invested, it does not insure against the low interest rates that are often part of a slow-growth environment. Therefore it has only minor effects on gender differentials and high/low education differentials, compared with our baseline fast-growth scenario (compare table A8 in appendix 4 with tables 6.5 and 6.7).

More important, when wage growth is zero due to slow growth, a price-indexed minimum pension is equivalent to a wage-indexed minimum pension, so the MPG becomes much larger relative to the workers' own annuity. Average women in all education categories except the top one now fall below the MPG. However, most of these women fail the eligibility test—they do not have twenty-four years of work.

Dispersion in Work Experience and Low Density of Contributions

Not all men and women are "average"; a dispersion exists in work experience, as well as wages, around the mean. Some women may meet the eligibility criterion and get the top-up, while some men may fall below the MPG pension level and get the top-up. Therefore, we estimated the dispersion around the average work experience by using the observed dispersion (coefficient of variation) of the accumulated years of work for each group at ages sixty-one to sixty-five and applied it to the mean value of number of years worked and estimated annuity. Assuming a normal distribution around the mean, we can estimate the percentage of the observations that would fall above or below a specified number of years of work and annuity value (table A9 in appendix 4).

Not surprisingly, the proportion of women who would fulfill the eligibility requirement is very sensitive to number of work years required. For women with the lowest education, only 25 percent are estimated to work fewer than ten years, but 48 percent work less than twenty years, and 57 percent less than twenty-four years. The numbers are similar in education categories two and three. This implies that under the old system eligibility rules, only one-quarter of these women would fail to qualify for the minimum pension, compared with 57 percent who fail to qualify in Mexico's new system. If the rules were adjusted to twenty years, as in Chile, another 9 percent of these low-educated women would become eligible.

We estimate that in the moderate-growth (baseline) scenario, 53 percent of the lowest-education women will have a personal pension below the MPG level, compared with 5 percent of the women with the highest education. However, women whose own pensions are below the minimum are probably those who worked less than twenty-four years and are therefore ineligible for the minimum pension guarantee.

By contrast, 100 percent of the men who contribute regularly when they work are eligible for the MPG, whether the number of years required is ten, twenty, or twenty-four. Men are less heterogeneous than women, as their work careers are clustered more tightly over a much higher number of years. In a moderate-growth environment (our baseline), men who contribute regularly would not use the minimum pension guarantee because they would have an estimated pension above the MPG level. But many men who work do not contribute. Low-density men, like women, may end up with pensions below the MPG, but they are the same men who are likely to fail the eligibility test.

This discussion demonstrates the extreme importance of choosing eligibility criteria for the public benefit with great care. It also raises the policy issue of to what extent countries want to subsidize women and men who have not worked in the labor market or have not contributed toward their retirement saving accounts when they worked. Is there some other affordable, efficient way to maintain women's living standards as they age?

Like Chile and Argentina, Mexico is grappling with this issue. But it has come up with a different solution from the other countries. In 2006, Mexico introduced a small cash transfer for the elderly as part of its antipoverty Oportunidades program (formerly called Progresa). This program is means tested both at the community level and the household level: first the poorest (mostly rural) localities are identified, and then the poorest households within the localities are found. A monthly cash supplement of 250 pesos (about US$25) is given to these households if they have elderly members (over age 70). While means testing is not done at the individual level, it is unlikely that a member of these households receives a pension from the contributory system. Other parts of this program apply to the children in these households. So the most vulnerable members of the poorest families are targeted for assistance. Means testing involves considerable administrative cost (see chapter 8), but by piggy-backing on an existing program, these costs are minimized. By the end of 2006, almost a million elderly in more than 30,000 communities were receiving this benefit. Elderly women whose husbands have died are likely to be the major beneficiaries if Oportunidades is expanded. This cash benefit will turn them into an asset to their extended families, rather than a liability.[5]

Replacement Rates

Since pensions are designed to replace wages at a point when the individual is too old to work, they are often compared with the wage that the individual earned as an indicator of whether the standard of living while working can be maintained after retirement. Mandatory pension systems typically target a replacement rate (pension/wage) of 40 to 60 percent, expecting that living costs will fall during retirement and that individuals who want more can save more voluntarily. By comparing gender ratios of replacement rates, we determine whether women have a greater or lesser ability than men to maintain their previous standard of living as they age. Women may have lower replacement rates than men because of their shorter work periods during which contributions are accumulated. But actually, as we saw in the cases of Chile and Argentina, the situation is much more complicated. While at first glance women have lower replacement rates than men in the new systems, under some scenarios it turns out that they have higher replacement rates. Key variables are the definition of the reference wage and the behavior of the subgroup of women we are examining.

As the reference wage for Mexico, we use wage rates at ages fifty-one to sixty, which is close to the peak period for men and women. Pensions differ between men and women because of differences in wages and years of contributions. Since the replacement rate implicitly controls for wages, we expect it to be more similar for men and women than absolute benefits are, and indeed this is the case (compare the gender ratios in tables 6.7 and 6.8). But the gender ratios are still very low.

For men, the annuity from their own contributions replaces almost a half of the reference wage, and for women only a quarter (table 6.8, rows

Table 6.8: Simulated Replacement Rates in Mexico (pension/reference wage, %)

	Education				
	0–5	6–8	9	10–12	13+
Replacement rates for average married male					
1. Annuity only	57	47	47	45	42
2. Annuity + SQ	78	62	59	54	46
3. Annuity + SQ/adjusted reference wage	87	70	67	60	51
4. Annuity + SQ, low-density man	47	37	35	32	28
Replacement rates for females					
5. Annuity only	26	23	26	22	31
6. Annuity + SQ	42	35	37	29	36
7. Annuity + SQ, full-career woman	85	74	72	50	49
8. Annuity + SQ/adjusted reference wage	99	106	103	82	64
Female/male replacement rates					
9. Annuity only	45	49	55	49	74
10. Annuity + SQ	54	57	63	53	78
11. Full-career woman	110	120	122	93	106
12. Annuity + SQ/adjusted reference wage	114	152	154	136	125
13. Annuity + SQ, low-density	54	57	63	53	78

Source: Calculations by the authors.

Note: Replacement rates are defined as pension/reference wage. Reference wage is defined as monthly wage rate at ages 51–60. Wage is from table 6.4, indexed up by 2% wage growth. Annuity + SQ are from tables 6.6 and 6.7. Men and women are assumed to retire at 65. Low-density means worker contributes only 60% of time he or she works. For rows 3, 8, and 12 with adjusted wage: wage rate from table 6.4 is adjusted by percentage of time individual worked at ages 51–55 to obtain a measure of actual earnings (monthly wage rate * % time worked).

1 and 5). Adding the SQ raises these rates and narrows gender differences, especially for individuals with less education (rows 2 and 6). But overall, projected replacement rates remain low for the average woman, much lower than those of men, because of their low work propensities. For full-career women, who work as much as men, replacement rates reach 50 to 80 percent, considerably more than those of men (rows 7 and 11). The position of full-career women relative to that of comparable men is higher during the retirement period than it was during the working period because of the equalizing effect of the SQ.

Actually, very few women earn the wage rate that we are using as the reference wage. In any given period the average woman works less than half the time, so their annual earnings are only a fraction of the full time wage rate. We therefore change our reference wage to reflect actual earnings by adjusting it for proportion of time worked between ages fifty-one and sixty, similar to what we did for the other two countries. This raises women's replacement rates much more than men's, and gender ratios now far exceed 100 percent. In fact, using this definition, Mexican women have higher replacement rates and higher gender ratios of replacement rates than those in Argentina or Chile (table 6.8, rows 8 and 12; figure 6.3)—because of the equal retirement age in Mexico.

In summary, average women get lower replacement rates of their full-time wage rates than men from their pensions, but this is only the beginning

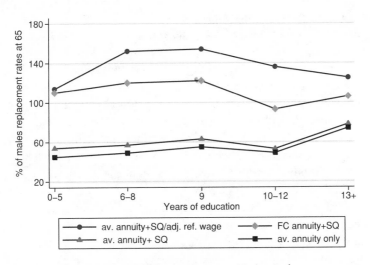

6.3. Female/male ratios of replacement rates, Mexico. Replacement rates for full-career women and average women with adjusted reference wage far exceed those for men in Mexico.

of the story. Full-career women have higher replacement rates than men. Moreover, when we use actual amount earned per year as the reference wage, by adjusting the full-time wage for proportion of time worked, replacement rates for women with primary or secondary schooling climb above 100 percent and, at all education levels, exceed those of comparable men. The SQ and equal retirement ages of men and women play key roles in achieving this outcome.

Joint Annuities

Joint Annuities for Widows

Mexico, similar to the other Latin American countries, requires men to purchase joint annuities that cover their wives at 60 percent of their own benefit. This imposes an implicit cost on married men while relieving single men of the obligation they had to finance widows' benefits from the common pool in the old system. Married men pay a price that takes the form of a lower monthly payout while they are alive. In Mexico, given the differences in age and life expectancy, the joint annuity requirement costs married men a 19 percent reduction in their own benefit, slightly more than in Chile but less than in Argentina, where a 70 percent joint benefit is required (table 6.9, row 1 vs. row 3). Of course, for men who would have purchased life insurance for their wives in any event, the real cost is much lower, as mandatory annuities simply replace voluntary insurance.

Women must also purchase a joint annuity, but the cost, in terms of lower monthly payouts to them, is only 5 percent. Joint annuities are cheap for wives to buy because, given the age and longevity differences, their husbands are less likely to survive them.

The widow's benefit exceeds her own pension in every education category. It more than doubles the personal pension of the average widow (compare rows 7 and 9). The two benefits combined maintain the household income after husband's death at about 70 percent of what it was before his death, roughly the amount needed to maintain the previous standard of living (table 6.9, row 11). It effectively keeps very old women out of poverty even if they were not affiliated with the social security system, so long as their husbands were covered. Passing this responsibility on to husbands rather than the common pool has helped Mexico to allocate scarce public resources to other purposes, such as the SQ, which benefits low-income men and women, or schooling and cash transfers for children from poor families.

Table 6.9: The Impact of Joint Annuities and Unisex Tables in Mexico[a]

	0–5	6–8	9	10–12	13+
			Education		
Males (in 2002 US$)					
1. Individual, gender specific	$448	$501	$589	$705	$1,120
2. Individual, unisex	409	457	537	643	1021
3. Joint, gender specific[b]	364	407	478	573	909
4. Joint, unisex	355	397	467	559	888
Females (in 2002 US$)					
5. Individual, gender specific	$133	$148	$187	$273	$502
6. Individual, unisex	143	160	201	294	541
7. Joint, gender specific[b]	126	141	177	260	477
8. Joint, unisex	131	146	184	269	494
9. Widow's annuity	218	244	287	344	545
10. Widow's + own annuity	345	385	464	603	1023
11. Widow's pensions as % of husband's plus wife's pensions[c]	70%	70%	71%	72%	74%

Source: Calculations by the authors.

[a] Based on 5% return during accumulation stage, 3.5% during annuity stage, real wage growth = 2%; 1997 data in 2002 US$. The SQ is included in annuity calculations. Joint annuity assumes 60% to survivor.

[b] These numbers are from table 6.7.

[c] Personal annuity of wife + widow's annuity after husband dies relative to personal annuities of husband + wife while husband was alive.

At the same time, divorced women get no legal protections from the joint pension requirement, as in the other Latin American countries. Divorce is very rare in Mexico, but it is likely to increase in the future. Men may desert their wives without going through a formal divorce procedure, and the wife may have a hard time enforcing the joint pension requirement in such cases. We discuss this issue further in chapter 8.

Unisex Mortality Tables

We also investigated the potential impact if unisex tables were required for annuity calculations. Insurance companies will generally place their clients into different risk categories for pricing purposes, and gender is an easily observable characteristic for these purposes. The greater life expectancy of women in annuity pricing is often cited as one reason for their lower pensions. One of the controversial issues in defined contribution plans is whether unisex mortality tables should be used, as they implicitly were in the old defined benefit systems. We calculated how much difference unisex tables would make to payouts on individual and joint annuities. After the switch to unisex tables, payouts on individual annuities fall by 9 percent for single men and rise by 8 percent for single women (table 6.9, row 1 vs. row 2, row 5 vs. row 6). This represents a modest-size redistribution between the genders.

However, the payouts on joint annuities are very close—they fall for men by only 2 percent and rise for women by 3 to 4 percent—when unisex instead of gender-specific tables are used, as we saw before for Chile and Argentina. Thus, the unisex requirement would imply a modest redistribution from single men to single women but would leave married individuals—the bulk of the population—largely unchanged (see figure 4.4). Although the use of unisex tables is highly contentious in many countries, it is important to realize that for joint annuities—which are the most common sort—their use hardly matters. Women's lower pensions stem primarily from their lower labor force participation, wages, and contributions, not from their greater longevity.

Lifetime Benefits and Imputed Taxes

Gross Lifetime Benefits

The pension from the worker's contributions and SQ is paid throughout the retirement period; the opportunity cost of the joint annuity is also incurred throughout the retirement years; and the widow's benefit begins, on average, about fourteen years after the woman's own pension starts. In order to compare these various costs and benefits it is necessary to convert them into expected present value (EPV) terms. We sum each benefit and cost over the individual's retirement lifetime and convert to expected lifetime values at age sixty-five using a 3.5 percent discount rate—the same interest rate as applied during the annuitization period (table 6.10).

The present value of the personal annuity and the SQ are far greater for the average man than for the average woman because he works many more days than she (table 6.10, rows 1 and 2 vs. rows 9 and 10). However, the SQ adds a much larger proportional amount to the lifetime flow of benefits for average women, especially low earners (row 6 vs. row 14; see also figure 4.5). The joint annuity adds even more than the SQ to most women (compare rows 10, 14, 20, and 25 to rows 11, 15, 21, and 26; see also figure 4.6). As a result, average married women get 65 to 85 percent as much as men in total lifetime benefits. And full-career married women get larger lifetime benefits

Table 6.10: EPV of Gross Lifetime Benefits from Personal Annuities, Joint Annuity, and Public Benefits in Mexico[a] (1997 data in 2002 US$000)

			Education		
	0–5	6–8	9	10–12	13+
Average man					
1. Own annuity if no SQ	$46.2	$53.7	$66.1	$83.3	$142.5
2. SQ to own account	16.8	16.8	16.7	16.0	15.0
3. Joint annuity paid for wife	–11.9	–13.3	–15.6	–18.7	–29.7
4. Joint annuity received	1.0	1.1	1.4	2.0	3.8
5. Total, average married man	52.1	58.3	68.6	82.6	131.6
6. *% increase from SQ*	*36*	*31*	*25*	*19*	*11*
7. *% increase from joint received*	*2*	*2*	*2*	*2*	*3*
8. *% decrease from joint paid*	*–19*	*–19*	*–19*	*–19*	*–19*
Average woman					
9. Own annuity if no SQ	$13.6	$16.2	$21.5	$34.8	$71.1
10. SQ to own account	8.5	8.5	9.5	10.6	12.3
11. Joint annuity received	13.2	14.7	17.3	20.7	32.9
12. Joint annuity paid	–1.1	–1.2	–1.6	–2.3	–4.2
13. Total, married woman	34.2	38.1	46.8	63.8	112.2
14. *% increase from SQ*	*62*	*52*	*44*	*30*	*17*
15. *% increase from joint annuity*	*97*	*91*	*80*	*60*	*46*
16. *% decrease from joint paid*	*–5*	*–5*	*–5*	*–5*	*–5*
Full-career woman					
17. Own annuity if no SQ	$28.3	$35.2	$43.1	$63.3	$97.5
18. SQ to own account	16.8	16.8	16.7	16.0	15.0
19. Total, full-career married woman	55.9	64.1	74.1	96.1	139.7
20. *% increase from SQ*	*59*	*48*	*39*	*25*	*15*
21. *% increase from joint annuity*	*46*	*42*	*40*	*33*	*34*
Ten-year woman					
22. Own annuity if no SQ	$8.2	$9	$10.7	$15.1	$21.8
23. SQ to own account	6.1	6.0	6.0	6.1	6.1
24. Total, ten-year married woman	26.7	29.0	33.2	40.9	59.4
25. *% increase from SQ*	*74*	*67*	*56*	*41*	*28*
26. *% increase from joint annuity*	*160*	*164*	*162*	*137*	*151*
Married woman/married man ratios (%)					
27. Average woman	66	65	68	77	85
28. Full-career woman	107	110	108	116	106
29. Ten-year woman	51	50	48	50	45

Source: Simulations by the authors.

[a] Based on 5% return during accumulation stage, 3.5% discount rate, real wage growth = 2%. EPV is given for men and women at age 65. EPV of individual annuity is same as fund accumulation given for panel A, table 6.5. EPV of individual annuity + SQ is same as fund accumulation in panel B, table 6.5. Husbands and wives are assumed to belong to the same education group. Absolute amount of joint annuity is same for average, full-career, and ten-year woman, but it varies as % of own annuity. % increase due to SQ and joint annuity received are based on individual annuity without SQ, in denominator. % decrease due to joint annuity purchased has individual annuity + SQ in denominator, since part of purchase is attributable to SQ received by the individual. (Also see notes to table 4.10.)

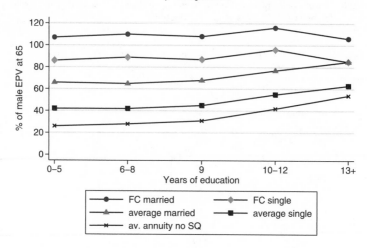

6.4. Female/male ratios of EPV of lifetime benefits, Mexico. EPV of full-career married women exceeds that of men in Mexico.

than men (figure 6.4). These results are very similar to those in Chile and Argentina. Lifetime gender ratios are much higher than monthly gender ratios because of the greater longevity of women but even more because of the value added by the joint annuity.

Net Benefits and Imputed Money's Worth Ratios

We move on to analyze patterns of redistribution in Mexico, employing the same three measures we used in previous chapters: (1) net benefits from the SQ (= the EPV of the SQ – the imputed tax cost of financing it); (2) the money's worth ratio from the SQ (MWR_{pub} = the EPV of SQ/EPV of imputed tax cost); and (3) the MWR from the public plus private benefits combined ($MWR_{pub+pvt}$ = (EPV of SQ + personal annuity)/(EPV of imputed tax cost + contributions)). In addition, for married women, we use a fourth measure, $MWR_{pub+pvt+jt}$, which adds the joint annuity into the numerator.

While we already know the EPV of public and private benefits for each schooling-gender group (from table 6.10), we now need to estimate the total tax bill and its allocation among various subgroups. As in the cases of Chile and Argentina, we assume that each cohort pays its own full cost, and within each cohort taxes are distributed proportional to lifetime earnings. This enables us to derive the uniform tax rate that everyone must pay to cover the public benefit, as well as the differential tax amount attributed to each subgroup (see appendix 3 for more details). In Mexico the imputed tax rate is 1.6 percent. This is much lower than the imputed rate in Argentina,

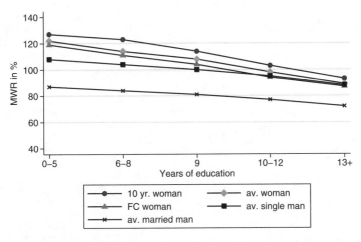

6.5. Money's worth ratios, public plus private benefits, Mexico [MWR calculated as (public + private benefit)/(tax + contribution)]. Low-earning women get highest money's worth ratios in Mexico.

despite the roughly similar total benefit payouts between Mexico and Argentina, because Mexico prefunds its public benefit by putting the SQ into each worker's account each year. The benefit is financed in part by investment earnings, so a lower tax rate is needed.[6] Instead, the required tax rate is closer to that in Chile, but compounds to a larger amount and covers much broader benefits.

Like Argentina (and unlike Chile), every subgroup in Mexico gets some public benefit (table 6.11). As in the other two countries, women, especially low-earning women, generally receive positive net benefits and money's worth ratios greater than 100 percent because of the redistribution they get from the public benefit (figure 6.5). In contrast, married men get MWRs less than 100 percent because they are financing that redistribution as well as the joint annuity. Thus, gender ratios in MWRs invariably favor women (table 6.11, rows 25, 26, and 27).

However, Mexico's gender ratios of MWRs are much more tightly clustered together than in Chile or Argentina (compare table 6.11 with tables 4.11 and 5.11). The main reason is that Mexico follows the principle of proportionality, whereas the discontinuities in Argentina's flat benefit and Chile's MPG produce unexpected leaps in MWR for certain subgroups of women The SQ is proportional to work since it is a constant payment per day worked. Imputed taxes, contributions, and private annuities are also proportional to work. Thus differences in work propensities do not translate into differences in MWRs. This narrows gender ratios in net benefits and

Table 6.11: Expected Lifetime Public Benefit, Imputed Tax Cost, and Redistribution from SQ in Mexico (in 2002 US$000)

	Education				
	0–5	6–8	9	10–12	13+
Average man					
1. SQ	16.8	16.8	16.7	16.0	15.0
2. Imputed tax cost	12.2	14.1	17.0	21.2	36.1
3. Net benefit	4.6	2.7	−0.3	−5.2	−21.1
4. MWR_{pub}	137%	119%	98%	75%	42%
5. $MWR_{pub+pvt}$, married man	87%	84%	81%	77%	72%
6. $MWR_{pub+pvt}$, single man	108%	104%	100%	95%	88%
Average woman					
7. SQ	8.5	8.5	9.5	10.6	12.3
8. Imputed tax cost	3.6	4.4	5.7	9.3	18.1
9. Net benefit	4.9	4.1	3.8	1.3	−5.8
10. MWR_{pub}	233%	195%	165%	114%	68%
11. $MWR_{pub+pvt}$	122%	114%	108%	98%	89%
12. $MWR_{pub+pvt+jt}$	198%	185%	172%	145%	126%
Full-career woman					
13. SQ	16.8	16.8	16.7	16.0	15.0
14. Imputed tax cost	7.5	9.3	11.3	16.5	24.7
15. Net benefit	9.3	7.5	5.4	−0.5	−9.7
16. MWR_{pub}	223%	181%	148%	97%	61%
17. $MWR_{pub+pvt}$	119%	111%	104%	94%	87%
18. $MWR_{pub+pvt+jt}$	156%	144%	136%	120%	114%
Ten-year woman					
19. Lifetime SQ	6.1	6.0	6.0	6.1	6.1
20. Imputed tax cost	2.5	2.7	3.2	4.6	6.6
21. Net benefit	3.6	3.3	2.8	1.5	−0.5
22. MWR_{pub}	249%	225%	188%	133%	92%
23. $MWR_{pub+pvt}$	127%	123%	114%	103%	93%
24. $MWR_{pub+pvt+jt}$	251%	249%	239%	208%	209%
Female/married male ratios of $MWR_{pub+pvt}$					
25. Average woman	139%	135%	133%	127%	124%
26. Full-career woman	136%	132%	129%	121%	122%
27. Ten-year woman	145%	145%	142%	133%	130%

Source: Calculations by the authors based on table 6.10 and assumptions described in appendix 3.

Note: Imputed MWR_{pub} = SQ/imputed tax cost. Imputed $MWR_{pub+pvt}$ = (annuity + SQ)/(imputed tax cost + contribution). All values are lifetime values discounted to age 65. Tax rate that covers SQ is estimated to be 1.6% of lifetime earnings (see appendix 3).

MWRs. Women get higher MWRs than men as a result of their lower wage rates and tax bills. But they do not get any added payoff from their fewer years of work. Nor do they get special treatment if they fall into certain niches, such as those in the twenty-year group in Chile or the ten-year group in Argentina. All these factors lead Mexico to miss out on the highest gender ratios but also to avoid some of the questionable equity and disincentive effects observed in Argentina and Chile.

Marginal money's worth ratios and work (dis)incentives

The discontinuously high returns for twenty-year women in Chile and ten-year women in Argentina imply negative marginal net benefits and low marginal MWRs, discouraging incremental work beyond those thresholds. In Mexico, in contrast, work is rewarded by a constant SQ. This translates into positive marginal net benefits and marginal MWRs greater than 100 percent for women who are considering a shift from ten-year to average status and from average to full-career status in the bottom three education categories— encouraging work. Marginal net benefits become slightly negative and marginal MWRs slightly less than 100 percent for the two top education groups because their marginal tax exceeds their marginal benefits, but the deviations are modest and less likely to deter work than the extreme deviations described above for Chile and Argentina (table 6.12, rows 1, 2, 4, and 5; see also figures 4.9 and 4.10). Because of the principle of proportionality, rewards for incremental work play a more consistent role here than in our other two sample countries, particularly for women.

Table 6.12: Marginal Net Public Benefits and MWRs for Incremental Work in Mexico

	Education				
	0–5	6–8	9	10–12	13+
Marginal net public benefit from incremental work (in 2002 US$000)					
1. Ten-year to average	1.2	0.8	0.9	−0.2	−5.3
2. Average to full career	4.4	3.4	1.6	−1.8	−3.8
3. Low-density to average married man	1.8	1.1	−0.1	−2.1	−8.4
Marginal MWR$_{pub+pvt}$ for incremental work (%)					
1. Ten-year. to average	114	103	101	94	87
2. Average to full career	117	108	101	88	84
3. Low-density to average married man	87	84	81	77	72

Note: Marginal MWR from work level i to j = $((SQ_j - SQ_i) + (\text{annuity}_j - \text{annuity}_i))/((T_j - T_i) + (\text{contrib}_j - \text{contrib}_i))$. Marginal net public benefits from work level i to j = $(SQ_j - SQ_i) - (T_j - T_i)$.

Who Gained or Lost Most from the Reform?

So far we have been analyzing the new system alone. We now move to a comparison of the new and old systems from the gender perspective. As in our earlier cases, we do not attempt to compare absolute gains or losses because the old system was nonsustainable in the long run, so it is difficult to establish the counterfactual. Instead, we focus on relative gains or losses.

The old system had certain features that were expected to help women, who tend to be low earners: modest eligibility requirements for a high replacement rate, a minimum pension, and generous widows' benefits (90 percent of the husband's benefit plus her own benefit). But it had other features that hurt women, such as a pensionable wage based on the last five years of earnings, the requirement of work for five years immediately prior to retirement, and the absence of indexation of the pensionable wage or of the pension itself in a highly inflationary environment.

The new system eliminated most of those features, both positive and negative, for women. It retains a public benefit (the social quota) targeted toward low earners and a minimum pension, but the latter requires twenty-four years of contributions for eligibility. It replaces the widow's benefit financed by the payroll tax with a somewhat less generous joint annuity purchased by the husband. Contributions to the accounts made by young women grow in real value by the time they retire, in contrast to the declining value of the old system's pensionable base salary. Whether women gained or lost relative to men from the reform therefore cannot be determined a priori; the question requires careful empirical analysis. We ask (1) how did gender ratios of lifetime benefits change due to the reform and (2) how did ratios of postreform to prereform lifetime benefits compare for various gender-education-marital subgroups?

How Gender Ratios Changed due to the Reform

In table 6.13 we compare gender ratios of lifetime benefits before and after the reform. A ratio of less than one indicates that the EPV for women was less than that of men—as of course it is in most cases. If the ratio in the new system is greater than that in the old system, the relative position of women has improved due to the reform.

Female/male ratios of benefits for single women invariably rise in the new system, with or without the SQ. Gender ratios are higher for married than for single women in the new system, due to the joint pension, but in

Table 6.13: Simulated Female/Male Ratios of Expected Present Value of Lifetime Benefits in New versus Old Systems in Mexico (%)

	Education				
	0–5	6–8	9	10–12	13+
Old system					
1. Average single woman	39	33	29	33	59
2. Average married woman	77	71	68	72	97
3. Full-career single woman	70	60	63	73	91
4. Full-career married woman	108	99	102	112	130
5. Ten-year married woman	69	57	52	46	44
New system (average woman/average man)					
6. Single, own annuity, no SQ	38	39	41	52	61
7. Single, own annuity with SQ	42	42	45	55	63
8. Married, own annuity with SQ + joint annuity	66	65	68	77	85
New system (full-career woman/average man)					
9. Single, own annuity with SQ	87	89	87	96	85
10. Married, own annuity with SQ + joint annuity	107	110	108	116	106
New system (ten-year woman/average man)					
11. Married, own annuity with SQ + joint annuity	51	50	48	50	45

Source: Calculations by the authors.

Note: Present values are measured at age 65 for both genders. Denominator is married man, with or without SQ as indicated. In old system, single and married men got same pension. In new system, married men get smaller pension than married men because married men must purchase joint pension. Single woman is assumed to have same work and wage history as married woman, but does not get survivors' benefit in old system or joint annuity in new system. She also does not have to pay for joint annuity for her husband in new system.

some cases they were higher still in the old system. (As noted above, widows were treated very well in Mexico's old system; they could keep their own benefit plus 90 percent of their husband's benefit.) For example, for single women with average work patterns and nine years of education, the gender ratio was 29 percent in the old system, while it rises to 45 percent in the new system; for married women it was 68 percent in both systems (table 6.13, rows 1, 2, 7, and 8). Full-career women register the most consistent gains. For example, full-career single women with nine years of education get a lifetime retirement income that is 63 percent that of men in the old system, compared with 87 percent in the new system; if married, the gender ratio rises from 102 percent to 108 percent (rows 3 and 4 vs. rows 9 and 10; figure 6.4). In contrast, the relative position of ten-year women falls, both for married and for single women.

Ratios of Postreform to Prereform Lifetime Benefits, Normalized

Finally, to capture differences in relative changes by each gender, education, marital, and labor force attachment subgroup, we calculate the ratio of EPV postreform to EPV prereform for each group, normalizing according to the ratio for married men with top education. A normalized ratio of 100 percent indicates that the relevant subgroup has gained (or lost) proportionately as much as highly educated married men, and the higher the normalized ratio the greater the gain in relative position (see table 6.14).

Many of the main results are similar to those we saw for Chile and Argentina:

1. Practically all subgroups gain more (or lose less) than top-earning men, but the biggest gains are registered among women.
2. For both men and women, relative gains are greatest for those with least education and earnings. Apparently, the redistributive SQ in the new system outweighs the formula in the old defined benefit system that seemed to favor the poor. Besides the positive impact of the SQ, compound interest in

Table 6.14: **Ratios of EPV of Postreform/Prereform Lifetime Benefits in Mexico (relative to ratio for married men in top education group, %)**[a]

	Education				
	0–5	6–8	9	10–12	13+
Average man					
1. Married	181	150	122	89	100
2. Single	219	181	147	107	120
Woman					
3. Average single	199	195	187	146	108
4. Average married	154	138	122	96	88
5. Full-career single	225	221	169	116	94
6. Full-career married	180	166	130	92	82
7. Ten-year married	134	130	114	95	103
8. Men + women: Average household	169	145	122	92	94

Source: Calculations by the authors.

[a] r = 5% during accumulation, 3.5% during annuity stage, real wage growth = 2%. Includes lifetime benefits from personal annuity and SQ. Also includes survivors' benefits and joint annuity if married. Each cell i shows $(PVnew/PVold)_i/(PVnew/PVold)_k$, where $(PVnew/PVold)_i$ = ratio of present value of lifetime benefits in new versus old systems for group i. This ratio is normalized (divided) by the ratio for reference group k, where k = married men in highest education category. If the number in a cell > 100%, it gained more than top married men.

the new defined contribution system benefits low earners and women with flatter age-earnings profiles.

3. Single men improve their positions relative to married men because they no longer have to finance the widows' benefit.

However, differences also appear compared with Chile and Argentina:

1. Married women gain less than single women. The reason lies in the treatment of the widows' benefit in the old system, which was much more generous than in Chile or Argentina.

2. Ten-year women lose position relative to most other groups, given the work-oriented nature of the SQ. This outcome is similar to Chile but unlike Argentina, where ten-year women are big gainers due to the flat benefit, which is not closely linked to work.

3. The biggest gainers from the reform are full-career women in the bottom half of the education distribution (figure 6.6). This outcome again contrasts with Argentina and is stronger than in Chile, where full-career women do not get the the public benefit. It is consistent with the underlying ethos of the Mexican reform—to reward work while partially equalizing pensions across earnings groups.

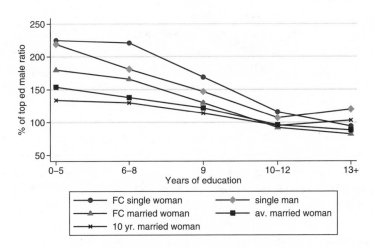

6.6. Postreform/prereform ratios of EPV by group, Mexico (normalized by postreform/prereform EPV ratio of top education man). Low-earning full-career women and single men are biggest relative gainers from the reform in Mexico.

What Do We Conclude from the Mexican Case?

Despite a defined benefit formula and survivors' benefits in the old system that seemed to favor low earners and women, many hidden details resulted in the opposite effect. In contrast, the defined contribution plans in the new systems have subtle features that favor women, such as the heavier weight given to earnings early in adulthood. These are reinforced by the joint annuity, which transfers income from husbands to wives, and the public benefit, the SQ, which redistributes to low earners. As the lowest earners in each education category, women will inevitably benefit from such redistributions.

We saw in Chile and Argentina that redistributing funds to low earners runs the risk of discouraging marginal work once eligibility has been established. Mexico has come up with a method for avoiding that disincentive, paying a flat amount per day worked; it is therefore proportional to time worked. In net benefit terms, the SQ is targeted toward those who are low earners by virtue of their low wage rates, not their low participation rates. This approach has the potential effect of encouraging workers to work and save for their own old age, narrowing projected gender differentials and also narrowing expected pension differentials between workers at the top and bottom of the education ladder. If women respond to these incentives by working more, gender ratios should rise further in the future. Mexico can afford the SQ, in part because it shifted the responsibility for supporting widows to their husbands rather than taxpayers.

The Mexican approach, however, does not avoid poverty for older women who did not work "enough" to benefit much from the SQ and do not have husbands who leave them large widows' benefits. The minimum pension is designed to serve this role, but eligibility conditions effectively exclude most women. Men and women with low density of contributions may be left with small pensions from contributions, small SQ benefits in their accounts, and lack of eligibility for the minimum pension guarantee. What are reasonable eligibility conditions for the public benefit in a contributory scheme, and what arrangements will keep out of poverty women who did not work enough to qualify for such benefits? Chile and Argentina have recently changed their systems to make the public benefit more accessible to such women, and Mexico is beginning to experiment with a noncontributory small or flat benefit to the elderly in poorer communities. We keep returning to this issue and discuss it further in chapter 8.

CHAPTER SEVEN

Gender Issues in Social Security Reforms of Other Regions

At the same time that the Latin American countries were reforming their systems, the transition economies of eastern and central Europe and the former Soviet Union were facing huge financial strains in their systems, which required them to reform also. Kazakhstan, Poland, Hungary, Latvia, Croatia, Kosovo, Bulgaria, Estonia, Lithuania, Macedonia, Slovakia, and Russia have instituted multipillar reforms or are in the process of doing so. Several Organisation for Economic Co-operation and Development (OECD) countries have also changed their systems to include a funded, privately managed defined contribution plan together with a public social safety net. We have not conducted the same detailed analysis for these countries as we have for Latin America, but using secondary sources we compare these new systems with those in Latin America from a gender perspective. We present data on Poland and, to a lesser extent, Kazakhstan and Latvia, from the transition economies, and on Sweden and Australia as examples of reforms in advanced industrial societies. This comparison allows us to enlarge the design features that we are able to explore.

In particular, many transitional economies have a public benefit that is larger, more closely linked to contributions, and less redistributive than those in the new Latin American systems. We would expect this to disadvantage women. In contrast, most OECD countries offer a noncontributory public benefit or minimum benefit that is based on residence rather than employment. Such a benefit should favor women. The joint annuity is typically not required in these countries, but unisex mortality tables are required for annuitization. Thus, each region has chosen a different strategy with different eligibility conditions, benefit-contribution links, work incentives, distributional effects, and costs. Finally, the wage and employment positions of women relative to men in the transitional and industrial countries are different from those in Latin America, with the gender gap in labor force participation rates generally less than 20 percent (OECD 2003). We would therefore expect—and in fact we find—different gender outcomes as a result of different initial conditions and policies.

The Transition Economies[1]

Old Age Security in the Old Systems

In the pension systems of the old Soviet Union and eastern and central Europe, the gender gap was small: Women worked almost as much as men, aided by state-provided child-care arrangements as well as a social expectation that everyone would work. Women earned almost as much as men, in part because of wage compression that minimized differentials and in part because the informal sector was very small. Typically, women were allowed to retire at age fifty-five, five years earlier than men, but this had little impact on their benefits as full pensions (55 to 85 percent of final wage) were awarded after only twenty years of work (twenty-five years for men), credit was given for child-caring years, and the defined benefit formula did not take age or future life expectancy into account. This system was implicitly expensive, but these costs were covered by the state and did not show up as explicit taxes, and in any event the impact of high taxes and distortionary benefit formulae on the labor supply did not seem to matter in a command economy.

The Multipillar Reforms

OVERVIEW Of course, this command economy was destined to fail (in part as a result of the disincentives it embodied), and as the conversion to a market economy took place, high pension costs and unrealistic formulae did matter. As a result, practically all countries in the former Soviet Union and eastern Europe have undergone or are now planning major structural reforms in their pension systems. While the details of the reforms vary across these countries, they have certain features in common: (1) a closer linkage between benefits and contributions through the adoption of a funded defined contribution pillar; (2) a public benefit that is smaller than it was before but is nevertheless (except in Kazakhstan and Kosovo) much larger and less targeted toward low earners than that in most Latin American countries; (3) a higher—but still quite low and not yet equalized—retirement age for women and men (fifty-eight for women and sixty-three for men in Kazakhstan, sixty for women and sixty-five for men in Poland, sixty for women and sixty-five in Croatia); (4) a benefit structure that gives lower annual pensions for early retirement and greater longevity, sometimes in the public as well as the private pillar; (5) a reduction in special privileges for women that previously existed, such as pension credits for time spent on maternity leave or child care;[2] (6) a weakening, and in some cases an elimination, of survivors' benefits and a continuation of the old system's prohibition on receiving personal pension and widow's pension simultaneously; and (7) an absence of firm decisions, so far, on how the annuity stage of the defined contribution plan will be handled.

PRIVATELY MANAGED FUNDED ACCOUNTS In all cases, these countries set up privately managed, funded defined contribution plans that mandated retirement saving and gave workers a choice of investment managers, much as in Latin America. While the size of these accounts varies widely, with contribution rates ranging from 2 percent (Bulgaria) to 10 percent (Kazkahstan), their structures are very similar.

PUBLIC BENEFITS—LARGE AND EARNINGS RELATED However, their public benefit structures are very different from those in Latin America.In all cases except Kazakhstan and Kosovo, the public benefit remains relatively large and more closely linked to contributions or years of work. In Hungary, Croatia, Bulgaria, and Macedonia, an earnings-related defined benefit plan that gives higher benefits to high earners—a smaller version of the old defined benefit scheme—was adopted for the public pillar. (In Croatia the formula was moderately progressive). In Poland and Latvia, a new form of public benefit was adopted—a notional defined contribution (NDC) plan. This system is pay-as-you-go, but it uses a benefit formula that mimics a funded defined contribution plan. That is, the contributions of each worker are recorded in an account and credited with a notional interest rate that is set by the government, but the contribution is immediately used to pay other retirees—no money remains in the account. When the worker retires, his or her "notional accumulation" is converted into a real annuity according to a formula that, in principle, takes life expectancy into account. Although they are allowed to retire early, women bear the full actuarial cost of doing so by getting a lower monthly pension. This system is discussed in greater detail in the following section on Sweden, which developed the NDC model and helped spread it to nearby countries.

Thus the public pillar was designed as an instrument of risk diversification rather than redistribution. In fact, basing benefits on contributions rather than redistribution to low earners is considered equitable in the transition economies, which have seen many idiosyncratic and perverse redistributions in the past—a reminder that the definition of *equity* varies with the cultural and historical experiences of a society. For similar historical reasons, rewards for work were given a high priority in these countries.

MINIMUM PENSIONS The public pillar did, however, include a minimum pension in most transition economies as a poverty prevention safety net. In Kazakhstan, deviating from the pattern described above, the minimum pension guarantee (MPG) (about 21 percent of the average wage) is the only public benefit. In Kosovo the residence-based public benefit is a flat pension pegged to the cost of a subsistence food basket. Estonia and Lithuania accompany their earnings-related public scheme with a small flat basic benefit that effectively sets a minimum. Beyond that, every country provides a minimum pension guarantee that varies between 17 percent and 30 percent of the average wage, with eligibility requiring ten to twenty-five years of contributions.

These eligibility requirements are modest in view of the high female labor force participation rates in the region. Most women will satisfy these conditions and are thereby insured against absolute old age poverty. At the bottom of the income distribution, gender differentials are compressed by the minimum pension. In Poland, 70 percent of recipients of the minimum pension are women, a result of their relatively low lifetime earnings and greater longevity (Woycicka et al. 2003). However, their high labor force participation rates also mean that the vast majority of woman will accumulate a personal pension that exceeds this minimum, so it will do little to reduce the gender gap, except for very low earners. Indeed, simulations show constant replacement rates across income categories and little redistribution beyond the bottom end, with Croatia, Lithuania, and Kosovo being the only outliers for reasons given above (Whitehouse 2003). This pattern is consistent with our prediction of lower pensions for and little redistribution to women. Moreover, the minimum pension is usually price-indexed, so it will decline through time relative to wages and become even less applicable in the future.

Changing Labor Market Behavior and Demography of Women and Men

Given the close linkage between benefits and contributions and the conversion of pension savings into an actuarially fair annuity, labor force participation rates, wage rates, and retirement age now matter much more than they did in the old systems. Yet, just as they began to matter, a growing gap

Table 7.1: Labor Market Patterns of Women and Men in Transitional Economies[a]

	Kazakhstan		Latvia		Poland	
	Female	Male	Female	Male	Female	Male
Formal Labor Force Participation						
Rates, Female/Male Ratios	85%		85%		78%	
Average Years of Work at						
Retirement.	35	40	32	39	32	42
Wage Ratio (Female/Male)	72%		80%		80%	
Retirement Age	58	63	60	60	60	65
Life Expectancy at Retirement	25	13	21	15	24	15
Unisex Life Expectancy at						
Retirement	19	16	17	17	20	16

Sources: Castel and Fox (2001), Woycicka et al. (2003), and additional data supplied by Paulette Castel. Life expectancy at retirement is from Whitehouse (2003).

[a] Years vary between 1996 and 1999.

appeared in work histories of men and women due to changing economic and social conditions and greater freedom to adapt to them.

In Kazakhstan, Latvia, and Poland participation rates in the formal labor market are now 15 to 20 percent lower for women than for men (table 7.1). Retirement age for women is typically five years earlier than for men. By the mid-1990s the average length of service for men was about forty years, compared with thirty-two years for women, and the latter number is expected to drop further as a result of growing informality (Castel and Fox 2001). While these disparities are small by Latin American standards, they are large compared with earlier Soviet Union days.

The gender gap in wages, too, is smaller than that in Latin America, but it is growing (Woycicka et al. 2003). Female wages are only 70 to 80 percent of male wages. Evidence from Poland indicates that occupational segregation has increased, with women concentrated in the public sector and in lower-paying fields such as health and education. In contrast, males are more likely to take jobs in industry, trade, and the private sector, which pay higher wages.

Meanwhile, life expectancy for men has actually been declining in much of the region, so female life expectancy at age sixty is five to seven years more than male life expectancy—a much larger difference than in Latin America, implying that women are even more likely to become widows. Taking into account their earlier pension ages, life expectancy for women at retirement is six to ten years more than for men, leading to much smaller annual benefits if gender-specific mortality tables are used (Whitehouse 2003). Unisex mortality tables are used for calculating the public benefit, but it is not yet known whether they will be required for the private funded benefit. However, even if they are used, the earlier retirement age for women implies a longer life expectancy at the point when the annuity is calculated.

Consequences for the Pension Gender Gap

Thus, reductions in female labor force participation and relative wage rates are taking place in a new system where these variables now matter. At the same time, implicit redistributions to women have decreased; for example, they do not get full credit for child-raising periods. Early retirement, which was a clear advantage in the past, results in mixed outcomes in the present systems as it simply trades off more leisure for less pension due to actuarial adjustments. As a result, the gender gap in pensions appears to be increasing. While detailed studies have not yet been made, estimated pension ratios for average women versus men have fallen from 95 to 100 percent under the old systems to 50 to 60 percent projected for the new systems (table 7.2). Also in the future more than in the past, full-career women will receive larger pensions than those with less labor market attachment.

A partial decomposition of the gender gap is available for Poland that is roughly comparable to the decomposition presented earlier for Latin America (table 7.2). Simulations (by Chlon-Dominczak in Woycicka et al. 2003) indicate that pensions received by average women will be only 45 percent as much as those of men if gender-specific mortality tables are used to purchase individual annuities. This percentage increases to 57 percent if unisex mortality tables are used for annuitization and 73 percent if retirement age is equalized at sixty-five. The remaining differential of 27 percent is due mainly to the growing wage disparities between men and women. This decomposition does not account for survivors' benefits, joint annuity, or minimum pension, which might raise these ratios for low earners and married women (but see below).

Simulations further compare these gender ratios with much higher female/male ratios under old system rules: 81 percent based on current labor market behaviors and 95 to 100 percent based on old behaviors. Thus, diverging work and wage patterns for men and women have led pensions to diverge by almost 20 percent, and new system rules have more than doubled this projected pension gap. It is sometimes argued that a large public benefit protects women. The experience of the transition economies suggests that the targeting of the public benefit matters more than its size. If the public benefit is large because it is positively related to work and earnings, it is unlikely to improve the relative position of women compared with the positions achieved by the private benefit.

Table 7.2: Female/Male Ratios in Pensions in the Transition Economies[a]

	Kazakhstan		Latvia		Poland
	New	Old	New	Old	New
Projected Gender Ratios in Pensions (Female/Male)	52%	95–100%	62%	98%	45% (no unisex) 57% (unisex) 73% (unisex, equal retirement age) 81% (old defined benefit formula, new work patterns)

Sources: For Kazakhstan and Latvia, see Castel and Fox (2001). For Poland, see Woycicka et al. (2003). Additional data provided in personal communications with Paulette Castel and Agniezska Chlon-Dominczak.

[a] Methodologies are different from those used for the Latin America study. These simulations are based on data for average man and woman presented in table 7.1. They do not use age-specific wage rates and labor force participations rates and were not disaggregated by education level or marital status. For Kazakhstan and Latvia, rate of return in funded pillar was assumed to be 3 percentage points higher than rate of wage growth. For Poland, interest rate and rate of wage growth were assumed to be approximately equal. This holds for notional defined contribution public pillar, but it underestimates rate of return in the private pillar. Higher rate of return would increase absolute pensions and replacement rates but leave the gender gap for average woman unchanged. Unisex mortality tables are assumed for NDC pillars in Poland and Latvia; they are also assumed for funded pillars in Kazakhstan and Latvia, although this has not yet been decided by policy makers. For Poland, results are given both for unisex and gender-specific mortality tables, assuming earlier retirement age for women. The third item in the Poland column gives results if unisex tables are used and retirement age for women is raised to 65 (equalized to that of men). The fourth item under Poland gives results of the old system formula based on new wage and work behaviors. The minimum pension was not included, but this will not affect average women.

Married Women and Survivors' Benefits

The position of married women will probably change even more than that of single women. In most countries in the region, survivors' benefits were reduced or eliminated by the pension reform. This was done to save money for the public treasury and to underscore the ethos of personal responsibility. The latter point of view, however, overlooks two important facts: (1) the husband probably contributes about 70 percent of total household income, which is lost when he dies, and (2) due to scale economies, the widow requires about 70 percent of previous household income to maintain her previous standard of living.

Latvia eliminated survivors' benefits for spouses entirely. In Kazakhstan the widows' benefit is small and flat, financed out of general revenues. In Poland the widow is paid a benefit from the public pillar after she reaches age fifty, but when she retires at sixty she must choose between her own public pension and the widow's pension; she cannot keep both. Since the public benefit is quite large, this is a large opportunity cost to the widow.

It depresses the widow's potential income and also the wife's incentive to work. Widows inherit part of the husband's account, if he dies before retirement. But we do not yet know if joint annuities will be required upon retirement. If not required, this would be a major blow to the lifetime retirement income of married women.

Divorce, Part Timers, Unisex Tables, and Indexation

Many issues that will affect women have yet to be decided in the transition economies. In Poland the new system includes provision for account splitting in case of divorce, but it is not yet clear how that will be implemented. It also extends coverage to part-time workers—disproportionately women— but this may simply stimulate part timers to shift to the informal sector to avoid the high payroll tax rates. The possible requirement of indexed annuities and unisex tables for the private benefit are still under discussion in the region. The public benefit is usually indexed to a combination of prices and wages, which means that it will increase faster than inflation over the retirement period—a provision that is favorable to older women who live longer. But it is as yet unknown whether indexation will be required for the private benefit or whether the insurance industry will be able to provide it, if required. Unisex tables, again, are implicitly used in calculation of the public benefit, but the decision for the private benefit has yet to be made. Given the earlier retirement age of women, insurance companies could circumvent a potential unisex rule by charging a higher price for early retirees to achieve a higher price (lower payouts) for women.

Summary

Details of the reformed systems matter a lot. The magnitude of the gender gap in monthly pensions is smaller in the transition economies than in Latin America due to higher female work propensities and smaller wage disparities. But women do not benefit from transfers from the public benefit or regulations over payouts from the private accounts to the same extent as in Latin America. In most cases the public benefit is far larger—but more earnings- and contribution-related—than in Latin America. Unlike Latin America, survivors' benefits have been reduced and the joint annuity has not become an equalizer of lifetime retirement income between the genders. Meanwhile, gender disparities in wages and employment have been increasing, and gender disparities in legal retirement ages remain. As a result, projected monthly and lifetime pensions for women are lower than those for men in the new systems and the gender ratio is lower than it was in the old systems. Older women who become widows may be faced with a declining standard of living relative to their previous life and relative to younger people around them. Equalizing retirement ages and requiring joint annuities would help avoid this outcome without costing public funds.

Sweden

Sweden has also adopted a multipillar reform. The gender impact has been analyzed by Stahlberg, Kruse, and Sunden (2006) and Stahlberg et al. (2006) following our methodology. We draw on that study in this section. In Sweden the labor force participation rates of men and women are very similar—in 2002, participation rates were 80 percent for men and 75 percent for women. However, women are more likely to work part time (21 percent of women's employment versus 7 percent of men's employment) and to take a year's maternal leave upon the birth of a child. Their earnings are only 91 percent those of men. Thus a gender disparity still exists, but it is smaller than we observed in Latin America.

Despite this difference in initial conditions, the simulations by Stahlberg, Kruse, and Sunden (2006) and Stahlberg et al. (2006) reinforce our policy conclusions: the relative position of men and women varies, depending on which indicator you focus on. Women's own annuities are smaller than those of men, but their lifetime benefit/contribution rates and replacement rates exceed those of men, because they are disproportionate recipients of redistributions through the minimum pension guarantee and unisex tables, which are required in both the public and private pillars. Sweden does not have a joint annuity requirement, nor does the public pillar offer widows' benefits, except on a temporary basis. Moreover, Sweden's reform moved from a flat benefit for all old people to a minimum pension guarantee that is price-indexed and therefore will be small relative to wages by the time today's young people retire. As a result, the relative position of women deteriorated in the shift from the old to the new system. Details of policies determine the gender impact.

The Old System

The old system in Sweden consisted of a basic (flat) pension received by all residents over the age of sixty-five, a portion that was based on previous wages (called the ATP), and a special supplement to those with a low or no ATP (predominantly women). The basic benefit was about 40 percent of the average wage, indexed to prices. The earnings-related part was a defined benefit, with the person's fifteen years of highest earnings as the reference wage. The reference wage, and therefore a person's benefits, had a ceiling, but contributions did not have a ceiling. Thirty years of labor force participation were required for a full pension. Retirement age for both genders was sixty-five, but earlier or later retirement was allowed, with actuarial adjustments. A widows' pension that existed prior to 1989 was being phased out and largely eliminated for cohorts born after 1945. The system was financed by a payroll tax and supplemented by general tax revenues.

We would expect the flat pension as well as the special supplement, the ceiling on benefits and the absence of a ceiling on contributions, to be heavily redistributive toward women. However, basing the defined benefit on the fifteen highest-wage years favored men, who are likely to have steeper age-earnings profiles and higher peak wages. Earlier analyses by Stahlberg (1990, 1995) showed that the ratio of expected lifetime benefits/lifetime contributions from the earnings-related system was 6 percent lower for women than for men, lowest of all for low-level, white-collar and blue-collar women, but it became 35 percent greater for women once the basic benefit was included in the calculation.

The Private Pillar in the New System

The new system in Sweden, as in Latin America, consists of a pay-as-you-go public pillar and a funded, privately managed pillar. The funded pillar in Sweden, like Latin America, is a defined contribution plan, with the funds privately managed and investment managers chosen by the worker. Unlike in Latin America, the contribution rate is very small—2.5 percent—and the number of asset managers among whom workers can choose is very large—more than six hundred. Upon retirement, the account balance is turned over to the government, which issues an annuity. The annuity may be fixed or variable, but it is not indexed for inflation. Unisex mortality tables are used, but joint annuities are not required. Contribution transfers between the accounts of spouses are allowed but not compulsory, either while married or upon divorce. Single women are protected by the unisex tables, but the standard of living of married women falls when the husband dies, as the household income falls by much more than the fall in the cost of maintaining the same standard of living due to household economies of scale.

The Public Pillar in the New System

THE NOTIONAL DEFINED CONTRIBUTION PLAN The public pillar in Sweden is different from and much larger than that in Chile, Argentina, or Mexico: 16 percent of wages is contributed to a notional defined contribution plan. Sweden pioneered the NDC plan, which was then copied by Poland and Latvia, as discussed above. Like a funded defined contribution plan, the worker's pension in an NDC plan ultimately depends on contributions plus the rate of return on the account. However, in the case of an NDC, the money does not really accumulate; it is not invested and does not earn a return that stems from the productivity of capital. Instead, the money paid in by workers today is used to pay benefits to retirees today. But the worker is nevertheless credited with those contributions plus a notional interest rate determined by the government, which in Sweden is the average nominal growth rate of wages (much lower than the rate normally expected on funded accounts). While contributions are only credited up to a ceiling, the contributions continue at an 8 percent rate on all wages above the ceiling—a provision that should produce a higher rate of return to women who are less likely to reach the ceiling.

When the worker retires—any time after age sixty-one—the notional balance in the account is turned into a monetary annuity, on actuarial terms, by the government, which then pays the benefit out of contributions that other workers are making at that time. The initial payout is based on expected real wage growth of 1.6 percent per year as the annuity interest rate. If this rate is realized, the annuity maintains its real value over time; that is, it is price-indexed. But if the actual rate of real wage growth is less than 1.6 percent, the individual's annuity payout goes down; that is, it does not keep pace with inflation. The potential absence of full price indexation will hurt women disproportionately because they live longer.

The notional defined contribution plan replaced the ATP system to eliminate perverse redistributions (such as those to workers with steep age-earnings profiles), incentive and equity problems stemming from the weak link between benefits and contributions, and higher costs for defined benefits as longevity of retirees increased. In the NDC system, benefits are directly linked to contributions, and expected longevity of each cohort of retirees is taken into account in the annuitization process. However, low-earning women get low pension entitlements.

To remedy this outcome, special provisions were included that redistribute to women. Unisex mortality tables are used in the conversion to an annuity. Notional defined contribution credits are given for parental leave benefits, periods of unemployment, and having preschool children.

However, the NDC annuity calculation does not allow for joint pensions, and survivors' benefits are only temporary—paid for only one year or until the widow's youngest child reaches age twelve if she is under age sixty-five, and paid nothing if she is over sixty-five.

THE MINIMUM PENSION GUARANTEE The public pillar in Sweden contains another component, which is potentially more redistributive—a minimum pension guarantee. If the NDC annuity is small, or if the individual does not have any NDC, sufficient money is paid by the public treasury to bring that person's pension up to the MPG level. In other words, eligibility for the MPG is residence-based rather than contribution-based, which favors women. As we discussed for the case of Chile, an MPG can generate work disincentives for low-earning women, who get no extra pension for incremental contributions. This work disincentive begins at a lower point in Sweden because of the country's universal eligibility—twenty years of work are not necessary in order to qualify.

Countering this effect is the fact that Sweden's MPG is price-indexed. Therefore, although the MPG starts out as 40 percent of the average industrial worker's wage, this percentage will be cut in half by the time today's young worker retires due to real wage growth in the interim. In that case, very few workers will have personal pensions that fall below the MPG level, so it will be of little help to women. More realistically, the MPG will be increased on an ad hoc basis, as in Chile. If it turns out to be wage linked, it should be heavily redistributive to women.

Simulations of Gender Ratios in the New System

Stahlberg et al. (2006) follow our procedure and simulate the impact of new system rules on four types of women:

1. Full-career women, who have the same labor force participation rates and retirement age as men
2. Full-time/part-time women, who work full time until having children, then take parental leave and work part time until the children are in school, at which point they return to full-time work (this might be the "average" woman in Sweden)
3. Ten-year women, who participate in the labor force for ten years early in life, before giving birth to children, then withdraw permanently (this is rare in Sweden)
4. Part-time women, who work part-time for most of their careers

For each case, Stahlberg and colleagues construct an earnings profile for five levels of education appropriate to the Swedish situation (no upper secondary school, upper secondary complete, undergraduate education less than or equal to two years, undergraduate education more than two years, postgraduate education). They examine monthly personal annuities, lifetime benefit/contribution rates, and replacement rates, comparing these indicators for women with those for full-career men.

Consistent with our findings for Latin America, women's monthly personal annuities in the new systems are lower than those of men in all cases (table 7.3, panel A). The average full-time/part-time woman gets about 80 percent as much as men, ten-year women get only 35 to 40 percent as much, and even full-career women get only 83 to 99 percent as much as men—because of their lower wages. Notice, however, that the gender gap in personal annuities is much smaller in Sweden than in Latin America because the wage gap and employment gap are much smaller and women do not have an earlier retirement age than men. The differential in lifetime annuities is less than for monthly annuities because of the greater longevity of women. Nevertheless, even for lifetime annuities, gender ratios remain below 100 percent, except for full-career women (panel B).

However, women get higher lifetime benefit/contribution rates than men because of redistributions through the MPG and the use of unisex tables (panel C). As in Argentina, ten-year women fare particularly well. Their lifetime benefit/contribution rates are three to four times as great as those of men because they consistently qualify for the minimum pension guarantee while contributing for only a short time. One might question whether subsidizing women who have low pensions when old because they chose not to work when young is a socially desirable use of public funds. Also worth noting is the fact that lifetime benefit/contribution rates for women compared with men are highest for women with a university education. This is because men with comparable education are likely to hit the ceiling on benefits but must continue to pay contributions.

Panel D in table 7.3 shows that women also get higher replacement rates than men, mainly due to the use of unisex tables. When gender-specific tables are used instead, as in panel E, women once again fall below men due to women's greater longevity, which reduces their annual pension. But for women with a university education the female/male ratio in replacement rates remains greater than 1 because of the ceiling on benefits faced by men. The child credit, by contrast, has only a negligible effect (compare panels F and D).

The current Swedish system does not mandate a joint annuity from the

Table 7.3: Female/Male Ratios of Monthly Annuities, Lifetime Benefit/Contribution Ratios, and Replacement Rates in the New Swedish System

	Education				
	No Upper Secondary	Upper Secondary	Undergraduate < 2 Years	Undergraduate > 2 Years	Postgraduate Education
A. Monthly annuities					
Full-career woman	0.88	0.83	0.88	0.91	0.99
Full-time/part-time woman	0.82	0.79	0.84	0.84	n.a.
Ten-year woman	0.41	0.40	0.35	0.35	0.40
Part-time woman	0.66	0.62	0.66	0.67	n.a.
B. Lifetime annuities					
Full-career woman	1.00	0.94	1.00	1.03	1.03
Full-time/part-time woman	0.93	0.90	0.95	0.95	n.a.
Ten-year woman	0.47	0.45	0.40	0.40	0.45
Part-time woman	0.75	0.70	0.75	0.76	n.a.
C. Lifetime benefit/contribution ratios					
Full-career woman	1.16	1.15	1.21	1.28	1.28
Full-time/part-time woman	1.18	1.17	1.23	1.23	n.a.
Ten-year woman	3.69	3.22	3.65	3.92	3.07
Part-time woman	1.19	1.19	1.25	1.32	n.a.
D. Replacement rates—with unisex tables and child credits					
Full-career woman	1.02	1.12	1.00	1.22	1.21
Full-time/part-time woman	0.98	1.07	0.96	1.17	n.a.
Ten-year woman	1.45	1.31	1.22	1.42	1.43
Part-time woman	1.04	1.17	1.04	1.25	n.a.
E. Replacement rates—with gender-specific tables and child credits					
Full-career woman	0.89	0.97	0.90	1.03	1.04
Full-time/part-time woman	0.86	0.95	0.85	1.00	n.a.
Part-time woman	0.98	0.97	0.90	1.03	n.a.
F. Replacement rates—with unisex tables, no child credits					
Full-career woman	1.02	1.12	1.00	1.22	1.21
Full-time/part-time woman	0.94	1.05	0.93	1.14	n.a.
Part-time woman	1.00	1.12	1.00	1.22	n.a.

Source: Stahlberg, Kruse, and Sunden (2006); Stahlberg et al. (2006).

Note: Replacement rate is pension/final wage. Benefit/contribution ratios are calculated in present value terms at age 65. Replacement rates and benefit/contribution ratios include own annuities + minimum pension guarantee. Denominator is average full-time man with same education as women for all gender ratios. See text for definition of four types of labor force attachments.

private account, which was largely responsible for bringing the gender ratios of lifetime retirement income for women above that of men in Latin America.[3] However, this provision would in any event be much less effective in Sweden, where cohabiting rather than marriage or formal registration is common. It is difficult to mandate future financial transfers to compensate for current services in the absence of some formalized arrangement. To the degree that women provide the current services (such as childbearing and child care) their future financial position will be in jeopardy. Many women are responding by cutting back on these services and having fewer children.

Comparisons of Gender Ratios in New and Old Systems

Comparing gender ratios in the new and old systems, we find that the relative position of women has deteriorated in virtually every case except for ten-year women (compare table 7.3 and table 7.4). The main reason is the replacement of the flat basic benefit by the minimum pension guarantee. In the old system, everyone got the basic benefit plus a special supplement for those with little or no ATP, which favored women. In the new system, these benefits have been eliminated and most groups (except ten-year women) will have a personal pension that exceeds the MPG. The high labor force participation of women, equal retirement age for both genders, and price-indexation of the MPG explain this result. Despite the high participation rates and equal retirement ages, women's pensions are smaller than those of men because of their lower wages and greater prevalence of part-time work. A price-indexed MPG does not counteract these forces. Gender ratios would be much higher and might exceed old-system ratios if the MPG were wage-indexed, as it is in Chile on an ad-hoc basis. Lifetime gender ratios for married women and the welfare of very old widows would also be higher if Sweden mandated that joint annuities be purchased for married (or registered) couples, as in Latin America. Many analysts expect that once the MPG has fallen to a less costly level, wage or Swiss indexation (50 percent wage indexation, 50 percent price indexation) will resume.

Australia[4]

The Old System

We make a final comparison with Australia—an example of a high-income country that adopted a multipillar system fifteen years ago. Unlike all the other countries we have studied, the old mandatory system in Australia

Table 7.4: Female/Male Ratios of Annuities, Lifetime Benefit/Contribution Ratios, and Replacement Rates in the Old Swedish System

	Education				
	No Upper Secondary	Upper Secondary	Undergraduate < 2 Years	Undergraduate > 2 Years	Postgraduate Education
Monthly annuities					
Full-career woman	0.96	0.98	1.00	1.00	1.00
Full-time/part-time woman	0.94	0.98	1.00	1.00	n.a.
Ten-year woman	0.35	0.37	0.35	0.34	0.42
Part-time woman	0.72	0.75	0.93	0.94	n.a.
Lifetime annuities					
Full-career woman	1.10	1.11	1.14	1.14	1.14
Full-time/part-time woman	1.07	1.11	1.14	1.14	n.a.
Ten-year woman	0.40	0.42	0.40	0.39	0.48
Part-time woman	0.82	0.85	1.05	1.07	n.a.
Lifetime benefit/contribution ratios					
Full-career woman	1.27	1.41	1.43	1.54	1.54
Full-time/part-time woman	1.31	1.44	1.47	1.47	n.a.
Ten-year woman	11.51	10.79	13.72	14.81	13.35
Part-time woman	1.31	1.49	1.83	2.04	n.a.
Replacement rates					
Full-career woman	1.12	1.33	1.13	1.32	1.21
Full-time/part-time woman	1.14	1.33	1.16	1.39	n.a.
Ten-year woman	1.24	1.20	1.24	1.35	1.54
Part-time woman	1.16	1.33	1.16	1.39	n.a.

Source: Stahlberg, Kruse, and Sunden (2006); Stahlberg et al. (2006).

Note: Replacement rate is pension/final wage. Benefit/contribution rate is calculated in present value terms at age 65. Replacement rate and benefit/contribution rate include own annuities + minimum pension guarantee. Denominator is average full-time man with same education as women for all gender ratios. See text for definition of four types of labor force attachments.

consisted of a means- and asset-tested old age benefit that was based purely on residence rather than employment and financed out of general revenues. Augmenting this simple public system, Australia had a system of voluntary, privately managed, funded pensions, mostly defined benefit, which resulted from collective bargaining and industrywide pay awards.

The Mandatory Employer-Sponsored Private Pillar in the New System

In 1992 this network of voluntary plans became mandatory—employers were required to make a minimum specified contribution (starting at 3 percent but rising to 9 percent) into each worker's pension plan. This was, in part, an attempt to increase worker remuneration without increasing inflationary pressures. In addition, it was a way to increase national saving and avoid a huge burden on the means-tested pension as the population aged over the coming years. If workers were required to save today, they were less likely to be eligible for the public means- and asset-tested old age pension in the future. The outcome was that Australia became one of the first countries outside of Latin America to develop a multipillar system.

The private pillar, known as the Superannuation Guarantee, consists of funded plans that are arranged by the employer, usually defined contribution and usually with some investment choice. Defined contribution plans allow employers to escape from the investment and longevity risk that is bringing an end to private defined benefit plans everywhere, and giving workers investment choice allows them to select the degree of risk they are willing to take. When these pensions were voluntary, men were much more likely to have them, and to have larger pension amounts, than women. Making the private pillar mandatory therefore incorporated in the social security system a pension that would be smaller for most females, but it greatly increased their coverage. This is likely to happen in other countries, such as the United States, that are considering the adoption of mandatory retirement saving accounts. In 1984, 51 percent of male full-time workers, but only 35 percent of females, were covered by private pensions. By 1994 coverage exceeded 85 percent for full-time workers of both genders. And for women working part time, coverage increased from 6 percent to 70 percent.[5]

Projected private pension amounts are much lower for women than for men in Australia, as in Latin America and the transition economies, and for similar reasons. Currently, the female labor force participation rate is 60 percent, of which 40 percent is for part-time work, and women are permitted to retire at age sixty, earlier than men. (Women's retirement age is gradually being raised to equality with men at sixty-five). Women who enter the labor force today are projected to accumulate twenty-eight years of work, compared with thirty-nine years for men (i.e., 72 percent as much as men). Females are concentrated in low-paid occupations and earn only 88 percent per hour as much as men, on average.[6]

A recent survey provides information on the superannuation accumulations of women compared with men as of 2002 (Clare 2004; table 7.5). For older workers these data include savings from time periods when retirement savings were voluntary, but for younger workers the data mainly reflect the period after superannuation became mandatory. On average, women's accounts were only 55 percent as large as men's accounts among those who had accounts (and men were more likely to have accounts). However, the

Table 7.5: Balances in Retirement Savings Accounts in Australia, 2002 (in thousands of Australian dollars)

Age Group	Full-Time Workers	Part-Time Workers	Not in Labor Force	Low Income	High Income	Average for Those with Accounts
			Men			
15–24	8	1	0.3	0.5	8	7
25–34	29	15	6	9	39	27
35–44	70	24	9	14	93	65
45–54	122	67	43	35	165	122
55–64	166	160	85	56	252	184
Total	72	39	42	17	123	79
			Women			
15–24	7	1	0.5	0.6	7	4
25–34	27	14	8	8	50	21
35–44	54	24	13	10	82	38
45–54	83	44	20	18	156	68
55–64	77	58	42	23	127	95
Total	47	24	17	9	100	43
			Women/Men (for workers with accounts)			
15–24	.88	1.00	1.67	1.20	.88	.57
25–34	.93	.93	1.33	.89	1.28	.78
35–44	.77	1.00	1.44	.71	.88	.58
45–54	.68	.66	.47	.51	.95	.56
55–64	.46	.36	.49	.41	.50	.52
Total	.66	.62	.40	.55	.82	.55

Source: Clare (2004), based on Household, Income and Labour Dynamics in Australia Survey, 2002.

Note: Low income means gross income < A$15,000 in last financial year. High income means gross income > A$50,000 in last financial year (medium income group is omitted). Average gender ratio would be less than 50% if women without accounts were included. In 2002 the exchange rate varied between US$.51 and US$.56 = A$1.00.

gender disparities are much smaller once employment status is controlled. Among full-time workers, women's accounts were 66 percent as large as men's, and among high-income employed workers, they were 82 percent as large (probably because women with high incomes are likely to have a history of high labor force participation).

Perhaps most important, gender disparities are much smaller among women under age forty-four within each employment category. In fact, for some young subgroups, women's accounts are larger than men's. We do not know the degree to which this is an age effect that will dissipate or a cohort effect that will continue. But the fact that the education and labor force participation of women has risen over the past three decades, female retirement age is rising, and retirement saving has become mandatory all lead us to expect that behavior changes will remain among younger cohorts.

Recent simulations have projected future fund accumulations for men and women based on their estimated lifetime earnings profiles. The gender ratio of accumulations is projected to be 55 percent for baby boomers born in 1950, almost 60 percent for baby boomers born in 1960, and 80 percent if women in the latter group increase their employment rates compared with earlier cohorts (Jefferson and Preston 2005; Preston and Austen 2001). In another simulation covering both old and young workers, gender ratios for aggregate fund accumulations are expected to reach 70 percent by 2020 (Kelly, Harding, and Percival 2002a, 2002b). These numbers are larger than in Latin America and larger than applied in the past before superannuation became mandatory, but still far from 100 percent. The remaining gap is due mainly to the prevalence of part-time work among women in Australia and to wage differentials by gender. Moreover, the smallest accounts occur among older individuals who are out of the labor force, the unemployed, or low-income workers—groups that are disproportionately women. The clear message is that mandatory saving improves gender ratios, but full equality in contributory pensions will not be achieved until the labor force role of women changes. This seems to be happening, but very slowly.

The Flat Means-Tested Public Pillar

HOW IT WORKS The public pillar in Australia's multipillar system is the old residence-based, means- and asset-tested benefit. Many OECD countries have such a benefit. Australia offers a good example of how a noncontributory old age benefit might work. The benefit is flat but is gradually phased out for those with incomes above a threshold.[7] The phaseout is apparently slow enough so that 80 percent of the population over age sixty-five receives at least part of the benefit. It provides single persons with an income that is 25 percent of average male earnings and provides couples with 40 percent— close to the poverty line. Retirement age is sixty-five for men and sixty (gradually being raised to sixty-five by 2014) for women. Unlike the public benefit in Latin America and the transition economies, it is indexed to wages, hence it will retain its relative value over time. Its cost is in the neighborhood of 3 percent of gross domestic product, which in Australia is roughly equivalent to a 5 percent payroll tax. In addition, recipients get other benefits such as discounts on medical expenses and taxes.

Despite the family income and asset tests, women are more likely to qualify than men in view of their lower personal incomes, earlier retirement, and greater longevity. Even if they do not qualify immediately upon retirement, women are likely to do so as they age, use up their own resources, and become widows. Women are also more likely to get the full benefit. In 2004, 60 percent of all recipients, including three-quarters of recipients over the age of eighty-five, were women. The majority of female recipients were single, divorced, or widowed (while the majority of male recipients were part of a couple). Many were women who had limited labor force experience—women who would have been excluded from the public benefits in Latin America or eastern Europe (Department of Families, Community Services and Indigenous Affairs 2004, tables 3 and 5).

STYLIZED SIMULATIONS OF PUBLIC PLUS PRIVATE BENEFITS Projected pensions for the future using micro data are not available, but we have carried out simple stylized simulations with rules similar to those in Australia to show how the public benefit modifies gender ratios from the private benefit alone. Gender ratios from private pensions are assumed to be 60 percent within all groups to focus attention on the equalizing role of the public benefit. All workers in the bottom education group are assumed to get the full public benefit. Based on the phaseout rule, workers in the middle group get partial benefits. Average single women, widows, and married couples with nonworking wives also get some public benefit at the top end. But top-earning single men, full-career single women, and married couples who both work get no public benefit. Gender ratios that combine public plus private benefits range from 80 percent for low-income singles to 60 percent for high-income married couples, with 68 percent for the modal middle-income married group who work. Thus, Australia's public benefit redistributes, especially to low-earning women, widows, single women with limited labor force experience, and married couples with nonworking wives At low education levels the public pension exceeds the women's own pension and cuts the gender gap in half (table 7.6).

The public benefit in Australia has a similar impact to the flat benefit in Argentina, but with some differences among subgroups that indicate important differences in concepts of equity. Both redistribute heavily to low earners and to women with limited labor force attachment. However, since Australia's eligibility test is based on residence rather than employment, it greatly benefits women who have stayed out of the labor market for their entire lives, a group that gets no protection in Argentina. The public benefit is wage-indexed, hence it will continue to provide protection for future cohorts of women (unlike Argentina's benefit, which is neither price-indexed nor

Table 7.6: Stylized Pensions from Public and Private Benefits by Gender, Education, and Marital Status in an Australian-Type System (as % of average male wage)[a]

	Education/Income Category		
	Low	Middle	High
Average Married Couple, Wife Worked			
Private pension	40	80	160
Public benefit	40	24	0
Total pension	80	104	160
% increment by public benefit	100%	30%	0
Average Married Couple, Wife Did Not Work			
Private pension	25	50	100
Public benefit	40	36	16
Total pension	65	86	116
% increment by public benefit	160%	72%	16%
Average Single Man			
Private pension	25	50	100
Public benefit	25	15	0
Total pension	50	65	100
% increment by public benefit	100%	30%	0
Average Single Woman and Widow Who Worked			
Private pension	15	30	60
Public benefit	25	23	11
Total pension	40	53	71
% increment by public benefit	167%	77%	18%
Full-Career Single Woman and Full-Career Widow			
Private pension	22	44	88
Public benefit	25	17	0
Total pension	47	61	88
% increment by public benefit	114%	39%	0
Gender Ratios (Female/Male)			
Private pensions	.60	.60	.60
Private + public pension, average married man and woman	.78	.68	.60
Private + public pension, average single man and woman	.80	.81	.71

Source: Calculations by the authors.

[a] These are hypothetical numbers, designed to show impact of an Australian-type means-tested benefit. Assumptions: Men in low, middle and high education categories earn 50%, 100%, and 200% of average male earnings, respectively. Average man gets 50% replacement rate of his wage from private retirement savings account based on 9% contribution rate. Average woman's private pensions are 60% those of average man in same education category if they have done some work, based on table 7.5. But some married women do not work at all. Full-career women work as much as men but earn and accumulate only 88% as much due to wage differentials. Men and women marry within same education class. Phaseout rule is $1 of public benefit lost for every $2.5 increment in private pension, beyond 25% of average male wage for single individuals, 40% for married couples. In calculating gender ratios for married men and women, each individual is assumed to get own private pension but half of the couple's public benefit. Private pensions for married men and women are same as private pensions for single men and women.

wage-indexed) and therefore is less likely to decline in importance through time.

HOW COSTS ARE CONTROLLED   Of course, these features are costly. To help pay the bill, Australia withdraws the benefit from the very groups that get the largest flat benefits in Argentina—high-earning men and women with full labor force participation—while taxing them to cover the system's costs. This approach potentially poses a disincentive to formal-sector work—an efficiency cost that must be added to the monetary outlays. However, Australia, unlike Argentina, has the administrative capacity to compel compliance and to contain the size of the informal economy. Australia's strategy might not be feasible in Argentina and would lead to greater informality and inefficiency because of evasion by those who are expected to finance the expensive old age pension without receiving any of its benefits.[8]

Australia also saves money by basing eligibility on family rather than individual income and assets. Thus, low-earning women do not get the full public age pension if they are married to high-earning men. Australia avoids giving substantial public funds to women from high-income families who have low personal incomes because they can afford to stay at home rather than work in the labor market. Chile's MPG, which is based on the individual's own pension income, has been criticized for subsidizing women from high-income families. But if the high-earning spouse wields power over the allocation of household resources, a family test as in Australia may mean that some older women end up with little resources for themselves yet no access to public funds. Finally, in the future, qualification for and costs of the means- and asset-tested old age pension will be cut by the growth of mandatory retirement saving accounts, which began in 1992.

OTHER DESIGN FEATURES THAT MAY HELP WOMEN   The Australian system has other design features intended to help women without imposing a large cost on the public treasury, including (1) tax advantages for contributions into accounts of low-income or nonworking spouses; (2) the possibility of contribution splitting between husbands and wives; (3) the option to continue making contributions to one's superannuation account for two years after leaving a job (during interrupted careers, to which women are prone); and (4) the requirement that divorce settlements take pension assets into consideration and division of the assets is allowed (although not mandated). However, the absence of a required use of unisex mortality tables has the opposite effect on women.

Perhaps the most important problem for women is that annuities, in particular joint annuities, are not required, and, in fact, the money can be taken out as lump sums as early as age fifty-five (now being raised to sixty). This factor has led to fears that retirees will use up their retirement saving quickly in order to qualify for the public pension. In particular, it will leave little saving or insurance for the wives when they become widows. Joint annuities would reduce the eligibility of women for the means-tested old age benefit, but neither joint nor individual annuities seem likely to be mandated in the near future. In Australia this burden is borne by the larger public benefit that widows receive, rather than by the joint annuities that are financed by husbands in Latin America.

Summary

The multipillar reform in Australia has helped women in absolute and relative terms by giving them much greater access to private funded pensions than they had before. Retirement age is gradually being equalized between the genders, which will raise women's own retirement income. The residence-based, means- and asset-tested public pillar that reaches 80 percent of the older population redistributes to low-earning and single women and eliminates old age poverty. Women are not excluded by eligibility rules based on contributions. Given its broad coverage and wage indexation, the Australian age pension has a much more equalizing impact than the public plans in other regions. The comparison with Latin America shows that if the public plan is redistributive, a larger benefit will equalize gender ratios more than a smaller one while the comparison with the transition economies shows that size alone does not accomplish this.

On the downside, the tax cost of the public benefit is potentially high in Australia, because it reaches most old people whether or not they have worked in the labor market and it rises on par with wages. The cost is cut by means testing and mandatory private retirement saving. But taxes, means testing, and mandatory saving pose a possible disincentive to formal-sector work and voluntary saving. Fiscal costs could be reduced in the future, while maintaining protection for men and women, if pension withdrawals over the lifetime of both spouses, as in joint annuities, were required.

CHAPTER EIGHT

Design Features That Determine Gender Outcomes

Multipillar social security systems consist of two parts: a privately managed funded defined contribution (DC) plan that handles workers' retirement saving and a publicly managed, tax-financed defined benefit (DB) plan that prevents poverty, equalizes more broadly, and diversifies risk. The DC plan is, by definition, contributory and designed to ensure that workers' standard of living will not drop dramatically in old age, as it might for short-sighted individuals if they relied simply on voluntary saving. Some countries impose few constraints on investments or payouts, while other countries impose large constraints to protect ill-informed or myopic workers from making mistakes. The public benefit has varying degrees of links to contributions in different countries. In some cases (e.g., Australia) it is mainly redistributive and financed by general revenues, while in other cases (e.g., the notional defined contribution plans in Sweden and Poland) a stronger link exists between benefits and payroll contributions. The Latin American public pillars offer a mixed approach that falls in between these two extremes. This chapter summarizes the key policy choices a country must make that strongly affect gender outcomes, pulling together the data and arguments presented previously in this book. Ultimately, value judgments are indispensable in making these choices and designing the system.

Policy Choices in the Public Pillar

We start by discussing basic design choices in the public pillar of multipillar systems. Of course, the most basic questions are, How large should the public benefit be? What proportion of the average worker's wage is it meant to replace? The answers to these questions determine the tax rate needed to finance the benefit. Thus, these questions reflect the country's benefit/cost trade-off, as well as its preferred division of responsibility between the public and private pillars. However, size alone has a surprisingly small impact on the relative welfare of men and women, as we saw in previous chapters. Instead, the structure of the public pillar matters much more, and we focus on this here.

Should eligibility for the public benefit be based on contributory history, or simply on age? If based on contributions, how many years of work should be required for eligibility? Or should the link be proportional? How targeted should the public benefit be toward low earners or other groups; that is, how redistributive, and to whom? Should disparities between benefits and contributions depend on marital status? On decisions to work in the home versus the market? On family income? On the individual's private pension amount? Should the benefit be price-indexed or wage-indexed? The less eligibility is employment related, the more redistributive to low earners, and the more generous the indexation rule, the more women are likely to gain and the less likely they are to fall into poverty in old age. However, these practices also break the benefit-contribution link and require taxes that may discourage formal work and output.

Thus, the design features that a country chooses reflect its fundamental objectives—old age poverty avoidance, broader equality, or risk diversification for everyone—and how much weight is placed on minimizing fiscal costs and work disincentives. As we have seen, the emphasis in Chile is on poverty prevention and tax minimization, in Mexico on broader pension equality and work incentives, and in Argentina on a partial and inconsistent mixture of poverty prevention, equality, and risk diversification, with less regard for fiscal costs or incentives. Many of these same issues and trade-offs are relevant to traditional, single-pillar, pay-as-you-go defined benefit schemes.

Should Eligibility Be Age Based or Contribution Based?

In a multipillar system, financing of and access to benefits from the private defined contribution pillar are, by definition, based on contributions. However, eligibility for the public benefit may be based on an entirely different set of characteristics, such as age and income rather than contributions, and, in either case, it may be financed out of payroll taxes or the government's general budget. In this section, we focus on the choice of eligibility conditions—a key factor that determines whether the public benefit is relevant to women.

Traditionally, pensions were designed to replace wages. Therefore it seemed logical to restrict eligibility to people who earned wages and contributed based on these wages for much of their adult lives. Restricting public benefits to people who have contributed may deter evasion from the system as a whole—which is particularly important in low- and middle-income countries where evasion is high. Contributions that are earmarked to a pension scheme may be evaluated politically differently from a nonearmarked tax, so pensions may not cut into the provision of other public services as much as they would if general-revenue financing were used.

However, if access is contribution based, many workers will fail to qualify for a meaningful benefit. Typically, these include the poorest workers and women. This exclusion is particularly acute in low- and middle-income countries, where small-firm, self-employed, rural, agricultural, and informal workers dominate. These groups work, but it is practically impossible for governments to capture payroll taxes from them on a regular basis, hence the low density of contributions we observed in our three Latin American countries. Women—who are more likely to work in the home or the informal sector—are less likely to qualify for a contribution-based public benefit. While extended families often care for their older members, the family system does not always function well (as we saw in chapter 2). As a result, some older men and, more often, women will end up without access to resources from either the family or a contribution-based social security system. If the object of the public benefit is to prevent old age poverty and increase equality, some other basis for eligibility is needed. Some countries have chosen to base eligibility for the public benefit simply on age and national residence to achieve this goal. They keep the public benefit modest in size but universal, while building up the private pillar to increase the pension for contributors.

In age-based public plans, costs are usually borne by general revenues, and the general population is eligible to receive the benefit once a specified age is passed. The benefit itself may be a universal flat benefit or a means tested benefit. An age-based program is more likely than a contribution-based program to prevent old age poverty, but it will cost the public treasury more, thereby involving a potential trade-off with fiscal discipline. The tax needed to finance the program may discourage people from working when young, the promised benefit may discourage voluntary saving, and eligibility rules may encourage workers to retire as early as possible. But everyone is covered.

The Netherlands, Denmark, Kosovo, and Australia are examples of multipillar countries whose public benefits are based primarily on age. In

Kosovo each person over sixty-five gets a subsistence-level basic benefit from the government; this is the simplest model. Many more women are eligible than would be the case if eligibility were based on contributions. Using Australia's plan as a more complex example, its age-based pension is means and asset tested, flat up to a threshold and phased out thereafter, and received in whole or part by 80 percent of all old people. Women who work at home receive positive redistributions, while men and women who work in the market receive smaller amounts and pay higher taxes to finance these transfers. Women in Australia may have less incentive to enter the formal labor force than they would otherwise, due to the income effect from getting the public benefit, the explicit tax cost of financing it, and the implicit tax cost from the phaseout if their own pension grows. Australia spends more than 3 percent of its gross domestic product on the old age pension, and this proportion was projected to rise much higher in the future—until the government mandated private retirement saving accounts. Meanwhile, Australia contains its costs by partially phasing out benefits for households in the third and fourth quintiles and cutting off access completely for the top quintile, an excluded proportion that should rise as the mandated personal retirement accounts grow.

Latin America has been grappling with the trade-off between the efficiencies of contribution-based eligibility for the public benefit versus the greater coverage if it is age based. Initially, even though the public benefit was general-revenue financed, all three countries in our sample tied eligibility to contributions. Chile required twenty years of contributions to be eligible for the minimum pension guarantee (MPG), Argentina required thirty years for access to its full flat benefit, and Mexico's social quota was paid into the account of each contributor per day of work. However, Argentina has moved away from this model, first by offering a reduced public benefit for only ten years of contributions and more recently by allowing retirees to pay these contributions ex post, out of their benefits; in effect, this makes almost everyone eligible. In 2006 Mexico launched a new initiative that will pay one million elderly, living in the poorest households in the poorest communities, an age-based pension. This benefit is expected to spread to other communities as well. In 2007 Chile's government proposed a major shift away from the MPG and toward a broad, age-based, means-tested benefit similar to Australia's that would be available to the bottom three quintiles of households.

Countries considering an age-based benefit for the elderly, financed out of general revenues rather than contributions, should ask themselves, how much will this cost in the long run, and is this use higher priority than other potential uses for these general revenues? The answers will likely depend on the ability of governments to collect taxes without evasion, the prevalence of poverty among the elderly, and the degree to which society can depend on extended families to support their older members. In some countries, the need for spending on schools, health systems, and other public goods exceeds its capacity to tax, so old age plans financed by general revenues would have to be very limited in scale. One size does not fit all—but more women are likely to gain more from an age-based public benefit that is not tied to contributions.

What Are Reasonable Eligibility Rules for a Contribution-Based Public Benefit?

If access to public benefits is based on contributory years rather than being universal based on age, details of eligibility rules are crucial. If set "too high," many women will fail to qualify and may end up below the poverty line, but if set "too low," the fiscal cost may be great. What is too high or too low is very country specific, depending on typical male and female work patterns. But often, twenty years seems to be an important cutoff point.

In Chile, where twenty years of contributions are required for eligibility for the minimum pension guarantee, the average woman affiliate who contributes regularly qualifies, and women with low education are projected to be the main beneficiaries. However, women who worked less than average or did not contribute regularly when they worked will fall below the cutoff point for eligibility, getting a small private benefit and no public benefit— and this turns out to be a sizeable group, given the low density of contributions. In contrast, even the average woman fails to meet the twenty-four-year eligibility rule for Mexico's MPG. And if thirty years are required, as for Argentina's full flat benefit, only women in the top educational categories, who work the most, will qualify. Argentina tried to resolve this issue by making workers eligible for a reduced flat benefit if they have contributed for only ten years. But this solution is problematic because it costs the public treasury a lot and provides a large lifetime subsidy to women who have worked little, including those from high-income families, while at the same time offering no protection to low-income women who have contributed for less than ten years. Argentina is now trying new approaches, discussed earlier.

One practical problem with these eligibility requirements is that it is difficult to define what is meant by *a year of contributions*. Does it mean every day in a year, one day per year, or something in between? Workers with a good knowledge of the rules could manipulate the system, while those who are not savvy could lose out. A more generic problem with "on-off" switches for eligibility is that a small difference in work histories can make a big difference in access to public transfers. Women who fall just beneath the bar may be totally excluded, while those who have just passed the bar may be discouraged from further formal work, especially if the public subsidy gets her up to a minimum and would simply be crowded out by further accumulations of her own.

An alternative approach would make the public transfer a continuous function of contributory days, as in Mexico's social quote (SQ), which pays a uniform amount into the account of each worker for each day worked. Eligibility starts at day one, but the amount of the benefit builds up for every additional day. An MPG could also be set with a low floor and discrete increments tied to number of years to reduce the cliff effects, strategic manipulation, and work disincentives that we feared in Chile. Making the public benefit proportional to days worked would redistribute to workers who work a lot, but at low wage rates. In that sense, it would subsidize most heavily those with limited potential earnings, rather than those who chose to work fewer years. However, it would not eliminate poverty among vulnerable groups such as informal sector workers or those engaged in home production. It also limits the achievement of broader gender equality, because men work more than women.

In fact, many multipillar countries that started with contribution-based eligibility rules have developed alternative definitions of contributory years to avoid poverty among noncontributors or low contributors, impelled by the large numbers who are excluded by these rules. For example, most European countries grant credit for time spent providing child care and elder care, which adds greatly to the years counted for women. This provision makes sense, in particular, if (1) bearing and raising children and caring for the elderly generate social benefits that exceed the private benefits, (2) society wishes to increase the time allocated to this activity, and (3) pension credits are an efficient way to achieve this result. With fertility rates below replacement levels one might argue that the answers to the first two conditions are "yes" in many countries—but it is worth noting that pension credits have not arrested this decline, so the third condition may not be satisfied. Several transition economies, faced with extreme fiscal pressures, have moved in the opposite direction, reducing child-care credits to economize on costs as they introduced their multipillar reforms, thereby trading off some poverty and equality objectives in favor of lower tax burdens and smaller work disincentives.

Targeting the Public Benefit: How Much and How Should It Redistribute to Low Earners?

Most of the public pillars in Latin American multipillar systems redistribute to low earners, although with different degrees of targeting. This contrasts with public benefits in traditional social security systems, which offer benefits that are positively related to earnings and often redistribute to high earners, who live longer, hence receive benefits for more years, and have steep age-earning profiles that are rewarded by the defined benefit formulae. Indeed, one of the reasons for separating the redistributive and saving functions into two different pillars of the system is to make it easier to track whether the subsidies from the public benefit are going in the right direction.

Women as a group gain from public benefits that are targeted toward low earners, because women tend to work and earn less than men. But, as we saw in our sample countries, women are a heterogeneous group. In fact, the wage and private pension differential between women with high and low education is far greater than the differential between men and women with the same education. Which is a higher priority: targeting the public benefit to protect low earners (which will be disproportionately but not exclusively female) or targeting it to equalize pensions between the genders (which will include middle-class women as beneficiaries)? We contrast three types of public benefits commonly found in multipillar systems—minimum pension guarantees, means-tested benefits, and flat (uniform) benefits—that place different emphases on poverty prevention, broader gender equality, and low tax costs.

MINIMUM PENSION GUARANTEES Most Latin American and eastern European countries offer a minimum pension guarantee as (part of) their public benefit. If the person's pension from other sources falls below a specified level, usually 17 to 30 percent of the average wage, the government provides additional resources to top it up and meet the minimum pension amount. The lower tail of the pension distribution is therefore raised. Since the pension itself must be calculated in any event, the marginal cost of calculating qualification for the MPG is small, making this benefit relatively easy to administer.[1]

Generally this kind of public benefit is for contributors only (although in Sweden it also covers noncontributors). If it is financed out of general revenues, as is typically the case, this implies that noncontributors (who pay taxes) are subsidizing contributors (who receive benefits). Because non-contributors as a group tend to be poorer than contributors, this perverse redistribution from outsiders to insiders runs counter to the progressive redistribution among the insiders.

The degree of protection provided by the MPG, as well as its fiscal cost, depends on the contributory years required for eligibility and the nature of indexation. In most cases the cost will be modest, because it only applies to workers who have contributed fairly regularly and the bulk of their pensions come from their own accounts. Thus the tax supporting it will also be modest and relatively nondistortionary. (For Chile we estimated this cost to be less than 1 percent of wages.) Nevertheless, low earners may be discouraged from working in the formal sector and contributing once they meet the eligibility conditions, because additional contributions will simply crowd out the public benefit.

As we saw in the case of Chile, women are expected to be major recipients of the MPG top-up, both because of their transient labor and low wages—providing they meet the eligibility conditions. But only the poorest women inside the system get it; it does nothing to achieve broader gender equality, unless it is set at a high level and is wage indexed. Women also benefit from the focus on individual rather than family income. Some of the women who receive Chile's minimum pension are from high-income households, not in danger of living below the poverty line but with small personal pensions because of their transient labor force attachment (Valdes 2002). These women would be ruled out by a means-tested program that took family income into account, as in Australia. At the same time, poor women who fail to meet the eligibility conditions (the "outsiders") get nothing from Chile's MPG, while they would be covered by Australia's plan.

MEANS-TESTED BENEFITS In principle, the most cost-effective way to prevent poverty among the elderly is to apply a universal means and asset test so the benefit goes only to those with meager family resources and it goes to all in the population who meet this criterion. A means-tested program is like an MPG, except that all income and assets of all household members are usually included in the means test. Also in contrast to the MPG, this type of benefit is generally age based, not contribution based, as it aims to aid those who need it most, who are likely to be outside the contributory system. It is almost always financed by general revenues rather than a payroll tax.

Australia's public benefit is an example of a very inclusive means- and asset-tested scheme. It exemplifies the point that if a high wage–indexed threshold is set for phasing out the benefit, means testing can achieve broader income and gender equality as well as avoiding poverty. Chile, in contrast, offers a very small, narrowly targeted, means-tested scheme (PASIS) for the poorest noncontributors. The PASIS benefit is only half that of the MPG and, until 2006, was severely rationed (rationing was removed and funding increased in 2006). Chile's proposed new public benefit will also be means tested, but it will be more like that in Australia—much more generous and inclusive than PASIS or the MPG.

The disadvantages of a means-tested benefit are well known: Because all income sources count, it is more difficult to implement than an MPG, where only pension income must be evaluated. It requires much greater administrative resources than flat benefits, where only age counts. If not well executed, many people will be miscategorized. Because case-by-case appraisals must be made, opportunities for bribery abound, particularly in low-income countries where a culture of corruption often prevails.[2] Some people who qualify may not even realize that and may not apply—the well-known stigma and take-up problems. Mexico is trying to solve these problems by piggybacking a new means-tested benefit for the elderly onto an existing antipoverty program (Oportunidades) that already has targeted the poorest households.

In an extended family setting, difficult decisions must be made about which household resources to include and how to measure the "need" of households that differ in size and composition of members. In chapter 2 we saw that several different equivalence scales exist and yield different results. Right now Chile is grappling with these questions in connection with its proposed new public benefit. Older members, especially women, may not have control over all the household income that is attributed to them, so their "means" may be overestimated. And the benefit they derive from the pension may also be overestimated if it is shared with other family members. In South Africa, for example, the broad-based, means-tested pension for the elderly reduces old age poverty in most rural black families and also raises school enrollment rates and health of children in those households, evidence of benefit sharing (Duflo 2000; Case 2001).[3] Furthermore, means testing may crowd out family support and reduce incentives to contribute and save voluntarily, in order to improve eligibility for public aid (for evidence on this point from South Africa see Jensen 2004). (The MPG does not have this distortionary effect, since saving outside the pension system and family transfers do not interfere with eligibility. The flat benefit is even less distortionary since everyone gets the same benefit regardless of other resources.)

Despite these disadvantages, means-tested programs have one big advantage over the MPG—they can readily be used even if no private contributory pillar is in place. And they have one big advantage over flat benefits—the limited money can be more clearly targeted toward those in need. For the same reason, women are likely to get a larger share of the total budget in a means-tested program than in a flat benefit plan. Means-tested programs therefore constitute a cost-effective way to alleviate old age poverty and gender inequality—providing they are well implemented.

FLAT BENEFITS A flat benefit pays a uniform amount (or uniform per day worked) to all eligible people once they reach a specified retirement age. Age-based flat benefits are found in the public pillars of Denmark, the Netherlands, Kosovo, and Bolivia. Argentina's two-tier flat benefit is a variation on this theme. Mexico's SQ, which puts a uniform amount into the account of each worker per day worked, attempts to combine the flat concept with work incentives. But this approach is unlike pure age-based flat benefits because it only reaches individuals who have worked and contributed in the formal labor market.

Age-based flat benefits are the simplest to administer. All individuals get the same benefit; its size is unrelated to wages, personal pension, or other income. Thus it does not discourage the worker from saving or the retiree from earning. It may seem to be nontargeted, but in fact it is redistributive to low earners if financed by taxes paid by high earners. Because women are relatively low earners, they are disproportionate recipients of net redistributions. The flat benefit equalizes gender ratios in the middle and high education categories as well as the bottom, as it constitutes a larger share of the total pension for women than for men with this same education. If eligibility is age based, women who have not worked in the market are the biggest net beneficiaries.

As a corollary, its tax cost is higher than that of an MPG or means-tested benefit pitched at the same level, because every eligible person gets the full flat benefit, not simply a top-up for a select group. Some of the recipients are middle and high earners who would not get the MPG or means-tested benefits. Further, this cost will grow over time, as populations age. The high and rising tax cost may discourage formal sector work as a secondary effect.

These costs and their growth could be contained by measures such as keeping the benefit modest; starting the benefit at a very old age, such as seventy or seventy-five, when retirees are more likely to have exhausted their other resources; and prescheduling an age increase each year in line with expected longevity gains. Also, part of the benefit could be recaptured from high earners through the income tax system. Nevertheless, some rich countries are now downsizing the relative size of their generous flat benefits by using price indexation rather than wage indexation. Sweden has completely eliminated it in favor of an age-based minimum pension guarantee.

WHICH IS THE BEST APPROACH? The choice among these alternatives depends in part on the country's fiscal capacity as compared with its administrative capacity, and by the relative weight it places on poverty prevention, broader equality, and lower taxes. It also depends on the degree of heterogeneity among the old. If old age poverty is pervasive, the case is strong for using the flat benefit. But if poor old people are less common than poor young people and if wide income disparities exist among the elderly population, it may be preferable to use the MPG or means testing. The latter are also less expensive because they are more selective. Hence they are preferred if fiscal resources are more scarce than administrative capacity and concerns about reduced incentives to save and work are small. Women benefit disproportionately from each of these options, as compared with traditional earnings-related benefits that are less redistributive to low earners.[4]

Should Low Labor Force Participation be Used as a Basis for Redistribution?

Low lifetime earnings, hence low pensions, stem from two possible factors: low wage rates and low labor force participation. While some people earn low wage rates because they have chosen jobs that offer nonpecuniary benefits, most earn low rates for other reasons over which they have little control—limited quantity and quality of education (perhaps because they came from disadvantaged backgrounds), lack of knowledge about how the labor market operates, and discrimination are three possible reasons. Relatively little volition is involved. Most people would prefer higher wage rates, ceteris paribus. Public benefits targeted toward recipients of low wage rates can be thought of as insurance against an event that was unavoidable by the individual.

Differential labor market effort is a different matter, at least for younger cohorts. In the past, strong social norms led women to work at home, without much individual thought, variation, or control. One reason some Organisation for Economic Co-operation and Development (OECD) countries adopted universal flat pensions was to redistribute to women who were expected to stay at home, with taxes paid by men who worked in the market. For the same reason, many traditional defined benefit systems that target public transfers to low earners, such as that in the United States, also implicitly subsidize low labor force participation of women, which was taken for granted when the social security system began seventy years ago.[5]

But social norms are now changing. Market work by women is allowed and even encouraged in many countries. Women are more likely to be educated, be single, and have fewer children, all of which increase that expectation. So the voluntary choice model may be increasingly applicable. Public benefits targeted toward those who have little labor force participation cannot be viewed as insurance against an unavoidable event. Rather, the benefits create an incentive to stay at home, and the taxes imposed to finance them are a disincentive to market work—even though this behavior may reduce labor supply and output for the broader economy (for evidence from the United States that women respond to such incentives, see Munnell and Soto [2005] and Munnell and Jivan [2005]). These undesired incentives may be one reason why some OECD countries have been shifting away from universal flat benefits toward less generous reliance on means testing in recent years.

Our three sample countries have taken very different positions on this issue. Of course, in all three countries the private annuity strongly rewards market work. But this is not always true of the public benefit. Mexico's social quota lets a person accept the consequences of his or her decision and gives a larger public benefit to those who work more in the market. Chile's MPG truncates the bottom end of the pension distribution, providing an income floor to those with a combination of low wages and partial labor force attachment. If those at the floor work more, their larger personal pension displaces the MPG. Argentina's flat benefit redistributes to those who have stayed out of the formal labor market for most of their adult lives. The high money's worth ratio (MWR) to ten-year women in Argentina and their low marginal MWR for incremental work may keep older women out of poverty but may also discourage younger women from market work. In contrast, in Chile and Mexico the danger of poverty exists for very old women who have not worked (but this is mitigated by limited means-tested programs and generous joint pension arrangements).

Should Marital Status Determine Access to and Size of Public Benefit?

In many traditional social security systems, married women have access to more generous benefits than single women. For example, once they reach retirement age, wives in the United States get a spousal benefit equal to 50 percent of the husband's pension from the social security system, and widows get a survivors' benefit that equals his full benefit, even if they have not worked in the labor market. While the spousal benefit is unusual, survivors' benefits are common. In our three sample countries, widows got 60 to 90 percent of their husbands' benefits in the old systems.

These provisions stem from an era when almost all men and women married and had children, wives were expected to stay at home, and husbands were expected to support them. However, in the modern era, in which marriage and childbearing are not universal and most women engage in substantial market work, these traditional arrangements create several anomalies. First, because married men have not paid additional contributions for spousal and widows' benefits, these pensions are really not financed by the husband but rather by the common pool. In effect, single people who contribute are subsidizing married people, and low-earning couples are subsidizing high-earning couples in which the wives receive larger benefits. Wives who stay at home often get larger benefits than single women who work and contribute. Being married raises the retirement transfer that women get from others outside the family. Married women seem to be treated well by these systems. In many countries, this situation has become a big drain on system finances.

However, to contain this cost, wives have usually been required to choose between their own benefit and the spousal or widow's benefit. This was true, for example, in the old system in Chile. Thus any contribution they made on their own was a pure tax; they got no incremental benefit in return. From this perspective, married women who worked were penalized. The largest net benefits went to married women who stayed at home. A recent study found that this provision led wives to work less and retire early in the United States (Munnell and Jivan 2005; Munnell and Soto 2005).

The treatment of marital status is different in multipillar systems. Marriage either decreases the public benefit paid to both partners or has no impact at all. But it may increase the payouts women receive from the private pillar.

In multipillar countries where the public benefit simply provides a pension floor to prevent old age poverty, the differentiated treatment of single versus married individuals stems from household economies of scale—two people who share a household can live more cheaply than two who live alone. Thus, the age-based flat benefit in the Netherlands is about 20 percent less per person for married than for single individuals. The same is true for the public benefit in Australia, and, moreover, the income and assets of both husband and wife count toward the means test that determines access. As a result, single women and widows receive larger public benefits than married women.

While this approach makes sense in principle, in practice many old people live together without marital formalities, and keeping track of such unofficial arrangements is difficult. Reducing the flat benefit for married people may discourage elderly people from getting married and encourage them to hide it if they do. Partly for these reasons, the minimum pensions in the new systems of Sweden, Chile, and most eastern and central European countries are independent of marital status.

As a corollary, in most of these countries we observe a movement away from survivors' benefits in the public pillar. The rationale driving this change seems to be that many women are single or cohabit without formal marriage, women are expected to work, any decision not to work is voluntary, so no reason exists for society to provide extra payment to widows—except to meet the poverty prevention goal of the system. Cutting survivors' benefits, especially those that are positively tied to the husband's earnings and pension, appears to be a reasonable way to economize on fiscal costs.

This reasoning is both right and wrong. On the one hand, the decisions to marry and to participate in the labor market are voluntary, and there seems to be no reason why others outside the family should subsidize or penalize them. On the other hand, the widow's standard of living is likely to fall drastically after the husband dies, even if she has worked. Typically, his income is greater than hers, so household income will fall by more than 50 percent. Yet, because of economies of scale, household costs for the same living standards will fall by only 30 percent. Widows often experience a drop in their living standard and are the poorest group of women as a result.

This dilemma can be resolved, without placing a burden on the public treasury, by requiring spouses to pay for survivor's insurance out of their retirement savings in the private pillar, by a joint pension requirement. Widow's benefits would then be provided, but the cost is largely internalized within the family. Scarce public funds could be targeted toward low earners, rather than middle- and upper-class widows. The joint pension requirement is basically the way widow's benefits are handled in Latin America, accounting in large part for the gains women have made in the new systems. We discuss this topic further below, in the section "Policy Choices in the Private Funded Pillar".

Should the Public Benefit be Price Indexed or Wage Indexed?

Price indexation of the public benefit promised to a retiree is essential in order to set a real floor to a retiree's standard of living and prevent real declines over his or her lifetime. (This argument applies also to the private benefit, as discussed in the section "Policy Choices in the Private Funded Pillar.") This is particularly important to women, who live longer. But price indexation poses problems as a method for determining the initial public benefit that will apply to successive cohorts, because it implies that the safety net will fall over time relative to wages. This trend, too, is especially relevant to women, who are major recipients of the public benefit.

For example, Chile's MPG is officially price indexed, currently at about 27 percent of the average male wage. But under price indexation, that percentage will fall to only 12 percent of the average male wage when today's young worker becomes a pensioner at age sixty-five, under our baseline assumption of 2 percent annual real wage growth. Although the safety net appears reasonably high today, it will be low compared with wages and the average standard of living in society at that time. It will also be low compared with the size of the annuity from the private accounts, so it will do little to counteract gender differentials in total pensions in the future. That expectation is part of the reason why very few future retirees get Chile's MPG top-up in our simulations with price indexation. In reality, the MPG has risen on par with wages on an ad hoc basis, both for new and old retirees, over the past twenty-five years. The protection afforded by a wage-indexed MPG is much greater and more widespread. But the cost will be correspondingly greater, so we do not know if this practice will continue.

Mexico plans to price index the public benefit—that is, maintain its real purchasing power—but we do not know how that will work, as no one has yet retired under the new system. The Argentine flat benefit has remained constant in nominal value over time. As prices rose due to devaluation of the peso, this situation became so untenable that Argentina had to add a minimum pension that exceeded the flat benefit on an ad hoc basis. An automatic adjustment rule would allow better planning by workers and retirees.

Australia and the United Kingdom provide an interesting comparison of the political impact of wage versus price indexation. Australia wage indexes its safety net. This enables retirees to share in the economic growth that occurs over time, and it affords the same level of relative protection to present and future cohorts. It particularly benefits women. But it is much more expensive than price indexation. Australia established a multipillar system with a large mandatory defined contribution plan, which will reduce the number of retirees qualifying for its means- and asset-tested public benefit, in part to enable it to continue this indexation policy.

In contrast, the basic (flat) benefit in the United Kingdom has been price indexed for more than twenty years. Its value has fallen from more than 20 percent to less than 15 percent of the average wage. As a result, the United Kingdom is the one OECD country that projects low fiscal costs despite the growth in its older population. However, this reduction in relative value of benefit provides pensioners an unacceptably low standard of living compared with current workers, so the United Kingdom has had to expand its provision of means-tested benefits. These, in turn, suffer from take-up and poor incentive problems. Very old women have relatively high poverty rates and are disproportionate recipients of these means-tested benefits. The United Kingdom is considering major changes in its system, in part because of widespread dissatisfaction with the low relative level of its safety net.

Switzerland tries to stay on the fence between these two approaches by indexing its public benefit half to price growth and half to wage growth. Most transition economies follow this example. Sweden is currently using price indexation to draw down its minimum pension to more reasonable levels, after which many analysts expect it to resume wage, or Swiss, indexation.

If the objective of the public benefit is poverty prevention and if the poverty line is defined in absolute terms as the cost of purchasing a fixed market basket of goods, price indexation satisfies this criterion. But if poverty is defined as a socially determined concept and if broader equality between pensioners and workers matters, some degree of wage indexation of the public benefit for successive cohorts is needed, even though it costs more. One possibility is to wage index the public benefit for successive cohorts but to price index during the retirement period of each pensioner. (This could be accomplished by revaluing the pensionable salary base according to wage growth, as is done in the United States.) Another possibility is to use Swiss indexation. Otherwise, future generations of low-earning pensioners will fall further below the average standard of living in society. The outcome of this debate is of particular concern to women, who are most likely to be recipients of the public benefit, and for the longest retirement period.

Policy Choices in the Private Funded Pillar

A similarly long list of policy choices must be made regarding the design of the defined contribution plan in multipillar systems. These choices become particularly critical when a country makes these plans mandatory, instead of voluntary as they are in the United States. What restrictions should exist during the accumulation stage to prevent overly risky or expensive investments? At what age should payouts be allowed? Should requirements be imposed to purchase annuities? Price-indexed annuities? Joint annuities? To use unisex mortality tables in the calculation of annuity payouts? What should be done in the case of divorce? While the answers to these questions affect all older people, they affect women in particular, because of their greater longevity and, traditionally, their lesser financial experience.

The Accumulation Stage: Portfolio Choice and Risk Aversion

Defined contribution plans have an accumulation stage and a payout stage. The main gender-related issue during the accumulation stage concerns the possibility that women may invest more conservatively than men, therefore getting a lower expected rate of return and ending up with lower balances and pensions. This gender difference in risk aversion has been found in several studies. However, it is reduced when other factors, such as income, education, and marital status, are taken into account (U.S. GAO 1997; Hinz, McCarthy, and Turner 1997; Jianakoplos and Bernasek 1998; Sundén and Surette 1998; Bajtelsmit, Bernasek, and Jianakoplos 1999; Bernasek and Shwiff 2001; Lyons and Yilmazer 2004; Save-Soderbergh 2003). Moreover, the differential would be much smaller if measured in risk-adjusted terms (the conservative portfolios that bring lower returns also imply less risk and could come out ahead if markets experience a prolonged downfall). The gender gap in riskiness of portfolios is likely to be reduced still further as women and men gain more financial experience, as they will in a mandatory plan.

Nevertheless, public policies can also cut the variance in rates of return due to unwise portfolio choice—through financial education, simple and limited investment options, and careful selection of the default portfolio, into which workers are placed who do not make an active choice of their own. These policies, in particular choosing the "right" default portfolio, are especially important for women. Most analysts believe that the default should be broadly diversified and age related, starting with a relatively risky portfolio that has a higher expected return when workers are young and gradually shifting into more conservative investments as the date of conversion to annuities and other payouts approaches.

We did not encounter this issue in our three sample countries, because they offered workers little choice of investment strategy in their early years. In our simulations we therefore assumed the same rate of return for everyone. Over the long run, and even more so in richer countries, workers will face greater choice, so variance will develop in rates of return among workers and possibly between the genders. Then, these policies take on strong relevance. In Sweden, where the funded DC plan is only a small part of the total pension, the default is a widely diversified, high-equity portfolio. The majority of workers entering the system—both men and women—are in the default. However, most of the gender-related policy choices occur at the payout stage, and we turn to these now.

Should Retirement Age be Raised and Equalized for Both Genders?

Two key questions in social security system design are, at what age should workers be permitted to start withdrawing their benefits, and should retirement age be equalized for men and women? These questions apply both to the public DB plans and private DC plans, but the answers have different implications in each.

In many countries, women are permitted to retire earlier than men. Perhaps this practice stems from the fact that wives tend to be younger than their husbands; a lower retirement age allows them both to retire at the same time. But this "special privilege" is anomalous, given that women have worked less, have smaller pensions, and are likely to live longer than men. It is a costly privilege, which adds to the financial woes of defined benefit plans and reduces pensions in DC plans.

In public DB plans, monthly benefits are usually not adjusted upward in an actuarially fair manner for postponed retirement, so women have an incentive to retire as early as legally allowed. Even if early retirement reduces their monthly pension a bit, it increases their lifetime benefits and gives them additional years of retirement leisure. This effect is accentuated for married women, whose pensions depend on their husband's rather than their own earnings, and in countries with minimum pensions, where continued work and contributions would reduce the MPG top-up. The high cost of early retirement is borne by the public treasury or the system's general pool in these cases. The cost is also borne by the broader economy, which loses valuable experienced labor. As a result, most OECD countries are now moving toward higher and equal retirement ages for men and women, and the transition economies are also narrowing the retirement age gap.

In contrast, in funded defined contribution plans, which annuitize on an actuarially fair basis, individual women bear the cost of their early retirement. The younger one is upon retirement, the less interest one accumulates, the more years one's accumulation must cover, and, therefore, the smaller the resulting monthly pension. Thus earlier retirement translates into substantially lower monthly benefits for women.[6] Chile and Argentina may appear to be favoring women but actually are not, when they permit them to start withdrawing their retirement saving at sixty rather than sixty-five. Early access to the private benefit, combined with delayed access to the public benefit, is a major reason for the exceptionally low gender ratio of monthly personal pensions in Argentina. The monthly pension for women in Chile would be increased by almost 50 percent if age of normal withdrawal were raised to sixty-five. Also, the projected fiscal cost of the MPG would fall, because personal annuities would then be more likely to exceed the minimum. Yet Chile's government did not include this step in its recent proposals for reform, a measure of its political unpopularity. Mexico's equal retirement age for men and women is likely to save money for the public treasury and augment its gender ratio and labor force at the same time.

Women can, of course, postpone retirement voluntarily. One of the advantages of a defined contribution plan is the hope that actuarially fair penalties will induce them to do so. But legal floors on retirement age exist because of the likelihood that many workers are myopic and will not respond to these incentives. The possibility of more leisure financed by faster access to their retirement savings may be attractive to women when they are in young old age. But they may regret their decision as they live longer than expected and find themselves with a very low income, compared with male pensioners and workers around them, in very old age.

Should Annuitization be Required?

In a defined contribution plan, workers accumulate savings while working and consume these savings during their retirement period. Workers who are myopic may use up their savings before their actual or expected age of death, if flexible withdrawals are permitted. Women are especially prone to outlive their savings, because of their greater longevity. This risk is accentuated in households where husbands have dominant decision-making power over family resources and place greater weight on consumption during their own shorter lifetime. Moreover, expected lifetime has been increasing by about one year per decade—that is, an average person born a decade later will probably live at least a year longer. This longevity increase is heightened in middle-income countries that are catching up with medical technologies used in richer countries. Workers may not take this additional longevity into account in their calculations, basing their expectations on the experience of their parents, who had much lower expected life spans.

Annuities, which provide longevity insurance, are therefore important to all workers, but especially to women, who may otherwise be left with meager resources in very old age. With annuities, retiring workers turn over their accumulations to an insurance company, which takes on longevity risk and agrees to pay them a specified monthly benefit for the rest of their lifetime. Public policies that limit payout options, with annuitization required or strongly encouraged, protect women from uncertainty as well as from their own myopia. Such policies protect society from the liability of supporting very old women who have outlived their retirement saving. Thus they are consistent with the objectives of avoiding poverty and controlling fiscal costs.

Of course, everything has its cost, and the cost of mandatory annuitization is that some people who expect to die young or are overannuitized from other sources (such as company pension plans) will be worse off than they would have been if they could withdraw their funds more quickly. Money tied up in annuities cannot be drawn on to meet emergency needs that might arise shortly after retirement. Bequests cannot be left to children or other heirs, as the worker's saving has already been turned over to an insurance company. These constraints increase the implicit tax component of the pension contribution.

How can these implicit costs be reduced? One possible approach is to mandate only partial annuitization—up to, say, 150 percent of the poverty line—allowing the individual to take the remaining part of his or her money in a lump sum or other flexible manner. Another possible solution is to offer a one-time partial withdrawal at any time during the course of the annuity; this would relieve pressure stemming from an unexpected emergency. Still another option is to give the retiree choice with regard to type of annuity. Annuities come in many types—individual annuities that cover a single retiree, joint annuities that cover a designated beneficiary as well, and annuities with a guaranteed payout period that continue making payments to the estate for a specified number of years even after the primary beneficiary dies. People who wish to purchase annuities but also want to protect their heirs may choose the latter two types.[7]

The three Latin American countries we analyzed offer annuitization or gradual withdrawals as two alternative payout options from their defined contribution plans. In our simulations we assumed annuitization. Two-thirds of all current pensioners have annuitized in Chile's new pension system, in part because annuities offer a good rate of return for a safe investment, in part because of aggressive marketing by insurance companies, and in part because preferred options (such as lump-sum withdrawal of the entire amount) are not permitted. In contrast, lump-sum withdrawals are allowed in Australia to make the accounts less restrictive and more attractive—but this will probably raise future financial pressures on the public old age pension. And, at the opposite extreme, annuitization is mandated in Sweden to ensure that everyone has a lifelong income without imposing an additional cost on the public treasury.

Should Annuities be Price Indexed?

Indexation is crucial for both genders. It is particularly important for women, who live longer than men and might be left with low purchasing power late in life if the annuity is not price indexed. With price indexation the monetary value of the private annuity increases each year, just enough to compensate for price increases. This allows the elderly to maintain a stable standard of living. With wage indexation it increases still further, enough to keep up with wage growth, which is generally higher than price growth, owing to productivity increases. Of course, in an actuarially fair annuity market, the higher future payout of the annuity means that retirees must accept lower initial payouts—this is the trade-off. The question is, which time stream of payouts would male and female workers prefer, and which is best for society?

In general, long-lived retirees benefit from annuities that keep pace with prices or wages, while retirees who expect to die young benefit from nominal annuities. Women and high-earning men, whose life expectancies are above average compared with the overall population, are major beneficiaries of indexation requirements if they are put into the same pool with low-earning men, who would do better with front-loaded payouts implied by nominal annuities.

But many women do not realize this fact. To these individuals, higher initial payouts through nominal (nonindexed) annuities may be very appealing at first; but this preference may turn out to be myopic, as the individual's standard of living falls in the future. With an inflation rate of, say, 4 percent per year, the real value of the annuity will be cut in half over the retirement period of the average male worker, who lives eighteen years after retirement, and to one-quarter of its initial value for very old women who sometimes live as much as thirty-six years after retirement. This could easily bring such a woman below the poverty level. Clearly, policy makers face a trade-off between avoiding poverty and avoiding tax distortions, as the lower initial payout due to the indexation requirement increases the perceived tax by workers.

Inflation protection is an expensive product for insurance companies to provide because of the reinvestment risk and nonhedgeable inflation risk they incur. In general, they cannot issue such insurance credibly unless they can invest in indexed financial instruments. But price-indexed financial instruments are rare in most countries, aside from occasional government bonds, and indexed bonds pay low interest rates. Companies then pass the higher cost of inflation risk along to annuitants in the form of a lower implicit rate of return. Wage indexation of private annuities is practically impossible because financial instruments linked to wage growth simply do not exist. It may be possible for the government, with its power of taxation, to wage index the public benefit, but it is unlikely that private insurance companies could wage index the private annuity.

What do countries do? In Chile, the private annuity is required to be price indexed. Chile is one of very few countries where indexed instruments of many sorts exist, and insurance companies therefore offer a high return on price-indexed annuities (James, Martinez, and Iglesias 2006). Indexed annuities are available in the United Kingdom, but a high load factor is charged to compensate the insurance companies issuing them for inflation risk.[8] Mexico intends to require that annuities be price indexed, but it is not clear that insurance companies will be able to offer that product at a reasonable price.

One possibility is for the government to require price indexation with a cap, such as the 5 percent cap in the United Kingdom, which is more manageable for insurance companies. Another possibility is for the government to reduce reinvestment and inflation risk to the insurance company by issuing indexed government bonds of varying durations, including very long term bonds. Indeed, if the government requires or encourages the use of indexed annuities, reducing such risk is an essential first step. In Sweden, the government has gone beyond this step and has taken over the responsibility for providing the indexed annuities in exchange for the funds in the accounts. In effect, the public agency that runs the system bears the inflation risk, but with an escape valve: if it is unable to cover that cost due to unexpectedly low economic growth or high inflation, benefits are cut; thus, risk is shared with retirees. In most of our simulations, we assumed that the annuity maintains a constant real value over the retiree's lifetime, which is equivalent to assuming actuarially fair price-indexed annuities or the absence of inflation.

Should Joint Pensions and Survivors' Benefits be Required?

As women are likely to outlive their husbands, survivors' benefits are crucial to their financial welfare. Because of household economies of scale, it costs one person about 70 percent as much to live as two, so the widow's standard of living is bound to fall when she loses her husband's pension, unless she receives survivors' insurance. As discussed earlier, for this reason traditional social security systems often provided public survivors' benefits, which were financed by the common pool. Married women got larger public subsidies than single women, and women with high-earning spouses got larger transfers than those with low-earning spouses. Many countries required women to give up their own pensions to get the widow's benefit, so married women who worked got little or no increment for their contributions. This kind of arrangement may induce wives to stay at home or to work in the informal sector where they avoid the payroll tax.

In contrast, the new systems of all three Latin American countries keep most of the cost of survivors' insurance within the family.[9] They require the husband to spread his retirement savings over the expected lifetimes of both spouses through joint withdrawals or joint annuities. This requirement reduces his pension by 15 to 20 percent, depending on the size of the survivor's benefit and the age of his wife. The theory behind this mandate is that wives have lower earnings and pensions because of the implicit contract they made with their husbands to allocate time toward household and child-care services in exchange for monetary income that he will provide. However, this flow of money often stops when he dies. The joint pension requirement enforces the wife's entitlement under the implicit family contract after his death.

In Argentina and Mexico this obligation is symmetrical—both spouses must purchase joint pensions. This approach emphasizes the concept of family co-insurance, more appropriate to situations where the wife also works (although the joint pension implies a much smaller reduction in personal pension for wives than for husbands). In Chile, only the husband is required to purchase a joint pension, based on the expectation that the wife is financially dependent on him but not vice versa.[10]

Most male retirees purchase joint annuities, producing the large intra-household transfer to their wives that we measured in tables 4.10, 5.10, and 6.10. This incremental transfer is overstated in families where husbands would have purchased life insurance voluntarily, as such voluntary arrangements may be crowded out by the mandatory arrangements. However, if households are myopic, or if the husband places greater weight on consumption during the period when he will be alive, the household will not save or insure an equivalent amount voluntarily (see Bernheim et al. 2003). Evidence from the United Kingdom, where a large voluntary defined contribution system has existed for some time, suggests that the vast majority of men purchase single life rather than joint annuities (Pensions Commission 2004). Apparently many widows can count on protection from their husband's retirement saving only if joint pensions are mandatory. Mandatory joint pensions avoid a moral hazard problem—that the husband will underinsure if he thinks he can pass this responsibility on to the public treasury.

The joint annuity requirement effectively extends a contribution-based system to cover married women who did not contribute—so long as their husbands did. It uses intrahousehold transfers instead of public transfers. Mandatory joint pensions are, therefore, a partial alternative to a noncontributory scheme, with much lower tax costs. They are likely to reduce poverty among very old women, because the money flows in just at the point where household income would otherwise be sharply cut.

Most important, in Latin America widows are allowed to keep this benefit from the joint annuity as well as their own benefit. Because the husband has paid for the joint annuity by taking a lower payout himself, this becomes his wife's property upon his death and no reason exists for her to have to pay twice by forgoing her own pension. This ends the high taxation of married women who work in the market and enhances the incentive for them to work. The widow's benefit plus her own personal benefit maintain household purchasing power at about 70 percent of the previous level, so her standard of living is roughly unchanged. The right to keep both benefits is the main provision in the new systems that raises the relative lifetime benefits of married women beyond that attained in the old systems. And it does so without placing a burden on the public treasury or on single men and women.

Yet the joint annuity is not always required—as we found in Sweden, Australia, and eastern Europe. The ethos in these countries seems to be that each individual's account is meant only for himself or herself. Mandatory joint pensions are considered "derived rights," which demean women (while public benefits are considered "entitlements"). This point of view ignores the value of family co-insurance as well as the objective facts that women earn less and have lower pensions than men, in part because they have allocated their time to the household. Given this division of family responsibility, women are bound to be financially dependent either on their husbands or on taxpayers at large. If public survivors' benefits are eliminated and not replaced by mandatory private joint pensions, women's relative position is likely to decline—as we found in several of these countries. Making joint pensions mandatory and allowing women to keep their own pensions as well maintains their standard of living, improves their position relative to men, and encourages them to work in the formal labor market, which is the only way they can become truly financially independent.

Unisex Tables

Even with laws requiring joint pensions for spouses and a redistributive public benefit, the problem of low monthly pension income remains for women, especially very old single women. One reason is the greater longevity of women, which means that their monthly pensions will be smaller than those of men who had similar accumulations in their accounts, if gender-specific mortality tables are used in calculating annuity payouts. The lower monthly pensions imply a lower standard of living for women—albeit for more years.

The mandatory use of unisex mortality tables has sometimes been urged to reduce the gender gap in monthly pensions due to longevity differentials. Unisex tables assume a common (average) survival probability, instead of differentiated mortality tables, for men and women. Because they treat both genders as if they have the same expected lifetimes, they equalize monthly benefits for men and women who have the same retirement accumulations. This raises annuity payouts for women and lowers them for men. It implies a redistribution of lifetime income to women, who get back more over their lifetimes than they paid for, and the opposite holds true for men.

The chief argument in favor of using unisex tables is that it tends to equalize the monthly benefits, therefore equalizing the standard of living of men and women. Those in favor of unisex tables also point out that the life expectancy distributions of men and women are wide and overlap, so it is unfair to attribute a higher average lifetime to all women, thereby penalizing them because of an average characteristic of their gender.[11] The chief arguments against unisex tables are that it implies a lifetime redistribution from men to women that is unwarranted and inequitable, and it poses implementation problems in competitive insurance markets.

In evaluating these arguments, it is worth recalling that the change in monthly income and the lifetime redistribution are very small—2 to 3 percent—in the context of joint annuities purchased by married couples. The effect is more noticeable—8 to 9 percent—for individual annuities purchased by single individuals (see tables 4.9, 5.9, and 6.9). Nevertheless, even in the latter case, mandating unisex tables would have a much smaller impact on living standards than mandating equal retirement ages for men and women. And it has a more perverse impact on redistributions than mandating a public benefit that is targeted toward the poor. Under unisex tables, the redistribution goes to women in all income classes, but especially to high earners, who are likely to live longer and receive the higher monthly benefit for more years. Using joint annuities and a targeted public benefit may be a fairer and more efficient way to raise the living standards of older women.

Traditional public defined benefit plans implicitly use unisex mortality tables, paying the same monthly benefit to men and women regardless of their differential mortality. This practice is also followed in the public pillars of multipillar systems. Some countries (e.g., Switzerland, Sweden) require that community mortality tables, including unisex, be used when accounts in the private pillar are annuitized, and this is likely to prevail in most European Union (EU) countries. Transitional economies use unisex tables in their defined benefit and notional defined contribution plans but still have not decided which way to go in their funded defined contribution plans. It is likely that pressures from the EU will push them toward unisex.[12] Most Latin American countries allow the use of gender-specific tables by insurance companies issuing annuities. However, the prevalence of joint annuities means that this allowance will make little difference in payouts to married individuals.

In competitive insurance markets, mandatory unisex tables pose a number of problems, including adverse selection by individuals and cream skimming by insurance companies. Men may avoid purchasing single life annuities, because they will get poor terms—this is a form of adverse selection, induced by rules that prohibit risk classification. In the extreme, men may forgo longevity insurance, and the market may end up dominated by the risky group—females—and their higher longevity rates. In the opposite direction, insurance companies will seek to attract the men, who are lower risk and therefore more profitable, and try to avoid female annuitants who will live longer. While they may not be legally permitted to exclude women, they may concentrate their marketing or offer better rates in occupations and industries where men dominate. If married men must purchase joint annuities while women must purchase individual annuities, as in Chile, insurance companies may charge more for the latter type of annuity, thereby obviating the point of the unisex requirement. In countries where women can retire earlier than men, higher rates might be charged for early retirees, who are predominantly women; this was a concern in Poland as it deliberated its new annuities law.

If nationwide unisex tables are required, companies that end up with a concentration of female annuitants will lose money. If companies are allowed to build unisex tables based on their own experience, those with a disproportionate number of females will offer lower pension payouts than others, effectively reintroducing gender-specific pricing. But potential future consumers will then seek out better rates elsewhere, so the high-rate companies with many females may find themselves without customers. Thus, unisex tables may not be compatible with voluntary annuitization and competitive insurance markets.[13]

What is the appropriate policy response to these pitfalls of unisex tables?

1. For women with very low old age income, most likely very old single women and widows, it would seem crucial to raise their monthly and lifetime benefits via redistribution—giving these women more in benefits than they contributed to avoid poverty. However, unisex tables are an inefficient way to prevent poverty, because most women who benefit are not poor while some men who implicitly pay by getting lower pensions are poor. A better alternative is to use a more transparent and targeted form of redistribution, financed by taxes on high-earning men and women, which would be the case if general revenues were used to finance a public benefit with this objective.

2. For married women in all income brackets, a joint annuity requirement may be thought of as a partial substitute for unisex tables. It may be a less distorting option, as husbands may recognize the grounds for supporting their widows. It increases lifetime retirement income at the point when it is most needed by the household, when the husband dies. Joint annuities virtually eliminate the gain to women and loss to men, as well as the distortionary impact on insurance companies, from using unisex tables. They therefore defuse the otherwise contentious unisex issue.

3. If unisex tables are required and individual annuities are allowed, countries might consider using a risk-adjustment mechanism to compensate insurance companies that end up with a disproportionate number of women.[14] Alternatively, countries might consider using a competitive bidding process that concentrates the entire annuity business in one company for a specified period, to avoid the selection and cream-skimming issues spelled out above. Poland has been considering these strategies. Some countries (e.g., Sweden) forgo the use of competitive insurance markets and simply resort to public provisions of annuities with unisex tables.

What Should be Done in Case of Divorce?

Women sometimes lose their partners—and the retirement income provided by those partners—through divorce. Traditional social security systems often make special provisions for divorced women. For example, in the United States they get the same benefits as a wife would, providing they were married for at least ten years and do not remarry. In this way, a man who sequentially marries four women for ten years each requires the social security system to support four wives. But women who are married for less than ten years before divorce have no right to any part of their husband's social security benefit. The plight of divorced women may be especially great in societies where the extended family plays an important role. Divorced women may become outsiders to their own families, unable to count on their support as they age.

The treatment of benefit and asset rights in divorce situations was not on the agenda in our three sample countries when they reformed their social security systems. Divorce is uncommon in Argentina and Mexico and was illegal in Chile until 2004. Thus regulations did not restrict what participants could or could not do with their accounts in case of divorce, and we did not deal with this issue in our case studies. However, divorce will probably be increasing there, just as it has increased around the world. In Mexico the divorce rate already doubled between 1970 and 2000. In the United States the divorce rate for the baby boom generation, born in 1946 to 1964, is double that of its parents, who were born in 1926 to 1930. According to projections for the United Kingdom for 2021, 38 percent of women aged fifty-five to sixty-four, just before retirement, will not be part of a marriage; about one-third of this group is never married and two-thirds are divorced (Pensions Commission 2004). And older women who are divorced have very high poverty rates (Munnell 2004).

The same logic that applies to joint pensions applies when marriages are split by divorce before retirement. Given the intertemporal exchange of services from the wife for financial support from the husband in a marriage, it seems reasonable that a mandatory system should require some compensation to the wife. Since retirement may be many years away, the joint pension is not the most appropriate instrument here. Instead, the money accumulated in retirement savings accounts could be considered community property, to be split upon divorce. Alternatively, account sharing could take place continuously, by splitting all contributions between the two spouses, on a monthly or annual basis, during the marriage. Each party could then use his or her share to purchase an annuity or other pension upon retirement. Similar procedures could be followed by registered partners; civil registration is a common arrangement in Europe. Yet practically no country with a multipillar system has adopted regulations requiring the splitting of contributions during marriage or of assets upon divorce or breakup of registered partners.

Informal cohabitation is increasingly replacing formalized arrangements such as marriage or registered partnership, both in Europe and the United States. Where the relationship is informal, it is even more difficult to enforce future compensation for past household services provided by the woman, which may have diminished her long-term earning and pension prospects. Whether through divorce of a formal arrangement or the breakup of an informal arrangement, it seems that the female partner bears the risk of low income in old age if the relationship should end. This risk is one rationale for structuring the defined contribution private pillar so that it does not discourage work by women, and accompanying it with a noncontributory benefit in the public pillar.

CHAPTER NINE

Conclusion

Summary of Results

Table 9.1 summarizes our main indicators for Chile, Argentina, and Mexico. Our empirical investigations and simulations show that women who work in the formal labor market have their own retirement saving accounts in the new systems. For many it is the first time they have had saving of their own. These accumulations and the pensions that they finance are smaller than those of men—only 30 to 40 percent as large—due to lower lifetime employment, earnings, and contributions, as well as earlier normal retirement age. However, because they tend to be low earners, women are recipients of net public transfers that raise their monthly and lifetime benefits. (This increase is larger and continues longer for future cohorts if the public benefit is wage indexed). As a result, pension income tends to replace a higher proportion of average annual earnings for women than for men, especially for low earners. And the imputed money's worth ratio (expected present value of lifetime public plus private benefits divided by present value of lifetime imputed contributions plus pension tax), a measure of redistribution, is much higher for women than for men.

Additionally, women are beneficiaries of regulations that require joint pensions in the private pillar. Women outlive men, on average, so joint pension requirements systematically redistribute from husbands to wives. Consequently, the lifetime retirement income of married women ends up being 70 to 90 percent as much as married men's. In most cases this gender ratio is higher than it was in the old system.

These results are partially due to the public benefits in the new systems, which redistribute heavily to low earners—and women are disproportionately low earners. But the joint annuity requirement accompanied by the removal of penalties for labor market work plays an even more important

Table 9.1: Comparing Gender Indicators (female/male ratios for average man and woman, %)[a]

	Education				
	1	2	3	4	5
Chile					
Monthly Benefits					
Own annuity	33	32	38	45	36
Own annuity + MPG	44	32	38	45	36
Own + wage-indexed MPG	96	66	45	45	36
Lifetime Benefits					
Own annuity	52	50	59	70	56
Own annuity + MPG	63	50	59	70	56
Own + wage-indexed MPG	121	88	67	70	56
Own + MPG + joint	87	73	83	94	79
Replacement Rates					
Own annuity + MPG	63	54	49	72	96
Reference wage adjusted	93	97	78	84	99
Own + wage-indexed MPG	139	112	57	72	96
MWR$_{pub+pvt}$	148	121	121	121	121
If MPG wage indexed	283	213	136	121	121
Post/Prereform	152	142	111	97	109
Argentina					
Monthly Benefits					
Own annuity	21	20	26	35	35
Own + flat benefit, age 65	14	15	21	29	42
Own + flat benefit, age 70	37	32	34	41	42
Lifetime Benefits					
Own annuity	33	31	42	56	57
Own annuity + flat benefit	41	37	44	56	67
Own + flat + joint + widows' benefit	68	65	72	83	93
Replacement Rates					
Own annuity + flat benefit	57	59	76	57	57
Reference wage adjusted	115	141	147	84	69
MWR$_{pub+pvt}$	178	170	143	130	149
Post/Prereform	325	281	144	143	137

role. In the new systems women do not have to give up their own benefit to qualify for the widow's benefit (that was purchased by their husbands in the form of a joint pension), as they often did in the old systems, so retirement income of working women rises substantially. Also, the actuarial connection in the new systems between lifetime contributions and benefits helps. Women get credit, compounded with interest, for their contributions made early in life, while old system benefits depended heavily on wages and contributions toward the end of the working career, a formula that favored men with rising age-earnings profiles. Women's pensions would rise much more—they would be 50 percent higher—if their normal retirement

Table 9.1: *continued*

	Education				
	1	2	3	4	5
Mexico					
Monthly Benefits					
Own annuity, no SQ	29	30	32	41	49
Own annuity including SQ	35	35	37	45	53
Lifetime Benefits					
Own annuity, no SQ	38	39	41	52	61
Own annuity including SQ	42	42	45	55	63
Own including SQ + joint	66	65	68	77	85
Replacement Rates					
Own annuity including SQ	54	57	63	53	78
Reference wage adjusted	114	152	154	136	125
$MWR_{pub+pvt}$	139	135	133	127	124
Post/Prereform	154	138	122	96	88

Source: Calculations by the authors.

[a] This table gives average female/married male ratios for each indicator, taken from earlier tables. For both men and women, own annuity and, when noted, public benefit are included. Denominator is married man, whose pension is lower than pension received by single man, because he pays in forgone benefits to finance a joint pension for his wife. Numerator is married woman. In Argentina and Mexico her own annuity would be slightly larger if she were single. Post/prereform indicator applies to married women and includes joint annuity in numerator. It compares ratio for women to ratio for top-educated men, as in tables 4.14, 5.14, and 6.14.

Men and women are assumed to retire at normal retirement age (65/60 in Chile and Argentina, 65/65 in Mexico). In Argentina, flat benefit starts at 60, 65, or 70 for different individuals, as discussed in the text. Monthly ratios are measured at age 65 in Chile and Mexico, age 65 and 70 in Argentina.

MPG = minimum pension guarantee; SQ = social quota.

Education categories are given as 1, 2, 3, 4, and 5 because relevant schooling levels vary across countries (see chapters 4, 5, and 6).

age were raised to sixty-five, which is the normal retirement age for men. (Mexico has already done this, but Chile and Argentina lag).

While women as a group gained in relative position due to the reform, different subgroups of women benefited the most in each country as a consequence of their differing policies. In all cases, the highest money's worth ratios and postreform/prereform ratios are received by women in the lower education groups, because of the equalizing role of the public benefit. Apparently the smaller public benefits in the new systems are more targeted toward the poor than the larger benefits in the old systems. In Chile only the lowest earners qualify for the public benefit, while in Mexico and Argentina it is received more broadly, across all income spectrums, although it is most redistributive to the bottom end.

In Chile and Mexico, full-career women gain more than ten-year women, consistent with the work incentives in their new systems. Work incentives are strongest in Mexico, where the size of the public benefit is directly proportional to days worked. These pro-work policies are likely to move average women closer to full-career woman status and further improve their relative position. In Chile, the position of ten-year women actually falls relative to men. But in Argentina, ten-year women register larger relative gains than other groups and also get the highest money's worth ratios, because of the flat benefit for retirees with only ten years of work. This subsidy to women who have not worked much in the formal labor market may slow down their shift to market work and thereby impede their financial independence in the long run, but it ensures that in the meantime these women can stay out of poverty.

In Chile and Argentina, married women gain more than comparable single women because they can keep their own pension in addition to the joint pension (in Mexico they did so in the old system as well). However, single women are not exactly comparable, because they work more, and this gives them an offsetting gain in systems that reward work; they may become full-career women.

Caveats

Some caveats and gaps arise in our analysis, including the following:

1. Single women and those cohabiting without a formal marriage contract receive lower annual and lifetime benefits than men or married women because they have lower wages and greater longevity than men and do not gain from the joint annuity, as do married women. Even if they work full career, their pensions will be low relative to men so long as their wage rates remain relatively low. Concerns about single women could be addressed through measures such as a wage-indexed public benefit or the use of unisex mortality tables in the private pillar. Moreover, they can improve their own situation substantially by raising their retirement age to parity with that of men and working like full-career women—and increasingly they are doing just that.

2. Some aspects of the system still discourage work by women. For example, the reduced flat benefit in Argentina and the minimum pension guarantee (MPG) in Chile could deter work by low-earning women after reaching the eligibility points of ten and twenty years of contributions, respectively, because their incremental net benefits are negative after that point. Moreover, the earlier allowable retirement age of women in Chile and Argentina reduces their years of work and contributions and increases their years of pensioning, hence it is a major reason for their relatively small pensions.

3. All workers, and especially women, benefit from automatic price indexation

of the social quota (SQ) in Mexico as well as the MPG and the private annuity in Chile. However, the public benefit is not price indexed in Argentina, and price indexation of the private annuity will be difficult in Mexico without the availability of indexed financial instruments in which insurance companies can invest. Price indexation of the ongoing pension after retirement is especially important to women given their greater longevity. Moreover, if the public safety net received by successive cohorts is not linked to wage growth, it will gradually diminish relative to workers' wage and the average standard of living in society, and its equalizing impact will disappear for future generations of women. (Chile has increased its minimum pension roughly on par with wage growth on an ad hoc basis, so its long-term impact will be much greater than for a price-indexed MPG.)

4. This study deals mainly with women who are in or who have husbands in the contributory social security system. It does not deal with the large group of rural women in low-income countries who do not meet these criteria and may have little income or saving when they become old. Recent data indicate that many urban men and women in our sample countries also fail to contribute regularly; instead, they become self-employed or work in the informal market. Adding a noncontributory, age-based component to the public benefit, which might be means tested or flat, financed out of general revenues, would solve this problem. Means-tested programs would be the least expensive way to ameliorate poverty because they target the lowest income groups, but they face daunting administrative hurdles as well as (dis)incentive problems. Flat benefits are easier to administer, less distortionary, and equalize across a broader range of education groups, but they are costly and must compete with other pressing social needs.

5. The favorable outcome we have described for women in Latin America contrasts with outcomes in the transition economies of eastern Europe and the former Soviet Union, where preliminary investigations suggest that women lost relative to men from the pension reform due to the earlier retirement age for women, the less targeted public benefit, the weakening of survivors' benefits, the failure to require joint pensions, and the continued requirement that working women must give up their own public benefit to get the widows' benefit if it exists (Castel and Fox 2001; Woycicka et al. 2003). Similarly, in Sweden the shift from a flat benefit to a minimum pension and the absence of survivors' benefits have hurt women (Stahlberg, Kruse, and Sunden 2006; Stahlberg et al. 2006).

Thus the relative gains to women are not inevitable—detailed design features matter. Several key lessons emerge for policy makers who wish to improve gender outcomes during a social security reform.

Lessons for Policy Makers

Rules of the System Should Not Penalize or Discourage Women's Work in the Labor Market

Specifically, the following measures should be taken to prevent penalties and disincentives:

1. *Retirement age should be equalized for men and women.* While earlier retirement for women was a privilege in the old systems, it creates a problem for them in the new systems. Women who underestimate their longevity retire early but may regret this decision when they age, their pensions are low, and their choice is irreversible. Equalization of normal retirement ages between the genders would increase women's accumulations by 30 percent and their monthly pensions by 50 percent in Chile and Argentina. It would ensure that lifetime retirement saving is allocated to old old age instead of young old age. It is especially important for single women who will not receive a boost from the joint pension. Equalizing the retirement age also increases the country's labor supply, savings, and gross domestic product.

2. *Women who have built their own pension should not have to give it up to get the widows' benefit.* In many traditional systems, working women must choose between the two pensions. Thus, women who work for much of their lives pay substantial contributions with no incremental benefit—the contribution is a pure tax. In contrast, in the new Latin American systems the widow keeps her own annuity as well as the joint annuity that her husband purchases. This raises her retirement income when she is old and also encourages her to work and contribute when she is young.

3. *Avoid eligibility conditions for public benefits that impose a high marginal tax rate on low earners,* as in the case of Chile's MPG and Argentina's reduced flat benefit. Instead, encourage their further work and thus help them escape their precarious position.

Individual Accounts Should Be Accompanied by a Strong Safety Net, which Protects Low Earners

Women are disproportionately low earners. The public benefit should do the following:

1. *If it is contribution based, avoid eligibility conditions that exclude most women* (as in the thirty-year contribution requirement for Argentina's full flat benefit)

or that impose a high marginal tax on women who qualify (as for Chile's
MPG). A continuous linkage to years worked (as in Mexico's SQ) is preferable to an on-off switch for eligibility.

2. *Be price indexed after the worker retires to enable retirees to maintain a stable
standard of living as prices rise.*

3. *Rise with wages for successive cohorts once it has reached the desired long-term level
relative to the average wage,* as is done on an ad hoc basis in Chile.

4. *Include a component that is based on age rather than contributions, designed to
keep out of poverty women who have not worked in the formal labor market.* This
may supplement or replace a contribution-based public benefit. The size of
this benefit, as well as its design as flat or means tested, depends on the administrative and fiscal capacity of the country and the relative priority given
to old age security versus other social needs.

Payout Provisions from the Individual Accounts Strongly Influence Women's Retirement Security

1. *Annuitization, which provides a guaranteed income for life, is especially important for women in view of their greater longevity.* Retirement and other savings
are more likely to be used up before death for women than for men, in the
absence of annuitization. Annuitization requirements—perhaps up to 150
percent of the poverty line—should be built into the defined contribution
system.

2. *Inflation insurance of annuities is crucial for women because it helps maintain
their real living standards as they age.* Private annuities are indexed in Chile,
but indexation will be difficult to achieve in other countries that do not have
many indexed financial instruments. Government issuance of long-term,
price-indexed bonds would help make indexed annuities feasible.

3. *Joint annuities purchased by the husband enable the widow to maintain the household's previous standard of living without imposing a burden on taxpayers.* A joint
annuity extends beyond the husband's death the informal family contract in
which he promises to provide the majority of monetary support while the
wife spends more time caring for the family. While this division of responsibility is changing, it will be many years before roles are totally equalized.
Even then, a symmetrical joint pension requirement would be desirable
to insure both spouses. Importantly, this extends system coverage to many
married women who have not worked in the formal labor market, without
imposing high fiscal costs.

4. *The use of unisex mortality tables needs to be carefully thought through.* Unisex
pricing of individual annuities helps to equalize the standard of living of

men and women in retirement. It redistributes from men as a group to women as a group, so a value judgment is needed on whether this redistribution is desirable and, if so, whether this is the best way to achieve it. It leads to cream skimming and adverse selection problems, but these can be mitigated by risk-adjustment mechanisms or concentrated annuity provision based on competitive bidding. The use of unisex tables reduces the opportunity cost of joint annuities, and joint annuities largely eliminate the impact on payouts of unisex tables for married couples.

5. *Legal protections are needed to split contributions and assets or provide a joint pension for divorced women and women cohabiting without formal marriage.*

Within this broad framework for gender-friendly policies, details of the "best" design pattern will vary, depending on a country's social objectives and budget constraints. Chile, Argentina, and Mexico have implicitly defined gender equity differently and have made different trade-offs between poverty prevention, broader pension gender equality, work incentives, and fiscal cost. These choices reflect different value judgments and political compromises.

Applicability to Traditional Systems

While our focus in this study was on multipillar reforms and most of our examples were from countries that had made such reforms, many counterpart policy choices could also be made in traditional pay-as-you-go systems, such as in the United States. For example, some traditional systems still permit women to retire earlier than men. Early retirement reduces the size of women's pensions, which contributes to the heavy incidence of female poverty in later years. At the same time it implies a larger aggregate public expenditure on women's pensions in young old age, which impedes the systems' fiscal sustainability and its ability to target assistance to those who need it most. Equalized retirement ages should surely be part of a program of gender equality. The United States already has equal retirement age, and other Organisation for Economic Co-operation and Development (OECD) countries either have it or are now moving toward it.

Many countries with traditional systems provide widows' benefits based on the husband's pension size without requiring the husband to finance it. Since the money then comes out of the public purse, women are often required to give up their own pension to get the widow's pension (which is larger). The United States is an example of countries that have such provisions. This is likely to deter women's market work, because the payroll tax has no corresponding benefit to them. While appearing to favor women, it really keeps them in a state of dependence, since their own work and contributions do not count. An alternative arrangement would require married men to finance the widow's benefit by taking a reduced pension of their own, which would then allow women to keep the widow's benefit in addition to their own pension. This arrangement would encourage women to work, helping to make them more independent and less likely to suffer a steep fall in standard of living when their husband dies. It would also save money for the public treasury.

A strong safety net that protects low earners and rises with the wage level for successive cohorts is essential for women. Most OECD countries, with traditional or multipillar systems, have such a safety net in the form of a flat or broad means-tested pension. The United States has no minimum pension and only a narrow means-tested benefit, and partly as a result, poverty among older women is higher in the United States than in other OECD countries. A wage-linked minimum pension for the very old would improve the situation of women at the low end of the income spectrum.

In some countries, such as the United States and United Kingdom, traditional public systems are accompanied by voluntary private pension plans. These private plans are not mandatory, but they are an important part of the country's old age security program. In these cases, it is important that legal protections give widowed and divorced women access to part of the retirement savings that were accumulated by their husbands during the marriage. Making these plans mandatory, with constraints on investments and payouts, would go further toward improving women's financial security in old age.

More broadly, policies that improve women's labor market role during the working stage will also improve their position during the retirement stage, both in the traditional and newer multipillar systems. Indeed, this is the only way to ultimately achieve gender equality.

Data Sources and Methodology

The Chile estimates are based on *Caracterización Socioeconómica Nacional 1994*, a nationally representative survey that provides information on current labor force participation, working status, affiliation to social security, and contributory status. The estimates used are based on the urban sample— approximately 100,000 individuals age sixteen or older. We report contribution patterns among affiliates (workers who have contributed at some point) in urban areas. The self-employed are not required to contribute. Our data indicate that 73 percent of all male workers and 55 percent of all female workers affiliate (most of the others are self-employed), and 90 percent of male affiliates (91 percent of female affiliates) who are employed contribute to social security. Thus, our estimates for Chile are close to the behavior of the average affiliate but do not apply to women who never worked in the formal labor market. Contribution experience is estimated based on current contributions of affiliates in different age and education cells. Wages reflect pay for full-time work (most work is full time, or thirty-five hours per week, in Chile). For some analyses, data on the distribution of wages within each cell were used to estimate dispersion of pension accumulations for that cell.

The Argentina data are based on the micro data set of the *Encuesta Nacional de Gastos de los Hogares* for 1996–1997, a nationally representative household survey. The sample contains 103,858 individuals, of whom 69,895 were sixteen years of age or older. All regions covered are considered urban. Our data do not allow us to distinguish between affiliates and nonaffiliates or between full timers and part timers. In Argentina all workers, including the self-employed, are supposed to affiliate and contribute. However, from other sources we learned that the overall contribution rate is only 23 percent of the economically active population, compared with 60 percent in Chile (AIOS 2005). Thus many work years may be noncontributing years. Work experience is estimated based on current employment status of the urban population, including both full-time and part-time workers. Wages reflect pay for full-time and part-time work and hence understate the true full-time wage rate. Because we cannot distinguish between nonaffiliates and affiliates, who have a higher labor force participation rate, we probably understate the labor force attachment of affiliates. However, we probably overstate contributions of affiliates when working, because of the high evasion rate.

The Mexico data come from the 1997 Mexican National Employment Survey (ENE97) completed by the Instituto Nacional de Estadística, Geografía e Informática, the Mexican statistical bureau. The sample contains information on 119,405 individuals age twelve or older. We use the subsample corresponding to more-urban areas (communities of 100,000 people or more), which is about 78 percent of the sample. This survey contained the standard employment survey questions and a module with employment history and job training questions. The ENE97 does not allow for the identification of social security affiliates (about 42 percent of the economically active population) or the contributions made to retirement plans. Work experience is estimated based on current employment (both part time and full time) of the more-urban population in relevant age-education cells. Wages reflect pay for full-time and part-time work in each cell. For some analyses we used the observed coefficient of variation on earnings for each cell as an estimate of the distribution of years worked and resulting annuity within that cell.

Using these cross-sectional statistical data, we divided men and women into gender-age-education–marital status cells. A typical cell, for example, might consist of all married women age thirty to thirty-five with a high school degree. For each cell we obtained the average employment rate and wage rate for the current population. Data on marital state enabled us to identify the age, M, at which the probability of being married > 50 percent. In constructing our synthetic men and women, we used the employment probability and wage rate of the single individual up to age M and the married individual after age M. The labor force participation rate of women typically declined sharply when they got married. In some (high education–older age) cells the number of single women is very small and is not broken down by marital status (divorced, widow, never married), so we could not profile women who remained single throughout life. However, to the extent possible we show the ratio of employment of single women to our representative women who marry. It appears that single women's work habits are much closer to those of men than is the case for married women.

We assumed that for each education level, an average man or woman who enters the labor force today proceeds through life with the age-specific employment probabilities and wage rates that were derived from the cross-sectional data. For simulations where positive economywide wage growth was assumed, we multiplied the age-specific wage rate by the projected growth factor. For all three countries our simulations use three different labor attachment patterns for women: *Full-career women* are those who have the same labor force participation rates and retire at the same age (sixty-five) as men. *Ten-year women* are women who work only ten years, early in their adult lives, before children are born. *Average women* have average work and wage for each education cell. *Average women if RA = 65* are women who start their annuity at age sixty-five but have the same work experience as average women up to age sixty. In some cases we simulate outcomes for low-density men and women who contribute only 60 percent of the time they work or for men who retire early. (Mismeasurement of the density of contributions affects the absolute amount of the pension but does not affect most gender ratios on which we focus, so long as the mismeasurement is in the same proportion for men and women.)

Contributions and fund accumulations are based on estimated annual earnings and work experience for each age-education-gender cell (see tables 4.5, 5.5, and 6.5). In our baseline, the real rate of wage growth is 2 percent annually and the rate of return is 5 percent during the accumulation stage; it is 3.5 percent during the payout stage. For Chile our data give us working years by affiliates. For Argentina and Mexico our data do not allow us to identify affiliates but instead give us data for all urban workers.

Annuitization upon retirement is assumed in order to achieve a stable lifetime income flow. Annuity payouts are obtained by dividing the accumulation by the actuarial factor, which depends on mortality and discount rates (see tables 4.6, 5.6, and 6.6). The actuarial factor for individual annuities at age sixty-five is the expected present value at sixty-five of a \$1 annual annuity payout, paid from age sixty-five to the end of life. It is derived by summing the expected present discounted values of the annual \$1 payout from each age, starting at 65 to some terminal age such as 100, at which point the probability of survival approaches 0.

$$A = \mathbb{C}_a[s_a/(1 + r)^{a-65},$$

where

A = actuarial factor

s_a = survival rate, which is the probability the individual has survived from age 65 to age a

$(1 + r)^{a-65}$ discounts the expected payout at age a back to age 65

Summing over all ages to 100 give us the expected present value (EPV) of the $1 payout, or the premium that will be charged for a $1 annuity payout. Dividing the accumulation by A then tells us the annual payout that can be purchased with that accumulation. Conversely, multiplying the annual payout by A tells us the EPV of that annuity and the premium that is necessary to purchase it in actuarially fair annuity markets. We derived A for each case discussed, with the help of a Stata program that was developed and shared with us by Edward Whitehouse of the Organisation for Economic Co-operation and Development (OECD).

Joint pensions with 60 percent to survivor (70 percent in Argentina) are required for married men, and also for married women in Argentina and Mexico. For the survivors' benefit in a joint annuity, instead of s we use s^w * $(1 - s^h)$ for each time period—the probability the husband will be dead and the wife still alive in each time period. The actuarial factor for the joint annuity is then the sum of two parts: the husband's benefit and the benefit for the surviving widow.

For the discount rate we use 3.5 percent, somewhat less than the 5 percent assumed during the accumulation stage because we assume that individuals purchase guaranteed fixed annuities, which require insurance companies to invest in a relatively conservative fashion. We use the World Bank mortality tables for the cohort retiring in 2040, which is approximately when today's young workers will retire. These tables incorporate projected mortality improvements for older people that are expected (with uncertainty) to occur over the next thirty-five years. Today's tables would have higher mortality rates, so they would yield larger annuities for a given accumulation. Gender-specific mortality tables are used, except where unisex is discussed. These tables do not differentiate expected lifetimes by socioeconomic group. Thus, they probably overestimate the progressivity of the system.

Wives are assumed to be three years younger than and have three to four years longevity greater than their husbands. In Chile males retire at age sixty-five, survive for 17.3 years, and, if married, purchase a joint annuity that covers their wives, who (at sixty-two) are expected to live another 23.5 years. Females retire at age sixty, at which point their life expectancy is 25.3 years. In Argentina men at age sixty-five survive 16.2 years while their wives (age sixty-two) are expected to survive another 22.7 years. Women survive for 24.5 years at age sixty. In Mexico both men and women retire at sixty-five. Male and female life expectancies at sixty-five are 15.9 and 19.7, respectively. Wives at sixty-two are expected to live another 22.3 years when their husbands retire.

For the public benefit, we get the annual pension directly from rules of the defined benefit and eligibility conditions of the individual, and we derive the EPV by multiplying this by the actuarial factor, A.

In all cases, pesos are converted into 2002 US\$ by multiplying by the accumulated inflation between data year and 2002 (1.43 for Chile, 1.235 for Argentina, 1.69 for Mexico) and then converting according to 2002 exchange rates: 1 US\$ for 688 Chilean pesos, 3.21 Argentine pesos, 10.1 Mexican pesos.

Changes in Education and How It Affects Women's Work and Pensions

Formal labor market participation of women has increased dramatically in recent years in Chile, Argentina, and Mexico, while that of men has remained stable. For example, between 1970 and 2000 in Mexico employment rates increased from 23 percent to 34 percent among women age sixteen to sixty-five, and it almost doubled for women age twenty-six to fifty-five. In contrast, employment rates for men were 82.1 percent in 1970 and 82.9 percent in 2000. In Chile labor force participation rates among women age sixteen to sixty-five increased by 25 percent between 1970 and 2000 and by more than 35 percent for women age twenty-six to fifty-five, while for men it fell slightly from 84 percent to 81 percent. In Argentina women's labor force participation rates doubled between 1975 and 2000 compared with a constant rate of 93–94 percent for men (table A1). We also notice that labor force participation is much higher among younger than older workers.

This leads to questions about whether the age-specific behavior we observed in our data will persist for women. In creating synthetic cohorts from a single cross-section we treated behavioral differences by age as age effects rather than cohort effects. We assumed that the age effects for the year of our surveys would continue as age effects into the future. But in reality the higher labor force participation rates of young female workers may be cohort effects. That is, these young women may stay in the labor force as they age, to a much greater extent than their mothers did. If this is the case, we have underestimated the gender ratios of lifetime retirement savings accumulations and pensions. In this section we explore the possible size of this bias in our analysis and how we handled it.

Our hypothesis is that increased education is associated with at least some of the increase in aggregate participation rates, particularly the higher participation rates of young women. More highly educated women are more

Table A.1: Change in Education Composition and Labor Force Participation Rates (lfpr) among Women Age 26–55 in Chile, Argentina, and Mexico, 1970–2000 (%)[a]

Chile

| | Education Groups | | | | | |
	Incomplete Primary	Incomplete Secondary	Complete Secondary	Up to 4 Years Postsecondary	5+ Years Postsecondary	Total
Labor force participation rates in each education group						
1970	37.5	41.1	45.4	70.0	75.8	41.7
2000	43.9	48.4	57.2	66.1	77.7	56.6
Shift in lfpr	6.4	7.4	11.8	-3.9	2.0	14.9
Share of total by education group						
1970	57.7	22.5	13.0	4.3	2.4	100
2000	15.1	28.5	28.6	16.1	11.7	100
Shift in education share	-42.6	5.9	15.5	11.8	9.3	0

Argentina

| | Education Groups | | | | | |
	Incomplete Primary	Incomplete Secondary	Complete Secondary	Some Postsecondary	University Degree	Total
Labor force participation rates in each education group						
1975	28.9	39.1	39.9	57.1	80.3	33.2
2000	53.3	58.6	64.3	70.1	83.4	65.2
Shift in lfpr	24.4	19.6	24.3	13.0	3.2	31.9
Share of total by education group						
1975	73.9	10.2	10.8	2.1	2.9	100
2000	28.7	15.6	21.8	11.6	22.2	100
Shift in education share	-45.1	5.4	11.0	9.4	19.3	0

(continued)

Table A.1: *continued*

| | Mexico | | | | | |
| | Education Groups | | | | | |
	0–5	6–8	9	10–12	13+	Total
Employment rates in each education group						
1970	15.3	22.3	26.8	47.3	39.0	19.1
2000	22.4	27.2	34.4	45.8	68.2	36.5
Shift in employment rate	7.0	4.9	7.6	-1.6	29.2	17.5
Share of total by education group						
1970	67.0	24.4	2.4	3.8	2.3	100
2000	24.1	25.8	18.4	17.2	14.6	100
Shift in education share	-43.0	1.4	16.0	13.3	12.3	0.0

Sources: Author's calculations using University of Chile Greater Santiago Area Employment Surveys, 1970 and 2000 for Chile; Encuesta Permanente de Hogares (urban areas), 1975 and 2000 for Argentina; 1970 and 2000 Census, IPUMS for Mexico

[a] For Argentina we compare 1975 and 2000; for Mexico we show employment rates, which are slightly lower than labor force participation rates.

likely to work in the labor market, while for men participation is much more stable across schooling groups. In general, women's labor market participation is more sensitive to wage incentives than that of men, possibly because women have the socially acceptable alternative of working at home. As women acquire more education, their market value increases; if their imputed value in the home does not increase as rapidly, a larger percentage of women will enter the marketplace. Causation may also run the other way. Having decided that their female as well as male children will work, perhaps because more "acceptable" jobs are available (Goldin 2006) the families of girls may encourage them to get more schooling, realizing that the market rewards education. In either case, the increase in participation rates within each education category should be less than the aggregate increase. By analyzing behavior separately for each education group, we have limited the size of the potential bias.

Also in either case the part of the aggregate change that is due to education shifts should remain and grow over time. Level of education is a characteristic that people carry with them through life. Thus if a young woman has more education, she is likely to continue working more as she ages. Women from older cohorts with less education will retire and be replaced with new entrants to the labor force, who will have more education than their predecessors, thereby shifting the entire education and participation distribution up. In that case, in the aggregate, women will accumulate more years of work and contributions than we have estimated; in effect, we have estimated a lower bound.

A cursory examination of the data shows they are consistent with this hypothesis. Table A1 depicts the changes in labor force participation rates by education and in education shares of the female population between 1970 and 2000 in Chile and Mexico and between 1975 and 2000 in Argentina. In each case, we see that employment rates among women increased over this period for practically every education category, but the aggregate increase in employment rates was much greater due to a shift of women into higher education categories between the 1970s and 2000. For example, in Mexico the employment rate increased less than 8 percent in each education category, but the aggregate increase was 17.5 percent. In each country, the vast majority of women were in the bottom education category (incomplete primary) in the early 1970s, but by 2000 the primary share had fallen drastically, the modal share had shifted to secondary, and many women had university degrees. In Mexico formal years of schooling for women doubled between 1970 and 2000. In Chile and Argentina, this measure increased by 44 percent and 60 percent, respectively, with the largest gains in all three country for those under age forty-five (tables A2, A3, A4). We also see that, across this entire period, propensities to work in the market were much higher for women who attended secondary school and even more so for those with higher education.

We seek to determine how much of the overall change is associated with increased education and how much is left over, indicating a change in work proclivities due to other factors. Our quantitative analysis described below indicates that education "explains" about one-third to one-half of the increase in participation rates in our three countries. Thus, separating our sample by level of schooling cuts down on the bias substantially but does not eliminate it.

We use two methods to carry out the decomposition between education and other factors that account for women's increased labor force participation. First, we use a regression approach based on the standard Oaxaca decomposition (Oaxaca 1973). This approach has the advantage that it allows us to account for changes in other variables that might be affecting participation (although the only other variable we include in our simple analysis is age as a continuous variable within each age group). The Oaxaca approach decomposes the difference into the effect of changes in the propensity to work within each education group and the effect of changes in education composition.[1]

Second, we use a simple accounting method to calculate the two sources of change in aggregate labor force participation (lfpr): First we assume that the distribution of the population by education (eddistrib) is the same in 2000 as in 1970 but that participation rates increased within each schooling group, as observed. In effect, we weight the change in participation rate of each schooling group by its share of the female population in 1970 to get the predicted aggregate change. This tells us how much the overall participation rate would have changed if education composition remained constant but work propensities within each group changed for other reasons. Next we assume that the education distribution of the population changed between 1970 and 2000 as observed, but that the participation rates of 1970 continued to apply within each education group (lfpri). In effect, we weight the change in education levels by the 1970 participation rate of each level to get the predicted aggregate change. This tells us how much the aggregate participation rate would have changed if education levels shifted but work propensities within each schooling category were unchanged. The overall change in participation rates is the sum of these two components plus an interaction term:

Table A.2: Decomposition of Increased Labor Force Participation Rates (lfpr) of Urban Women in Chile, 1970–2000: Increased Schooling vs. Increased Work Propensities within Schooling Groups (by age group)

	Age Groups					Total 16–65	Total 26–55
	16–25	26–35	36–45	46–55	56–65		
Differences in labor force participation between 1970 and 2000 (%)							
% in lf in 1970	39.2	45.7	41.6	35.3	18.5	38.6	41.6
% in lf in 2000	38.6	58.7	56.3	53.7	26.9	48.6	56.6
Change in lfpr	−0.6	13.0	14.7	18.4	8.4	10.0	14.9
% change in lfpr	−1.5	28.4	35.3	52.1	45.4	25.8	35.8
Differences in mean school years, 1970–2000							
Mean schooling in 1970	8.5	7.8	7.5	6.7	6.6	7.7	7.4
Mean schooling in 2000	12.1	11.9	11.0	9.9	9.0	11.1	11.1
Difference	3.6	4.1	3.5	3.2	2.4	3.4	3.7
% change in schooling	42.4	52.6	46.7	47.8	36.4	44.2	50.0
Decomposition of difference in lfpr using regression (Oaxaca) approach							
Difference due to change in propensity	5.0	5.8	7.4	17.8	8.7	9.4	9.4
Difference due to shift in schooling	−5.6	7.2	7.3	0.6	−0.2	0.6	5.5
Total	−0.6	13.0	14.7	18.4	8.5	10.0	14.9
% due to change in propensity	47.2	44.6	50.3	96.7	102.4	94.0	63.1
% due to shift in schooling	−52.8	55.4	49.7	3.3	−2.4	6.0	36.9
Total	—[a]	100	100	100	100	100	100
Decomposition of difference in lfpr using weighted proportions approach							
Difference due to change in propensity[b]	−6.5	1.2	9.0	11.4	6.8	3.0	6.8
Difference due to shift in schooling[c]	−4.4	11.2	9.2	3.6	−1.8	3.4	8.9
Difference due to interaction[d]	10.3	.6	−3.5	3.3	3.5	3.5	−0.7
Total	−.6	13.1	14.7	18.4	8.5	10.0	14.9
% due to change in propensity[b]	−30.7	9.5	61.4	62.2	80.3	30.4	45.5
% due to shift in schooling[c]	−20.7	86.0	62.3	19.8	−21.8	34.5	59.5
% due to interaction[d]	48.8	4.5	−23.8	18.1	41.5	35.1	−4.9
Total	[a]	100	100	100	100	100	100

Source: Calculations by authors based on data from University of Chile Employment Surveys 1970 and 2000.

[a] Because net change is small but component parts are large, percentages are calculated over sum of absolute changes. Therefore the sum of absolute values is 100%.

[b] Change in participation weighted by each group's schooling share in 1970.

[c] Change in schooling weighted by each group's participation rate in 1970.

[d] Residual = difference between total change in lfpr and the sum of (b) + (c).

Table A.3: Decomposition of Increased Labor Force Participation Rates (lfpr) of Urban Women in Argentina, 1975–2000: Increased Schooling vs. Increased Work Propensities within Schooling Groups (by age group)

Age Groups	26–35	36–45	46–55	56–65	Total 16–65	Ages 26–55
Differences in labor force participation between 1975 and 2000						
% in lf in 1975	37.4	34.0	27.0	15.2	30.4	34.0
% in lf in 2000	65.7	67.5	62.0	45.1	61.7	65.2
Change in lfpr	28.3	33.5	35.0	29.9	31.3	31.1
% change in lfpr	75.6	98.5	129.4	195.9	102.8	91.3
Differences in mean school years, 1975–2000 [a]						
Mean schooling in 1975	7.2	6.9	6.4	6.0	6.7	6.8
Mean schooling in 2000	11.9	11.1	10.2	8.8	10.7	11.1
Difference	4.7	4.2	3.9	2.8	4.0	4.3
% change in schooling	65.9	62.1	60.4	47.0	60.2	62.3
Decomposition of difference in lfpr using regression (Oaxaca) approach						
Difference due to change in propensity	13.4	24.8	26.5	27.8	22.1	11.1
Difference due to shift in schooling	14.9	8.7	8.5	2.0	9.2	20.1
Total	28.3	33.5	35.0	29.8	31.3	31.1
% due to change in propensity	47.3	74.0	75.7	93.3	70.6	35.5
% due to shift in schooling	52.7	26.0	24.3	6.7	29.4	64.5
Total	100	100	100	100	100	100
Decomposition of difference in lfpr using weighted proportions approach						
Difference due to change in propensity [b]	15.9	24.6	29.7	29.1	23.1	23.0
Difference due to shift in schooling [c]	16.0	13.2	13.1	.8	13.1	14.3
Difference due to interaction [d]	−2.9	−4.3	−7.8	.03	−4.8	−5.4
Total	29.0	33.5	35.0	29.9	31.4	31.9
% due to change in propensity [b]	54.8	73.5	84.9	97.3	73.4	72.1
% due to shift in schooling [c]	55.3	39.3	37.5	2.6	41.7	44.9
% due to interaction [d]	−10.1	−12.8	−22.4	0.1	−15.1	−17.0
Total	100	100	100	100	100	100

Source: Encuesta Permanente de Hogares 1975 and 2000.

[a] Years of schooling are authors' estimates. Data set gave school categories, and we converted into years by using midpoint for each schooling level.

[b] Change in participation weighted by each group's schooling share in 1975.

[c] Change in schooling weighted by each group's participation rate in 1975.

[d] Residual = difference between total change in lfpr and the sum of (b) + (c).

Table A.4: Decomposition of Increased Employment Rates of Urban Women in Mexico, 1970–2000: Increased Schooling vs. Increased Work Propensities within Schooling Groups (by age group)

Age Group	16–25	26–35	36–45	46–55	56–65	Total 16–65	Ages 26–55
Difference in employment rates between 1970 and 2000							
% employed 1970	27.8	19.8	18.8	18.0	14.5	22.7	19.1
% employed 2000	32.0	37.9	38.8	29.2	16.4	34.0	36.5
Change in % employed	4.3	18.1	19.9	11.2	2.0	11.3	17.4
% change in % employed	15.5	91.7	105.6	62.3	13.7	49.8	91.1
Differences in mean school years, 1970–2000							
Mean schooling in 1970	5.0	4.1	3.3	3.2	2.6	4.1	3.6
Mean schooling in 2000	9.3	9.2	7.8	6.1	4.6	8.2	8.1
Difference	4.2	5.1	4.5	2.9	2.1	4.1	4.5
% change in mean schooling	84.3	125.5	134.1	89.8	80.1	100	125
Decomposition of difference in % employed using regression (Oaxaca) approach							
Difference due to change in propensity	−2.2	7.7	12.1	6.2	−0.2	4.5	8.9
Difference due to shift in schooling	6.7	10.7	7.9	5.2	2.3	7.1	8.6
Total	4.5	18.4	20.0	11.4	2.1	11.6	17.5
% due change in work propensity	−49.9	41.8	60.5	54.4	−11.0	38.8	50.9
% due shift in schooling	149.9	58.2	39.5	45.6	111.0	61.2	49.1
Total	100	100	100	100	100	100	100
Decomposition of difference in % employed using weighted proportions approach							
Difference due to change in propensity[a]	1.7	6.6	8.5	5.1	0.1	3.5	6.7
Difference due to shift in schooling[b]	4.8	11.3	8.3	5.3	2.5	7.1	9.1
Difference due to interaction[c]	−2.1	0.4	3.2	1.0	−0.6	0.7	1.6
Total	4.4	18.3	20.0	11.4	2.0	11.3	17.4
% due change in work propensity[a]	38.3	36.2	42.6	44.6	6.4	30.7	38.5
% due shift in schooling[b]	108.8	61.8	41.6	46.9	122.7	62.7	52.1
% due to interaction[c]	−47.1	2.0	15.9	8.5	−29.1	6.6	9.3
Total	100	100	100	100	100	100	100

Source: Author's calculations using census samples, Mexico 1970, 2000, IPUMS.

[a] Change in participation weighted by each group's schooling share in 1970.

[b] Change in schooling weighted by each group's employment rate in 1970.

[c] Residual = difference between total change in employment rate and the sum of (a) + (b).

$$\Delta \text{lfpr} = \Sigma \Delta \text{lfpr}_i * 1970\text{eddistrib} + \Sigma \Delta \text{eddistrib} * 1970\text{lfpr}_i$$

$$+ \Sigma \Delta \text{lfpr}_i * \Delta \text{eddistrib}_i$$

summed over all education categories, i. Not surprisingly, since we did not add many variables in the Oaxaca approach, we get similar results in the accounting decomposition.

Appendix tables A2, A3, and A4 report the results of these decomposition exercises for the three countries studies. For Mexico, we use employment of women instead of labor force participation. We see that for the prime-age group twenty-five to fifty-five the increased employment of women is due about equally to both forces—greater education and greater propensity to work within a given education category.[2] This finding suggests that employment rates within education categories, on which we base our analysis, will be much more stable than the aggregate, but in the aggregate we will still understate future employment and contributions by young women so long as they retain their higher work propensities. For Chile, schooling shifts played the major role for ages twenty-six to forty-five, while changes in work propensities dominate for the older age groups. This again suggests that we have eliminated much of the problem for younger women when we disaggregate by education.[3] In Argentina, where labor force participation of women doubled, only about one-third of the increase was due to a shift in education composition, so a substantial increase in work propensities remains when we disaggregate by education.

We do not attempt in this study to explain the other half of the story—the increase in work propensities within each education category. We suspect that this is, at least in part, a cohort effect, stemming from changes in social norms regarding work versus childbearing. The dramatic decline in fertility rates among young women probably signals that they will stay in the labor force as they age, so our synthetic work histories within education categories understate the actual years of employment and contributions that they will accumulate. [Also see Duryea, Edwards, and Ureta (2004) for a related analysis across a larger number of Latin American countries.][4]

We conclude that it is likely that younger women today will continue to work more than their mothers and grandmothers did, partly as a result of increased education and partly because of social norms that increase work propensities of females. This trend toward higher labor force participation will continue as education levels continue to rise. Our simulation results for women with primary school education will become a much less important part of the total picture, and those for secondary and postsecondary levels will dominate. Therefore, the overall "average" women among younger cohorts will be in a different schooling group and have a higher accumulation of work years and retirement savings than we have estimated. She will be closer to the full-career woman.

Consequently, female/male pension ratios will be higher than we have estimated on the basis of these cross-sectional data. The new pension systems tend to reward work more than the old systems, so this cohort change should improve the gains to women from the reform.

Imputed Taxes, Net Benefits, Money's Worth Ratios, and Redistributions

In addition to calculating the expected present value (EPV) of lifetime benefits and contributions, we also measure redistribution through the public pillar (see Tables 4.11, 5.11, and 6.11). Some groups pay more in taxes than they receive in benefits, while others pay less. We use three imputed measures of redistribution: (1) net benefits equals gross lifetime public benefits minus taxes paid to finance them ($NB_{pub} = GB_{pub} - T$); (2) money's worth ratio from taxes paid for public benefit equals lifetime public benefits divided by lifetime taxes paid to finance them ($MWR_{pub} = GB_{pub}/T$); and (3) money's worth ratio from taxes plus contributions paid for public benefits plus private annuities ($MWR_{pub+pvt} = (GB_{pub} + ANN)/(T + C)$). The money's worth ratio is a benefit/cost ratio expressed in terms of EPV at age sixty-five. It is frequently used as a measure of actuarial fairness of annuities. If the MWR is above 100 percent for an individual or group, the individual or group expects to get back from the system more than her entire payments, in EPV terms, implying that the system offers a net benefit for her, and vice versa.

We also show, as a fourth measure, a money's worth ratio that includes the benefit from the joint annuity. This is not a return to one's own contribution and taxes, hence would not ordinarily be considered part of the net benefit or MWR, but it is of interest as an important benefit that women receive from the system, in this case from their husband's contribution. (In Argentina and Mexico men are also covered by the joint pension that their wives finance, but the amounts are very small in EPV terms because wives' pensions are smaller and the likelihood is greater that their wives will outlive them).

While we know the EPV of benefits and contributions, from the system rules and assumptions about rates of return, we do not know the tax burden that each subgroup pays, nor do we know the total tax burden for the system as a whole at any given point in time. The total tax burden depends on numbers of retirees who qualify for the public benefit and is, in our three countries, financed in whole or part by general revenues. This means it is financed by taxes levied against income from capital as well as labor, and from other sources such as sales or value-added taxes—to an unknown extent. Moreover, intergenerational transfers are involved, again to an unknown extent. Therefore, we need to impute each subgroup's tax share, and our measures are only imputed net benefits and imputed MWRs.

Our basic strong assumptions are that (1) each cohort pays for its own benefits (i.e., total taxes equal total benefits for each cohort and there are no intergenerational redistributions) and (2) each (education-gender) subgroup's share of that total is proportional to its lifetime earnings. Then we simply add up the total lifetime public benefit for a given cohort and divide by its total lifetime earnings to get the tax rate that will finance the benefit. We apply the resulting tax rate to the lifetime earnings of each subgroup and compare with the subgroup's lifetime benefits to get the redistribution through the public pillar. Some subgroups will have a tax cost that exceeds its public benefit, and vice versa, but overall, for each cohort, total tax costs = total public benefits, net benefits = 0, and MWR_{pub} = 100 percent.

We already know the EPV at age 65 of benefits for the average member of each subgroup. In order to get aggregate benefits and tax cost we need to weight each subgroup i according to its representation in the population, a_i. We make simple stylized assumptions here: The five education groups are weighted 10 percent, 20 percent, 40 percent, 20 percent, and 10 percent, respectively. Men are weighted as 60 percent of the total—divided equally between fully contributing men and low-density men. Women are weighted as 40 percent, half of whom are average women, 25 percent full-career women, and 25 percent ten-year women. Then net benefits for each subgroup i is calculated as follows:

$$NB_{pubi} = GB_{pubi} - \text{imputed } T_i$$

where i stands for a particular (education-gender–labor force attachment) subgroup, NB_i = EPV of net benefits, GB = EPV of gross benefits, and T_i = tax cost of that subgroup. The estimated tax burden, T_i, of each subgroup is obtained by multiplying the uniform tax rate calculated below by the group's total lifetime contributory wage, W_i:

$$T_i = tW_i$$

We calculate the uniform tax rate as the rate that will generate enough taxes to cover all benefits:

$$t = \sum a_i \text{GB}_{\text{pub}i} / \sum a_i W_i$$

In sum, the uniform tax rate, t, times W_i summed over all i, equals total imputed taxes, which in turn equals gross public benefits summed over all i, where a_i is the weight assigned to group i.

$$t \sum a_i W_i = \sum T_i = \sum a_i \text{GB}_{\text{pub}i}$$

We use the same estimated total benefits and taxes within each subgroup to calculate the corresponding MWRs.

In the cases of Chile and Argentina, where public benefits are financed on a pay-as-you-go basis, we assume that the entire tax payment by each subgroup is paid at age sixty-five. Summed over all subgroups, this entire tax payment is then used to finance the cohort's public retirement benefit. In the case of Mexico, we assume that the tax share is paid proportional to wages for each period that the individual works. We do this because Mexico's social quota (SQ) is funded, that is, put into the accounts of workers for each contributory period. We assume that these tax payments, which finance the SQ in each year, earn the same 5 percent rate of return that private contributions earn. This means that Mexico requires a smaller annual tax rate than Chile or Argentina to finance the same benefit, because that tax is paid earlier and invested. Our calculations using this method show that the simulated tax rate in Argentina is almost 6 percent and that in Mexico only 1.6 percent, while both finance public benefits that increase private benefits by roughly the same proportion. In Chile, if the minimum pension guarantee is price-indexed it will cost only 0.03 percent of wages. If it is partially wage indexed and partially price indexed—rising with wages for successive cohorts but price indexed after retirement—this results in a simulated tax rate of 1 percent, for a much smaller and more narrowly concentrated public benefit than that found in Mexico or Argentina.

It should be emphasized that all the above assumptions are gross simplifications. They are made simply to allow us to estimate what redistributions would take place, subject to these assumptions. For example, it is possible that future generations will subsidize present generations, so the latter can all have positive net benefits and MWRs exceeding 100 percent, while this could not happen under our assumptions. Similarly, it is possible that high earners will pay a lower tax rate than low earners, in which case we have overestimated the progressivity of the system and the extent to which it redistributes to women.

Finally, we estimate the incentives for incremental work by calculating the marginal net public benefits and marginal $MWR_{pub+pvt}$. The marginal net public benefit in moving from ten-year to average status is $(GB_{pubav} - GB_{pub10}) - (T_{av} - T_{10})$, and similarly for the shift from average to full-career work. The marginal $MWR_{pub+pvt} = ((GB_{pubav} + ANN_{av}) - (GB_{pub10} + ANN_{10}))/((T_{av} + C_{av}) - (T_{10} + C_{10}))$, and similarly for the shift from average to full-career work.

Additional Appendix Tables

Table A.5: Estimated Fund Accumulations Based on Wage Dispersion, Chile (estimated accumulations given for deciles that accumulate less than MPG target)

	Education				
	Incomplete Primary	Incomplete Secondary	Secondary	Up to 4 Years Postsecondary	5+ Years Postsecondary

Baseline: (real r = 5% during accumulation, 3.5% during annuitization, real wage growth = 2%)

Men at 65: Fund needed for annuity > MPG: 2002 US$11,662

All deciles >MPG target for men

Women at 60: Fund needed for annuity > MPG: 2002 US$15,360

	Incomplete Primary	Incomplete Secondary	Secondary	Up to 4 Years Postsecondary	5+ Years Postsecondary
1st decile	$4,293	$6,675	$10,374		
2d decile	$6,412	$9,541	$14,331		
3d decile	$8,205	$11,020			
4th decile	$9,731	$12,541			
5th decile	$10,688	$13,672			
6th decile	$11,880	$15,914			
7th decile	$13,302				
8th decile	$15,470				

Women at 65: Fund needed for annuity > MPG: 2002 US$13,525

	Incomplete Primary	Incomplete Secondary	Secondary	Up to 4 Years Postsecondary	5+ Years Postsecondary
1st decile	$5,599	$8,689	$13,264		
2d decile	$8,363	$12,346			
3rd decile	$10,711	$14,089			
4th decile	$12,711				
5th decile	$13,955				

Slow growth: (real r = 3% during accumulation, 1.5% during payouts, wage growth =0)

Women at 60: Fund needed for annuity > MPG: 2002 US$19,488

	Incomplete Primary	Incomplete Secondary	Secondary	Up to 4 Years Postsecondary	5+ Years Postsecondary
1st decile	$1,973	$3,069	$4,767	$7,802	$14,838
2d decile	$2,946	$4,384	$6,581	$9,745	$18,614
3d decile	$3,770	$5,062	$7,400	$12,046	
4th decile	$4,470	$5,762	$8,406	$14,234	
5th decile	$4,911	$6,281	$10,051	$16,594	
6th decile	$5,459	$7,312	$11,833		
7th decile	$6,112	$8,248	$14,116		
8th decile	$7,108	$9,620	$17,389		
9th decile	$9,022	$12,220			

Women at 65: Fund needed for annuity > MPG: 2002US$16,577

	Incomplete Primary	Incomplete Secondary	Secondary	Up to 4 Years Postsecondary	5+ Years Postsecondary
1st decile	$2,336	$3,632	$5,533	$9,094	
2d decile	$3,488	$5,087	$7,664	$11,353	
3d decile	$4,468	$5,877	$8,633	$14,020	
4th decile	$5,302	$6,690	$9,800	$16,563	
5th decile	$5,821	$7,295	$11,717		
6th decile	$6,475	$8,491	$13,800		
7th decile	$7,244	$9,590	$16,467		
8th decile	$8,436	$11,181			
9th decile	$10,704	$14,209			

Source: Calculations by the authors. Accumulation dispersion estimates are based on actual wage dispersion and average labor force participation rates within schooling groups. Data are from 1994 and 1994; MPG is used in 2002 US$; MPG assumed to be price indexed.

Table A.6: Slow Growth Scenario: Accumulations, Annuities, and Impact of Public Pillar on Gender Ratios in Chile[a]

	Education[b]				
	Incomplete Primary	Incomplete Secondary	Complete Secondary	Up to 4 Years Postsecondary	5+ Years Postsecondary
Accumulations (in 2002 US$000)					
Men at 65	$13.5	$19.5	$29.1	$40.5	$93.3
Women at 60	5.4	7.5	13.2	21.8	40.1
Women at 65	6.4	8.7	15.4	25.4	47.7
Full-career women	9.8	13.3	21.4	29.5	50.6
Ten-year women	3.2	3.8	5.0	8.0	12.8
Annuities and MPG (in 2002 US$)					
Married man					
Annuity at 65	$60	$87	$130	$180	$415
Annuity + MPG	78	87	130	180	415
% increase by MPG	30	0	0	0	0
Average woman					
Annuity at 60	$22	$30	$53	$87	$161
Annuity + MPG	78	78	78	$87	$161
Annuity + MPG if wage indexed	78	78	78	$87	$161
% increase by MPG	261	160	48	0	0
Full-career woman					
Annuity at 65	$46	$63	$101	$139	$238
Annuity + MPG	78	78	0	0	0
% increase by MPG	69	25	0	0	0
Ten-year woman					
Annuity at 60	$13	$15	$20	$32	$51
% increase by MPG	0	0	0	0	0
Female/male ratios (%)					
Average annuity only	36	35	41	48	39
Average annuity + MPG	100	90	60	48	39
Full career annuity + MPG	100	90	78	77	57
Ten-year annuity only	16	18	15	18	12

Source: Calculations by the authors.

[a] Based on 3% return in accumulation stage, 1.5% in annuity stage, 0% real wage growth; 1994 data in 2002 US$.

[b] Minimum pension guarantee (MPG) is converted to actuarially equivalent monthly top-up. See appendix 1 for more details about data and methods.

Table A.7: Slow Growth Scenario: Accumulations, Annuities, and Impact of Public Pillar on Gender Ratios in Argentina[a]

	Education				
	Incomplete Primary	Incomplete Secondary	Complete Secondary	Some Postsecondary	University Degree
Accumulations (in 2002 US$000)					
Men at 65	11.5	17.6	26.3	27.3	52.8
Women at 60	3.0	4.3	8.5	11.8	23.1
Women at 65	3.5	5.0	9.9	13.8	27.0
Full-career women	7.6	10.4	17.1	17.8	31.0
Ten-year women	2.1	3.1	4.0	4.8	8.2
Annuities and flat benefits (in 2002 US$)					
Married man					
Annuity at 65	$51	$79	$117	$122	$236
Annuity + flat	128	156	194	199	313
% increase by flat	150	98	66	63	33
Average woman					
Annuity at 60	$12	$17	$33	$46	$90
Annuity + flat (60/70)	66	71	87	100	167
% increase by flat	462	322	163	117	86
Full-career woman					
Annuity at 65	$35	$47	$78	$81	$142
Annuity + flat at 65	112	124	155	158	219
% increase by flat	222	162	99	95	54
Ten-year woman					
Annuity at 60	$8	$12	$16	$19	$32
Annuity + flat at 70	62	66	70	73	86
% increase by flat	660	447	346	289	169
Female/male ratios (%)					
Average annuity only	23	21	28	38	38
Annuity + flat at 65	9	11	17	23	53
Annuity + flat at 70	51	46	45	50	53
Full-career annuity + flat at 65	87	80	80	80	70
Ten-year annuity + flat at 70	48	42	36	37	28

Source: Calculations by the authors.

[a] Based on 3% return in accumulation stage, 1.5% in annuity stage, 0% real wage growth; 1996 data in 2002 US$. Full flat benefit begins at age 60 for women, 65 for men. But most women are eligible for reduced flat, which begins at 70. Full-career woman retires and begins full flat at 65. See text for discussion of eligibility for flat and reduced flat. See appendix 1 for more details about data and methods.

Table A.8: Impact of Public Benefit on Gender Ratios of Accumulations and Monthly Pensions in Mexico under Slow Growth[a]

	Education				
	0–5	6–8	9	10–12	13+
Accumulations (in 2002 US$000)					
Men at 65, no SQ	$20.1	$23.4	$28.6	$35.9	$61.5
Men at 65, with SQ	29.1	32.3	37.6	44.5	69.7
Women at 65, no SQ	5.9	7.1	9.4	15.2	30.7
Women at 65 with SQ	10.3	11.4	14.2	20.6	37.2
Annuities including SQ (in 2002 US$)					
Married man at 65					
Annuity, no SQ	94	110	134	168	288
Annuity including SQ	137	151	176	209	327
% increase by SQ	45	38	31	24	13
Average woman at 65					
Annuity, no SQ	28	33	44	71	144
Annuity including SQ	48	53	67	96	174
% increase by SQ	74	61	51	35	21
Female/male ratios (%)					
Average annuity, no SQ	29	30	33	42	50
Average annuity including SQ	35	35	38	46	53

Source: Calculations by the authors.

Note: The public pillar takes the form of the social quota (SQ), a uniform payment per day worked into the account of each worker. The SQ was set equal to 5.5% of the minimum wage initially, and thereafter was indexed to prices. Mexico also has an MPG = $133 in 2002 US$, but for men this is exceeded in every education category after the SQ is added. Women in the bottom four education categories have an annuity that is less than the MPG, but they do not reach the 25-year eligibility requirement.

[a] Based on 3% return in accumulation stage, 1.5% in annuity stage, 0% real wage growth; 1997 data in 2002 US$.

Table A.9: Eligibility for MPG Taking Account of Dispersion in Years of Work in Mexico (percentage eligible for MPG and percent with pension under MPG)[a]

	Education				
	0–5	6–8	9	10–12	13+
Woman					
Mean years worked	20.9	19.9	21.9	24.4	31.7
% under 10 years	25.5	28.5	24.5	16.8	5.9
% under 20 years	47.8	50.2	45.6	38.5	19.9
% under 24 years	57.3	59.2	54.8	49.0	28.9
% over 24 years, eligible for MPG	42.7	40.8	45.2	51.0	71.1
Average pension with SQ (2002 US$)	$126	$141	$177	$260	$477
% with pension under MPG	52.6	47.3	37.5	21.1	4.9
Man					
Mean years worked	45.0	44.3	44.6	43.9	42.8
% under 10 years	0.0	0.0	0.0	0.0	0.0
% under 20 years	0.0	0.0	0.0	0.0	0.1
% under 24 years	0.0	0.1	0.0	0.1	0.7
% over 24 years, eligible for MPG	100.0	99.9	100.0	99.9	99.3
Average pension with SQ (2002 US$)	$364	$407	$478	$573	$909
% with pension under MPG	0.0	0.0	0.0	0.0	0.0

Source: Calculations by the authors based on data in ENE97.

[a] MPG = $133 in 2002 US$. ENE97 respondents were asked how many years they had worked in total. Based on answers from women and men age 61–65, we calculated coefficient of variation. We then applied this coefficient to the mean accumulated experience estimated for our synthetic cohort. Assuming a normal distribution, we could then calculate percentages of our cohort that would have various years of experience and percent with experience of 24 years or more, therefore eligible for the MPG. This assumes all working years are contributory years. Based on 5% real rate of return during accumulation, 3.5% during annuitization, 2% real wage growth.

NOTES

INTRODUCTION

1.   For example, in the United States, for which such data are readily available, 60 per-
     cent of people over the age of sixty-five and 72 percent of those over age eighty-five
     are women, and this disparity has been increasing through time. In the eighty-five-
     and-over group, only 9 percent of women are still living with their spouses (Posner
     1995). The poverty rate of women over age sixty-five is 15 percent, compared with 7
     percent for men over age sixty-five. The poverty rate for women over age eighty-five is
     20 percent. For divorced, separated, or never-married elderly women the poverty rate
     is 27 percent (Shirley and Spiegler 1998; also see Munnell 2004; Street and Wilmoth
     2001). Using the Luxembourg Income Study database, Smeeding and Sandstrom
     (2004) conclude that poverty in old age is almost exclusively a problem of older
     women living alone due to widowhood or divorce. Women sixty-five and over and
     living alone have poverty rates of 30 percent in the United States and 12 percent
     across seven representative OECD countries if poverty is defined as 40 percent of
     adjusted national median disposable income. These numbers increase to 46 percent
     and 27 percent, respectively, if the threshold is defined as 50 percent.
2.   For examples, see World Bank (2004).
3.   For a list of the countries that had adopted multipillar reforms as of 2000 and an
     analysis of the political reasons for their reform choices, see James and Brooks (2001).
     Among the countries that adopted the new type of system in the 1980s are Chile,
     Switzerland, the Netherlands, and the United Kingdom; those adopting this type of
     system in the 1990s include Australia, Denmark, Sweden, Hong Kong, Argentina,
     Uruguay, Peru, Colombia, El Salvador, Costa Rica, Mexico, Bolivia, Hungary, Poland,
     and Kazakhstan. Since 2000 the new system was adopted or is currently under con-
     sideration by Slovakia, Lithuania, Russia, Estonia, Croatia, Romania, Latvia, Bulgaria,
     Macedonia, and Kosovo. A plan to include individual accounts as part of social secu-
     rity has also been under discussion in the United States.
4.   Other papers have discussed the projected replacement rates of men and women
     in Chile and Argentina, but none has systematically used current labor market be-
     havior to construct a variety of synthetic individuals and their expected pensions
     under the new and old systems, nor has any examined multiple indicators. See Ber-
     tranou (1998, 2001), Arenas de Mesa and Montecinos (1999), and Barrientos (1998).

Edwards (2002) and James, Edwards, and Wong (2003, 2007) present data on some of these indicators, but not all.

CHAPTER TWO

1. Possibly for similar reasons, widows are also more likely to live alone in wealthier countries. For example, in Australia 34 percent of all women age seventy to seventy-four live alone, and this proportion rises to 46 percent for women age eighty to eighty-four. In contrast, only 15 percent of men age seventy– to seventy-four live alone, and this proportion rises to 24 percent for those age 85 and older. Men are more likely to live with their wife or other partner (Schulz 2000).

2. In urban areas in Mexico, in 1995, elderly women who were not in the labor force spent thirty-four hours per week in domestic activities, compared with eleven hours among elderly men who were not in the labor force. The disparity is even greater in rural areas (Pedrero 1999).

3. Among men and women who receive a pension, 7 percent and 8 percent, respectively, receive a family transfer. Among those who do not receive a pension, 16 percent of men and 21 percent of women receive a family transfer.

CHAPTER THREE

1. Considerable controversy surrounds the magnitude of the work disincentive effects stemming from higher taxes and other measures that reduce the net wage. Studies in industrial economies indicate that the labor supply of prime-age males is relatively inelastic with respect to tax and wage rates. Women's labor supply may be more sensitive, as net wages may influence their allocation of time between market work, which is taxed, and home work, which is not taxed. A rise in tax costs may wipe out the margin that made market work attractive to women. The choice of retirement age seems to be especially sensitive to payroll taxes (Gruber and Wise 1999). In Chile the labor force participation of older workers increased dramatically after the reform, in part due to the exemption of pensioners from the pension payroll tax (Edwards and James 2005). Recent research shows that incentives in the U.S. system encourage women to work less in prime age and to retire early because their retirement income depends mainly on their husband's pension rather than on their own contributions (Munnell and Soto 2005; Munnell and Jivan 2005). Furthermore, higher taxes may push workers into the informal or underground economy. While informal work to evade taxes and regulations exists in all countries, it is particularly prevalent and accessible in low- and middle-income countries. If productivity is lower in the informal sector because of less access to capital, credit, and marketing channels, this becomes a source of inefficiency in the use of labor.

2. Specifically, using available cross-sectional statistical data, we divided men and women into gender-age-education–marital status cells. A typical cell, for example, might consist of all married women ages thirty to thirty-five with a high school degree. For each cell we obtained the average employment rates and wage rates for the current population. We then assumed that, for each education level, an average man or woman who enters the labor force today proceeds through life with the age-specific employment probabilities and wage rates that were derived from the cross-sectional data. For simulations where positive economywide wage growth was assumed, we multiplied the age-specific wage rate by the projected growth factor. Contributions depend on these employment histories. Data on marital state enabled us to identify the age, M, at which the probability of being married > 50 percent. In constructing

our synthetic men and women, we used the employment probability and wage rate of the single individual up to age M and the married individual after age M. A sharp decline in the labor force participation rate of women typically occurred when they got married.

3. The absence of longitudinal data meant that we could not vary wages as a function of experience, so the lifetime earnings and pensions of full-career women may be understated.

4. Interestingly, their wages are not like those of men; in fact, they are slightly lower than those of married women (perhaps because of selection bias—married women are more likely to work if they have a high-wage offer, while single women work even if they have a low-wage offer).

5. In Chile, which introduced portfolio choice in 2002, workers are required to invest in low-risk portfolios during the ten years prior to retirement. The earlier retirement age for women, therefore, in effect requires them to make more conservative investments with a lower expected return for a higher percentage of their adult lives. We abstract from this difference in our analysis, thereby slightly understating the expected gender gap in accumulations. For the U.S. literature on this topic, see Bajtelsmit, Bernasek, and Jianakoplos (1999); Bernasek and Shwiff (2001); Jianakoplos and Bernasek (1998); Lyons and Yilmazer (2004); Sundén and Surette (1998); and Hinz, McCarthy, and Turner (1997). On Sweden, see Save-Soderbergh (2003). For partial surveys of this literature, see U.S. GAO (1997), Burnes and Schulz (2000), and Shirley and Spiegler (1998).

6. In reality most adjustments to insolvency have not been distributionally neutral. For example, maintaining fiscal balance through inflation, with indexation applying only to a minimum pension, hurts high earners disproportionately, while raising the payroll tax rate subject to a fixed maximum hurts low earners and equalizing retirement ages for the two genders hurts women, especially in a defined benefit plan.

7. This bias is reduced, but not completely eliminated, in defined benefit systems such as that in the United States, which index up the earlier wages according to economywide wage growth and base the pension on total lifetime indexed wage.

8. In our calculations we abstract from inflation and deal only in real interest rates and wage growth. Yet in reality these countries had very high levels of inflation, and how they treated inflation varies a lot between the new and old systems. For example, pensions in the old systems were based on past wages that were usually not indexed up for inflation. This especially hurt women, who often had worked many years in the past before childbearing, at wage rates that became worthless after inflation. Once a person retired, the initial benefit was usually not automatically indexed for inflation. Ad hoc adjustments were made, but they were uncertain, they were only partial, and they lagged behind inflation. This imprecise system created problems for all workers, but particularly for women because of their greater longevity. However, some systems included a minimum pension that roughly kept pace with the consumers' price level. Low-earning women would have benefited disproportionately from such a minimum, while high-earning men may have found their pensions dwindling in real terms over time.

In the new systems, contributions made to the funded plan early in one's career are likely to rise faster than inflation because of the positive real rate of return on investments. Chile's annuities are indexed after retirement, and Mexico's public benefit is indexed. Chile's minimum pension guarantee formally rises with the price level, but it actually has been rising faster than prices as a result of political decisions. We abstract from inflation because of its uneven nature and the unpredictable ad hoc responses that were made by the old systems. This approach is equivalent to assuming zero inflation or full indexation in the old systems and biases our results against the new systems.

CHAPTER FOUR

1. By 1979 the old system was composed of thirty-two pension funds with more than a hundred different programs. It is difficult to obtain precise information about all these subsystems. These descriptions are based on SAFP (2003), Cheyre (1991), and personal communications with Augusto Iglesias, director, Primamerica Consultores. The defined benefit formula we present applied to the largest scheme, Servicio Seguro Social, which covered two-thirds of total contributors (mainly blue collar).

2. Data on administrative and insurance costs are from James et al. (2000) and James, Smalhout, and Vittas (2001). More recent data indicate that fees have fallen about 10 to 15 percent in the three countries studied (AIOS 2005). Fees in Chile were initially about 3 percent of payroll but more recently have fallen to 2.4 percent. Almost half of these fees are for a group survivors' and disability insurance policy that covers all contributing workers.

3. Formal employment is established by a written contract that employers and employees sign.

4. Of course, it is possible that some services are purchased on an independent contractual basis to avoid the contribution requirement, just as independent contracting has grown in many industrialized countries to avoid payroll taxes and fringe benefits. Given this possibility, it is interesting to note that 25 percent of self-employed workers make voluntary contributions to the pension system, even though they are not required to do so (table 4.2, panel A). They may do so, for example, in order to be covered by disability insurance or to acquire twenty years of contributions and become eligible for the minimum pension guarantee. By the same token, once employees have reached the twenty-year point they may be able to escape further contributions if they can switch their status to self-employed. We return to this issue below in our discussion of the MPG.

5. Including all workers is appropriate because the data show no significant correlation between wage levels and affiliation or contribution probabilities. Our method of estimating the applicable monthly wage rate, while simplistic, has several advantages: It does not impose a particular functional form, and it implicitly weights the sample according to its composition (by other characteristics) within each cell. The human capital earnings function, in which earnings are expressed as a quadratic in potential experience, might have appeared to be an alternative estimation method. However, it is not the most appropriate here, because we lack a good proxy for female experience (age is sometimes used as a proxy for experience, but the gist of the issue here is that it is a differential proxy for men and women, and we are seeking to identify the pension implications of this differential). We chose a five-year age interval as a compromise between increasing sample size in each cell versus keeping the age categories narrow, since estimated salaries for a range of years are likely to overestimate starting-period salaries and underestimate ending-period salaries.

6. We examined whether actual wage dispersion within each education cell would change these results significantly. We found that 80 percent of women in the bottom education category and 60 percent of those in the second category would qualify for some top-up under a price-indexed MPG (table A5 in appendix 4). If women do not

have enough money in their accounts to purchase an annuity above the MGP level upon retiring, they are required to withdraw their own savings at the MPG level until their accounts are empty, at which point the government subsidy takes over. For expositional purposes we assume they annuitize, and we calculate the monthly top-up needed to get them to the MPG point.

7. Basing the MPG on personal accumulation makes it easy and inexpensive to monitor, and it avoids issues concerning the intrafamily division of resources that arise in a means-tested program based on family income, but it may also mean that society's limited redistributional funds are being spent on women from middle-class families who can afford to forgo market work and income. This has been documented by Valdes (2002, table 1.1). Much of Valdes's data are from minimum pension eligibility in the old system, but this danger exists in the new system too. Similar observations have been made about the social security system in the United States, which has a progressive benefit formula that subsidizes middle-class women who have limited labor market earnings because they have spent much of their time working in the home rather than in the formal market (Coronado, Fullerton, and Glass 1999, 2000; Gustman and Steinmeier 2000).

8. Calculations are by the authors, based on data on annuities and programmed withdrawals supplied by the regulators of AFPs and insurance companies. For more information about payouts, see James, Martinez, and Iglesias (2006).

9. This analysis applies only to survivors' benefits during the payout stage. During the accumulation stage, husbands are also required to purchase survivors' insurance for their wives. A small amount of the total contribution (about 1 percent of payroll) is used for survivors' and disability insurance. We do not include the value of survivors' benefits during the working stage in our calculations; in this sense we understate the transfer from men to women in the form of survivors' insurance. Survivors' insurance during the accumulation stage is financed by a similar charge (as percentage of wage) to all workers, whether married or single, men or women. Women workers also must pay this premium although their husbands will not collect the benefit as widowers unless they are disabled or otherwise financially dependent on their wives. Thus, this is a pure tax to working women but a positive transfer to women in their roles as surviving wives.

10. The key assumptions determining payouts are age of wife and percentage to survivor—the younger the wife and larger the percentage to survivor, the more the husband's benefit will decline, even under unisex calculations, when a joint annuity is purchased.

11. This tax cost would be lower for a price-indexed MPG and vice versa for a fully wage-indexed MPG.

12. If the married man would have voluntarily purchased a joint annuity or the equivalent in life insurance for his wife, he would derive utility from the mandatory joint annuity, which simply displaces the voluntary insurance, so his own MWR is understated by this calculation; it is actually the same as that of the single man. Although the cost of the joint pension is subtracted from the husband's payout in this analysis, the joint annuity received by the widow is not included in MWRpub+pvt, because she gets that annuity by virtue of her husband's contributions, not her own. (Nonworking, noncontributing wives also get the joint pension). However, if we include the joint annuity as another component of her retirement income from the system as a whole, her MWR rises to more than 200 percent in some cases (table 4.11, rows 17, 23, and 29).

13. The ten-year woman in the bottom educational category doesn't get the MPG and pays practically no taxes. If she works an average amount she becomes eligible for the MPG, which yields a lifetime net public benefit of $3086 (table 4.11, rows 7–9; table 4.12, row 1). If she proceeds to work full career, however, she pays additional taxes while losing the MPG. Hence her net benefit becomes –$25 and her marginal net benefit from incremental work becomes –($3086 + 25) = –$3111 (table 4.11, rows 14–16; table 4.12, row 2). She also gets back the full value of her contributions to the private account. Then, marginal $MWR_{pub+pvt}$ is 155 percent for the shift from ten-year to average status and only 68 percent for the shift from average to full career status (table 4.12, rows 5 and 6).

14. Low-density men considering more regular contributory work also face work disincentives from a wage-indexed MPG. They would lose the MPG but would have to continue to finance it, as well as the joint annuity for their wives if they are married (table 4.12, rows 3 and 6). Their MWR ranges from 8 percent at the bottom end (due to the MPG loss) to 80 percent at the top end (due to the joint annuity requirement).

15. Taxes as well as benefits changed in the process of the reform. Contribution rates to the pension system were cut substantially when the new system was adopted. Transition costs have had to be covered out of general revenues as a result of the switch to the new system, much of them through cuts in government spending. Moreover, as we have seen, the MPG will put a burden on future general tax revenues. We assume that these tax changes are levied in a way that leaves relative positions unchanged.

16. If the minimum pension was indexed in the old system while pensions were not indexed generally, eventually most retirees would have gotten the minimum—thereby achieving gender equality, but at a very low level. This was the situation in some Latin American countries before the reform.

17. Specifically, for each subgroup i we calculate $(PVnew/PVold)_i/(PVnew/PVold)_k$, where $(PVnew/PVold)_i$ = ratio of present value of lifetime benefits in new versus old systems for group i and reference group k = married men in the top education category. We follow this complex procedure because we want to be able to compare relative gains or losses among all gender, education, and labor force attachment subgroups without assuming that the absolute value of promised benefits would have been paid under the old system. For example, suppose that expected lifetime benefits had doubled for the top-educated man and trebled for the low-educated man. Then their separate new/old ratios would be 2/1 and 3/1, respectively, and the normalized ratio for the latter would be 3/2 = 1.5, informing us that the man with low education improved his initial position 50 percent more than the man with high education. This relationship would hold even if the old system had to change to keep it solvent, so long as these changes maintained the same relative positions that existed initially. This contrasts with the approach in table 4.13, where we compared women with men in the same educational categories, and we did not compare men across educational cells.

CHAPTER FIVE

1. The original reform law 24241, as well as the modifications introduced in 2004 and 2007, can be found at http://www.safjp.gov.ar/SISAFJP/normativa.

2. In our simulations we assume that average women in the bottom two education categories who worked less than twenty years qualified for the ten-year option, while women in the top three education categories qualified for the more generous twenty-year option. Women in the bottom education category received the minimum pension, which exceeded their own pension. The average man in all education categories

was eligible for the twenty-year option, and his own pension exceeded the minimum pension.

3. Workers had a choice between a private account that is similar to the Chilean model and a public defined benefit (called PAP). Initially PAP was available only to workers with more than thirty years of contributions; workers who contributed for less than thirty years lost all their contributions, so PAP was particularly inappropriate for women. Workers who entered PAP could later switch to the private scheme, but not vice versa—one of the reasons why participation in PAP was less than 20 percent. More recently, Argentina has changed the public defined benefit option and opened it up to everyone, indeed made it mandatory for some, so its membership will undoubtedly increase in the future.

4. Payroll contributions toward pensions are part of a much larger package of payroll contributions for social insurance. Total payroll contributions range between 22 and 33 percent of gross wages in Argentina, compared with 16.7 percent of gross wages in Chile.

5. The sharp rise at age sixty to sixty-five for those with secondary or higher education is probably a result of selection bias among those who stay in the labor market at that point.

6. We do not know what the long-run costs will be on Chile's MPG or Argentina's flat benefit. However, simulations described in appendix 3, based on very stylized assumptions, suggest that a 6 percent payroll tax would be needed in Argentina but only 0.03 to 1 percent in Chile to cover their respective public benefits. The lower cost in Chile is due to the fact that the MPG is paid only to a narrow segment of retirees and is only a top-up to their own annuity rather than a full payment to all.

7. In fact, more than half of all current retirees are at the minimum (personal communication with Rafael Rofman, senior economist, World Bank, April 4, 2005). Most of them retired under the old system rules—but our simulations show that with a high minimum and low- contribution density, the same outcome is predicted for the new system.

8. Low-density men also face a marginal MWR of far less than 100 percent, hence a disincentive to increase their density of contributions, because of both the imputed tax on earnings and the joint annuity requirement. The higher tax rate needed to cover the flat and widow's flat benefits and the higher 70 percent survivors' share cuts the Argentine MWR much more than the low tax rate and 60 percent share in Chile. This may be part of the reason many remain as low-density men.

9. Law 18_037 (Dec 68) article 37 # 3 stated that the right to a widow's pension is conditional on "not receiving an old age benefit." However, in practice women often received both, in part because husband and wife were in different subsystems and in part because of poor records and uneven enforcement.

CHAPTER SIX

1. The requirement that the individual had to have worked the five years immediately prior to retirement in order to qualify for a pension would have excluded many women who worked when young and then withdrew from the labor force upon marriage and childbearing. In this chapter, we assume that ten-year women somehow managed to qualify for a pension. This creates a bias in favor of the old system. In the new system there is no doubt that they would have property rights to the money in their own accounts, including the social quota.

2. In 2004 the government made it more attractive for workers to stay in the old system

upon retirement. Defined benefit amounts were increased and indexed to prices. In addition, workers are allowed to withdraw about 30 percent of the balance in their accounts if they choose the old system.

3. Additionally, to avoid political opposition from organized groups, the government excluded federal employees (covered by ISSSTE), the armed forces, and oil worker systems from the reform. The current government is implementing plans to convert ISSSTE to a defined contribution system. Besides mandatory coverage, workers may make voluntary contributions, but less than 1% of all contributions are voluntary (Sinha and Yanez 2007).

4. Although ten-year women have not worked as much as our other prototypes, they get a large percentage increase in benefits from the SQ. This may seem surprising, given the close ties between the SQ and work. Two reasons account for this: the SQ is a constant reward for days worked, so it is a higher proportion for those with lower wage rates, and it does not rise with wage growth in the economy. Ten-year women work early in their adult lives, so the SQ they get is higher relative to their wage than it is for full-career women, some of whose wages come later and are much larger.

5. Starting in 2002, Mexico City also instituted a monthly cash transfer of 600 pesos (about US$60) to the elderly. This is a flat benefit provided to every resident over age 70. It is not means tested. This program is perceived as a political decision by the mayor of the city, who was campaigning for national office at the time. Its future is uncertain.

6. Since the SQ is paid monthly, we also assume that the tax needed to finance it is paid monthly by the worker—much earlier than the tax in Argentina that is paid upon retirement. We calculate the present value (PV) of this monthly tax at age 65, using the same 5% interest rate that is earned on the accounts, and these compounded numbers are presented as the imputed tax cost in Mexico in table 6.11. The PV of the total imputed tax and total public benefits in Mexico are slightly larger than those in Argentina, although Mexico's tax rate is much smaller, because the tax is paid much earlier in the worker's life.

CHAPTER SEVEN

1. Most data for the former Soviet Union countries are from Castel and Fox (2001) and personal communications with Paulette Castel and Louise Fox. Data for Poland are from Woycicka et al. (2003) and personal communications with Agniezska Chlon-Dominczak. Other data on eastern European countries are from Whitehouse (2003).

2. In Poland, women get credit in the public plan for years on maternity leave, but only at the minimum wage level. In Latvia, credit is given for a maximum of 1.5 years of maternity leave. In Kazakhstan, pension credit for maternity leave and child care were eliminated.

3. Collective agreements that cover most workers provide for survivors' benefits, but these vary by occupation and tend to be less generous for low-paid workers.

4. Data given below on Australia are from are from Ginn, Street, and Arber (2001); Shaver (2001); Schulz (2000); Kelly, Harding, and Percival (2002a, 2002b); Jefferson and Preston (2005); Preston and Austen (2001); and Clare (2004).

5. Coverage is less than 100 percent because workers earning less than A$900 per month are exempt, and many of these are women.

6. Similar numbers are found in the United Kingdom, where women's labor force

participation is only 65 percent that of men, and 40 percent of this participation is part time. Average hourly earnings for women are only 75 percent those for men, and most of this gap persists among full timers. The gap increases with age, as in Latin America. Employment and earnings gaps are especially great for women with children (Ginn, Street, and Arber 2001).

7.   Specifically, in 2002 the full flat benefit was approximately A$11,000 annually for a single person (A$18,000 for a married couple), but it was reduced by 40 cents for every dollar over A$3,000. The full phaseout would then occur when annual personal income exceeded A$31,000 for a single person (A$49,000 for a married couple). (See OECD 2005.) Apparently, only 20 percent of retired Australians had personal incomes that exceeded these amounts.

8.   The United Kingdom also offers a flat benefit and means-tested benefits as part of its multipillar system, but with different costs and targeting than either Australia or Argentina. In the United Kingdom the basic flat benefit requires thirty-nine years of contributions from women (forty-four from men). This eligibility requirement might at first appear to disqualify most women. However, years spent caring for children or frail or disabled adults can be substituted for paid employment and part-time work, so most women qualify. High earners are not excluded from the UK benefit, which makes it potentially more expensive than that in Australia. To offset these costs, the UK basic benefit is indexed to prices, not wages. Consequently, although it started at more than 20 percent of the average male wage, it is now less than 15 percent and projected to fall to 7.5 percent by 2050. This low level might leave many low earners, especially women, in relative poverty. To prevent this occurrence and to assist women who do not qualify for the basic benefit, the UK basic benefit is supplemented by narrowly targeted means-tested benefits; women are the major recipients. While this is meant to protect those on the low end, there is much concern in the United Kingdom about the stigma and take-up problems among this group.

Simulations that combine the private and public pension find that women in the United Kingdom receive total benefits that are 60 to 70 percent those of men after they claim the basic and means-tested benefits in addition to their own pension (Falkingham and Rake 2001). This percentage is much higher than the gender ratios of monthly pensions in Chile and Argentina, largely because of the more equalizing combination of basic and means-tested benefits as well as the higher gender ratios of employment and wages in the United Kingdom. However, it is lower than the gender ratios of lifetime benefits in Chile and Argentina when the joint annuity is included. (Joint annuities are not required in the United Kingdom.)

The UK system is now in the process of changing, with an increase in the basic benefit and automatic enrollment in private plans, in part because of dissatisfaction with the declining basic benefit and heavy reliance on means-tested benefits.

CHAPTER EIGHT

1.   Chile's MPG loses some of this advantage. Technically it is means tested against other income as well, because the individual is required to sign a statement that he or she has no other pensions or wages. This broader income test is supposedly monitored by the pension fund with which the individual is affiliated, not by the government. These funds have little incentive to spend resources on implementing the means test, and we have no evidence on how effectively this is done.

2.   One study found that many recipients of means-tested pensions in India were

required to pay bribes and high transaction costs in order to receive their benefits. Another study reported poor record keeping and long delays in establishing eligibility and obtaining pensions (Palacios and Sluchynskyy 2006).

3. These spillovers within the family may also be socially useful. However, transfers to families with children might be more effective if child welfare is the goal.

4. For a fuller examination of experience with age-based pensions, including flat and means-tested arrangements, in multipillar systems and monopillar systems, see Palacios and Sluchynskyy (2006).

5. For the recent empirical literature demonstrating this effect for the United States, see Coronado, Fullerton, and Glass (1999, 2000) and Gustman and Steinmeier (2000).

6. The new public notional defined contribution plans in the transitional economies similarly penalize women who retire early; in fact, this is one of the ways these schemes are expected to save money, compared with the old systems.

7. Annuities can also be fixed (the insurance company promises a constant payout stream) or variable (payouts each year depend on some factor such as investment returns that year). Which will be chosen depends on the retiree's degree of risk aversion or constraints imposed by a risk-averse government.

8. In the United Kingdom, the load (difference between initial premium and present value of future benefit stream) charged for indexed annuities is about 7 to 10 percent of the premium, while it is close to 0 percent for nominal annuities. In Chile, by contrast, loads for indexed annuities are close to 0 percent. The difference may stem from the fact that many indexed financial instruments are available in Chile, which enables insurance companies to insure against inflation while still earning a rate of return that exceeds the risk-free rate, while this is not true in the United Kiingdom. See James, Martinez, and Iglesias (2006).

9. Some public involvement remains. In Argentina the surviving spouse gets 70 percent of the other spouse's flat benefit when he or she dies. In Chile the MPG applies to the joint pension purchased by the husband to protect his widow.

10. In Chile women are required to purchase individual pensions upon retirement unless their husbands are disabled. In Argentina and Mexico both men and women must purchase joint pensions. In all three countries, workers of both genders are also required to purchase survivors' insurance during the accumulation stage, while working. This insurance, however, is financed as an equal percentage of wages—less than .5 percent—for all workers, so singles subsidize married couples in this case. In Chile, the wife is covered by survivors' insurance, but the husband is covered only if he is disabled. Nevertheless, working women have paid the same insurance fee as men. The government has recently proposed charging a lower fee to women, in the form of a rebate into their accounts, to reflect the lower costs they imply.

11. The same could be said of other criteria used by insurance companies for risk classification—age, health status, and the like. Insurance companies use these observable factors to divide people into risk categories that are priced differently in order to avoid adverse selection and keep good risks in the market. Without the ability to match price to differentiated risks of various groups, the insurance industry could not operate on a voluntary basis.

12. In the United States, voluntary employment-based defined benefit plans are legally required to pay equal monthly benefits to men and women, implying unisex tables. According to the Employee Retirement Income Security Act, the law that has governed employer-sponsored defined benefit plans since 1974, a joint benefit is also required, thereby providing survivors' benefits, unless the spouse specifically waives that right.

However, the most common type of private retirement plan today, 401(k) plans, are defined contribution plans that do not specify the benefit. Instead, the account balance is typically paid out in a lump sum upon retirement. If the worker later decides to annuitize, this takes place outside the employment relationship, so gender-specific tables may be used and individual annuities issued. The rules might be quite different if these accounts became part of the mandatory system.

13. These problems are accentuated if the pension is indexed, shifting payouts to later in life. Under indexation, women as a group gain more from a unisex regime, while men must forgo more early benefits for higher future benefits, which they do not survive to get. Consequently, men are more likely to oppose the use of unisex tables if indexation is required, they are more likely to oppose indexation under unisex plans, and they will try harder to avoid annuitizing if both unisex and indexation are mandatory. Insurance companies will try harder to avoid women if unisex table use is combined with indexation.

14. Companies with a disproportionate number of men would pay a premium to a central authority to absorb the profit they are making due to unisex table use, and this would be used to compensate companies with disproportionate females for their losses due to unisex tables. This premium payment would allow all companies to charge consumers the national unisex rate while remaining indifferent to the gender of their annuitants, so it avoids the cream skimming and instability issues mentioned above. However, such risk-adjustment procedures require good mortality data and considerable technical skills—both of which are in short supply in low- and middle-income countries.

APPENDIX TWO

1. This method estimates a regression equation as follows:

$$Y_1 = X_1 b_1 + e_1$$
$$Y_0 = X_0 b_0 + e_0$$

where Y_0, Y_1 are dummy variables for labor force participation at time 0 and time 1, respectively; X_0, X_1 are covariates of participation at time 0 and time 1; respectively; and the es are the corresponding error terms. In this analysis time 0 is 1970 and time 1 is 2000. We estimate the regressions using probit regression and obtain coefficient estimates for b_0 and b_1. We use these coefficients to estimate predicted values for employment, as follows:

$$X_0 b_0, X_1 b_0, X_0 b_1, X_1 b_1$$

Then we can express the difference in participation between time 0 and time 1 as:

$$Y_1 - Y_0 = (X_1 b_1 - X_1 b_0) + (X_1 b_0 - X_0 b_0)$$

The first term in the right hand side, $(X_1 b_1 - X_1 b_0)$, is the effect of change in coefficients, or the change in the propensity to be employed, holding the education composition constant. The second term, $(X_1 b_0 - X_0 b_0)$, is the effect of change in the education composition, holding constant the propensity to be employed.

2. For younger and older age groups the change in overall employment was much

smaller and entirely due to increased schooling. Possibly younger age groups do not work more in 2000 because more of them are still in school, while older age groups do not work more because more of them retire early, but those with more education are the ones who stay in the labor market.

3. Women under age twenty-five actually experience a decline in labor market participation due to a shift in education, possibly because they remain in school longer. This will offset some of the positive effect of schooling after they pass age twenty-five.

4. We carried out a similar decomposition for the United States, using labor force participation rates and education composition for 1970 and 1999, from Blau, Ferber, and Winkler (2002). We expected education to play a less important role here because the gains in schooling were less dramatic than in low-and middle-income countries. The aggregate female labor force participation rate for women age twenty-five to sixty-four was 49 percent in 1970 and 73 percent in 1999, an increase of 49 percent over this period. We found that 65 percent of the increase in aggregate female labor force participation was due to an increase in work propensities within education categories, 16 percent was due to a shift in education composition, and the remaining 19 percent was due to the interaction between the two. We observe a big shift in education composition away from those with high school education or less and toward those with some college education or a college degree. At the same time, the biggest increase in labor force participation occurred among those with college education—the association between education and participation rates grew over this period, hence a large role for the interaction effect.

REFERENCES

Arenas de Mesa, Alberto, and Verónica Montecinos. 1999. "The Privatization of Social Security and Women's Welfare: Gender Effects of the Chilean Reform." *Latin Amerian Research Review* 34 (3): 7–34.

Arenas de Mesa, Alberto, Jere Behrman, and David Bravo, 2004. "Characteristics and Determinants of the Density of Contributions in a Private Social Security System." Michigan Retirement Research Center Working Paper 2002-077. Ann Arbor, MI: Michigan Retirement Research Center.

Arenas de Mesa, Alberto, David Bravo, Jere Behrman, Olivia Mitchell, and Petra Todd. 2007. "The Chilean Pension Reform Turns 25: Lessons from the Social Protection Survey." In *Lessons from Pension Reform in the Americas*, ed. Stephen Kay and Tapen Sinha. New York: Oxford University Press.

Asociación International de Organismos de Supervision de Fondos de Pensiones (AIOS). 2005. "Los Regímenes de Capitalización en América Latina." *Boletín Estadístico* 14 (December).

Bajtelsmit, Vickie, Alexandra Bernasek, and Nancy Jianakoplos. 1999. "Gender Differences in Defined Contribution Pension Decisions." *Financial Services Review* 8 (1): 1–10.

Barrientos, Armando. 1998. "Pension Reform, Personal Pensions and Gender Differences in Pension Coverage." *World Development* 26 (1): 125–37.

Bernasek, Alexandra, and Stephanie Shwiff. 2001. "Gender, Risk and Retirement." *Journal of Economic Issues* 35 (2): 345–56.

Bernheim, Douglas, Lorenzo Forni, Jagadeesh Gokhale, and Lawrence Kotlikoff. 2003. "Mismatch between Life Insurance Holdings and Financial Vulnerabilities—Evidence from the Health and Retirement Survey." *American Economic Review* 93 (1): 354–65.

Berstein, Solange, and Andrea Tokman. 2005. "Are Women Relatively Better Off when Old? Gender Income Gaps during Active and Passive Life." Unpublished paper. Santiago, Chile: Superintendencia de Administradoras de Fondos de Pensiones.

Berstein, Solange, Guillermo Larrain, and Francisco Pino. 2006. "Chilean Pension Reform: Coverage Facts and Policy Alternatives." *Economía* 6 (2): 227–79.

Bertranou, Fabio. 2001. "Pension Reform and Gender Gaps in Latin America: What Are the Policy Options?" *World Development* 29 (5): 911–23.

Bertranou, Fabio, and Andrea Sanchez. 2003. "Características y determinantes de la densidad de aportes a la Seguridad Social en la Argentina 1994–2001." In *Historias Laborales en la Seguridad Social*. Serie de Publicaciones de la Secretaría de Seguridad Social, año 1, n 1. Buenos Aires, Argentina: Ministerio de Trabajo.

Bertranou, Julián F. 1998. "Mexico: The Politics of the System for Retirement Pensions." In *Do Options Exist? The Reform of Pension and Health Care Systems in Latin America.* ed. M. A. Cruz-Saco and C. Mesa-Lago. Pittsburgh, PA: University of Pittsburgh Press, 85–108.

Blau, Francine, Marianne Ferber, and Anne Winkler. 2002. *The Economics of Women, Men and Work*, 4th ed. Upper Saddle River, NJ: Prentice-Hall.

Burnes, Kathy, and James Schulz. 2000. *Older Women and Private Pensions in the United States.* Waltham, MA: National Center on Women and Aging, Brandeis University.

Case, Anne. 2001. "Does Money Protect Health Status? Evidence from South African Pensions." National Bureau of Economic Research Paper #8495. Cambridge, MA: National Bureau of Economic Research.

Casey, Bernard, and Atsuhiro Yamada. 2002. "Getting Older, Getting Poorer? A Study of the Earnings, Pensions, Assets and Living Arrangements of Older People in Nine Countries." Labour Market and Social Policy Occasional Paper No. 60. Paris: Organisation for Economic Co-operation and Development.

Castel, Paulette, and Louise Fox. 2001. "Gender Dimensions of Pension Reform in the Former Soviet Union." In *New Ideas About Old Age Security* ed. R. Holzmann and J. Stiglitz. Washington, DC: World Bank.

Cheyre, Hernan. 1991. *La Prevision en Chile Ayer y Hoy.* Santiago, Chile: Centro de Estudios Publicos.

Clare, Ross. 2004. *Why Can't a Woman be More Like a Man—Gender Differences in Retirement Savings.* Sydney, Australia: Association of Superannuation Funds of Australia Research Centre.

Coronado, Julia Lynn, Don Fullerton, and Thomas Glass. 1999. "Distributional Impacts of Proposed Changes to the Social Security System." In *Tax Policy and the Economy,* ed. J. Poterba, vol. XIII, 149–86.

———. 2000. "The Progressivity of Social Security," National Bureau of Economic Research Working Paper W7520. Cambridge MA: National Bureau of Economic Research.

Cruz-Saco, M. A., and C. Mesa-Lago, eds. 1998. *Do Options Exist? The Reform of Pension and Health Care Systems in Latin America.* Pittsburgh, PA: University of Pittsburgh Press.

Deaton, Angus. 1997. *The Analysis of Household Surveys: A Microeconometric Approach to Development_Policy.* Baltimore, MD: Johns Hopkins University Press.

Deaton, Angus, and John Meullbauer. 1986. "On Measuring Child Costs: With Applications to Poor Countries." *Journal of Political Economy* 94 (4): 720–44.

Deaton, Angus, and Christina Paxson. 1997. "Poverty among Children and the Elderly in Developing Countries." Development Studies Paper #179. Princeton, NJ: Woodrow Wilson School of Public and International Affairs, Princeton University.

Department of Families, Community Services and Indigenous Affairs, Government of Australia. 2004. *Income Support Customers: A Statistical Overview 2004.* Statistical Paper No. 3. Canberra, Australia: Department of Families, Community Services and Indigenous Affiars.

Duflo, Esther. 2000. "Grandmothers and Granddaughters: Old Age Pension and Intra-Household Allocation in South Africa." National Bureau of Economic Research Working Paper #8091. Cambridge, MA: National Bureau of Economic Research.

Duryea, Suzanne, Alejandra Cox Edwards, and Manuelita Ureta. 2004. "Women in the Latin American Labor Market: The Remarkable 1990's." Labor Markets Policy Briefs Series. Washington, DC: Inter-American Bank.

Edwards, Alejandra Cox. 2000. "Pension Projections for Chilean Men and Women: Estimates from Social Security Contributions" (translated to Spanish as "El Futuro de las Pensiones en Chile"). *Estudios Públicos* 79 (Winter): 237–85.

———. 2001a. "Social Security Reform and Women's Pensions." Policy Research Report on Gender and Development, Working Paper Series #17. Washington, DC: World Bank.

———. 2001b. "Gender Inequities in the Pension and Social Protection Systems in the Region." Paper presented at the Annual Meeting of the Board of Governors of Inter-America Development Bank and Inter-American Investment Corporation, Santiago, Chile.

———. 2002. "Gender Differentiated Effects of Social Security Reform: The Case of Chile." *World Bank Economic Review* 16 (3): 321–43.

Edwards, Alejandra Cox, and Estelle James. 2005. "Do Individual Accounts Postpone Retirement? Evidence from Chile." Michigan Retirement Research Center Working Paper 2005-098. Ann Arbor, MI: Michigan Retirement Research Center.

———. 2006. "Who Annuitizes and How do System Rules Shape These Choices?" Michigan Retirement Research Center Working Paper 2006-019. Ann Arbor, MI: Michigan Retirement Research Center.

Falkingham, Jane, and Katherine Rake. 2001. "Modelling the Gender Impact of British Pension Reforms." In *Women, Work and Pensions*, ed. Jay Ginn, Debra Street, and Sara Arber. Buckingham, UK: Open University Press.

Friedberg, Leora, and Anthony Webb. 2006. "Determinants and Consequences of Bargaining Power in Households." Working Paper 2006-13. Boston: Center for Retirement Research, Boston College.

Ginn, Jay, Debra Street, and Sara Arber. 2001. "Cross-National Trends in Women's Work." In *Women, Work and Pensions*, ed. Jay Ginn, Debra Street, and Sara Arber. Buckingham, UK: Open University Press.

Goldin, Claudia. 2006. "The Quiet Revolution that Transformed Women's Employment, Education and Family." *American Economic Review* 96 (2): 1–21.

Gómez de León, Jose, and Susan Parker. 1998. "Demographic Changes, Mortality Reductions, and the New Mexican Social Security Law." Paper presented at the Annual Meeting of the American Association for the Advancement of Science, Philadelphia, February.

Grandolini, G., and L. Cerda. 1998. "The 1997 Pension Reform in Mexico." Policy Research Working Paper No. 1933. Washington, DC: World Bank.

Gruber, J., and D. A. Wise. 1999. *Social Security and Retirement around the World*. Chicago: University of Chicago Press.

Gustman, Alan, and Thomas L. Steinmeier. 2000. "How Effective Is Redistribution under the Social Security Benefit Formula?" National Bureau of Economic Research Working Paper W7597. Cambridge MA: National Bureau of Economic Research.

Hagenaars, Aldi, Klaus de Vos, and M. Asghar Zaidi. 1994. *Poverty Statistics in the Late 1980s: Research Based on Micro-Data*. Luxembourg: Office for Official Publications of the European Communities.

Hinz, Richard, David McCarthy, and John Turner. 1997. "Are Women Conservative Investors? Gender Differences in Participant-Directed Pension Investments." In *Positioning Pensions for the Twenty-First Century*, ed. M. Gordon, O. Mitchell and M. Twinney. Philadelphia: University of Pennsylvania Press.

Instituto Mexicano del Seguro Social (IMSS). 1993. *Ley del Seguro Social*. Mexico, D.F. Mexico: Instituto Mexicano del Seguro Social. http://www.imss.gob.mx (accessed September 13, 2007).

Instituto Nacional de Estadística y Censos de la República Argentina (INDEC). 1996–1997. *Encuesta Nacional de Gastos de los Hogares.* Buenos Aires, Argentina: Instituto Nacional de Estadística y Censos de la República Argentina.

Instituto Nacional de Estadística, Geografía e Informática (INEGI). 1998. *Encuesta Nacional de Empleo 1997.* Compact disc. Aguascalientes, Mexico: Instituto Nacional de Estadística, Geografía e Informática.

James, Estelle, and Sarah M. Brooks. 2001. "The Political Economy of Structural Pension Reform." In *New Ideas About Old Age Security*, ed. Robert Holzmann and Joseph Stiglitz. Washington, DC: World Bank.

James, Estelle, and Xue Song. 2001. "Annuities Markets Around the World: Money's Worth and Risk Intermediation." Center for Research on Pensions and Welfare Policies (CeRP) Working Paper 16/01. Moncalieri, Italy: Center for Research on Pensions and Welfare Policies.

James, Estelle, and Dimitri Vittas. 2001. "Annuities Markets in Comparative Perspective: Do Consumers Get Their Money's Worth?" In *OECD 2000 Private Pensions Conference 2000.* Paris: Organisation for Economic Co-operation and Development.

James, Estelle, Alejandra Cox Edwards, and Rebeca Wong. 2003. "The Gender Impact of Pension Reform." *Journal of Pension Economics and Finance* 2 (2): 181–219.

———. 2007. "The Gender Impact of Social Security Reform in Latin America." In *Lessons from Pension Reform in the Americas*, ed. Stephen Kay and Tapen Sinha. New York: Oxford University Press.

James, Estelle, Gary Ferrier, James Smalhout, and Dimitri Vittas. 2000. "Mutual Funds and Institutional Investments: What Is the Most Efficient Way to Set Up Individual Accounts in a Social Security System?" In *Administrative Costs and Social Security Privatization*, ed. John Shoven. Chicago: University of Chicago Press.

James, Estelle, Guillermo Martinez, and Augusto Iglesias. 2006. "The Payout Stage in Chile: Who Annuitizes and Why?" *Journal of Pension Economics and Finance* 5 (2): 121–54.

James, Estelle, James Smalhout, and Dimitri Vittas. 2001. "Administrative Costs and the Organization of Individual Account Systems: A Comparative Perspective." In *New Ideas About Old Age Security*, ed. Robert Holzmann and Joseph Stiglitz. Washington, DC: World Bank.

Jefferson, Therese, and Alison Preston. 2005. "Australia's 'Other' Gender Wage Gap: Baby Boomers and Compulsory Superannuation Accounts." *Feminist Economics* 11 (2): 79–101.

Jensen, R. 2004. "Do Public Transfers Displace the Benefits of Private Transfers? Evidence from South Africa." *Journal of Public Economics* 88 (1): 89–112.

Jianakoplos, Nancy, and Alexandra Bernasek. 1998. "Are Women More Risk Averse?"_*Economic Inquiry* 36 (4): 620–30.

Kelly, Simon, Ann Harding, and Richard Percival. 2002a. "Live Long and Prosper? Projecting the Likely Superannuation of the Baby Boomers in 2020." Online Conference Paper CP 28. Canberra, Australia: National Centre for social and Economic Modelling, University of Canberra.

———. 2002b. "Projecting the Impact of Changes in Superannuation Policy: A Microsimulation Approach." Online Conference Paper CP 23. Canberra, Australia: National Centre for social and Economic Modelling, University of Canberra.

Lanjouw, Peter, Branko Milanovic, and Stefano Paternostro. 1998. "Poverty and Economic Transition: How Do Economies of Scale Affect Poverty Rates of Different Households?" Washington, DC: World Bank.

Lee, Haeduck. 2000. "Poverty and Income Distribution in Argentina: Patterns and

Changes." Washington, DC: World Bank Poverty Reduction and Economic Management Unit, Latin America and the Caribbean Region.

Lyons, Angela, and Tansel Yilmazer. 2004. "How Does Marriage Affect the Allocation of Assets in Women's Defined Contributon Plans?" Center for Retirement Research Working Paper 2004-28. Boston: Center for Retirement Research.

Mexican Census. 2000. Available from the Integrated Public Use Series International (IPUMS) Minnesota Population Center. http://international.ipums.org/international (accessed September 13, 2007).

Ministerio del Trabajo y Prevision Social. 2002. *Encuesta de Proteccion Social (EPS) 2002—Metodologia y Primeros resultados de la Encuesta de Proteccion Social 2002.* Santiago, Chile: Gobierno de Chile Ministerio del Trabajo y Prevision Social, Subsecretaria de Prevision Social.

Munnell, Alicia. 2004. "Why Are So Many Older Women Poor?" *Just the Facts on Retirement Issues* 10 (Brief). Boston: Center for Retirement Research, Boston College.

Munnell, Alicia, and Natalia Jivan. 2005. "What Makes Older Women Work?" Issue Brief, Series 1. Boston: Center for Retirement Research, Boston College.

Munnell, Alicia, and Mauricio Soto. 2005. "Why do Women Claim Social Security Benefits so Early?" Issue Brief #35. Boston: Center for Retirement Research, Boston College.

National Economic Council (NEC). 1998. "Women and Retirement Security." Washington, DC: National Economic Council.

Oaxaca, Ronald. 1973. "Male-Female Wage Differentials in Urban Labor Markets." *International Economic Review* 14 (3): 693–709.

Organization for Economic Co-operation and Development (OECD). 1982. *The OECD List of Social Indicators*. Paris: Organisation for Economic Co-operation and Development.

———. 2003. *The Effects of Partial Careers on Pension Entitlements*. Paris: Organisation for Economic Co-operation and Development.

———. 2005. *Pensions at a Glance*. Paris: Organisation for Economic Co-operation and Development.

Palacios, Robert, and Oleksiy Sluchynskyy. 2006. "The Role of Social Pensions." Washington, DC: World Bank.

Parker, Susan, and Rebeca Wong. 2001. "Welfare of Male and Female Elderly in Mexico: A Comparison." In *The Economics of Gender in Mexico: Work, Family, State, and Market.* Washington, DC: World Bank.

Pedrero, Nieto Mercedes. 1999. "Situación económica en la tercera edad." *Papeles de Población* 5 (19): 77–102.

Pensions Commission. 2004. *Pensions Challenges and Choices: First Report of the Pensions Commission.* Norwich, UK: Published with the permission of the Pensions Commission on behalf of the Controller of Her Majesty's Stationery Office.

Posner, Richard. 1995. *Aging and Old Age*. Chicago: University of Chicago Press.

Preston, Alison, and Siobhan Austen. 2001. "Women, Superannuation and the SGC." *Australian Bulletin of Labor* 4 (December 27): 272–95.

Save-Soderbergh, Jenny. 2003. "Pension Wealth: Gender, Risk and Portfolio Choices." Dissertation Series No. 59. Stockholm: Swedish Institute for Social Research, Stockholm University.

Schulz, James. 2000. *Older Women and Private Pension in Australia*. Waltham, MA: Brandeis University.

Shaver, Sheila. 2001. "Pension Reform in Australia: Problematic Gender Equality." In *Women, Work and Pensions: International Issues and Prospects,* ed. Jay Ginn, Debra Street, and Sara Arber. Buckingham, UK: Open University Press.

Shirley, Ekaterina, and Peter Spiegler. 1998. "The Benefits of Social Security Privatization for Women." SSP No. 12. Washington, DC: Cato Institute.

Sinha, Tapen, and Mario de los Angeles Yanez. 2007. "A Decade of Government Mandated Privately Run Pensions in Mexico: What Have We Learned?" In *Lessons from Pension Reform in the Americas*, ed. Stephen Kay and Tapen Sinha. New York: Oxford University Press.

Smeeding, Timothy, and Susanna Sandstrom. 2004. "Poverty and Income Maintenance in Old Age: A Cross-National View of Low Income Older Women." Center for Retirement Research Working Paper 2004-30. Boston: Center for Retirement Research, Boston College.

Soldo, Beth J., Rebeca Wong, Alberto Palloni, and the Mexican Health and Aging Study Team. 2003. *Mexican Health and Aging Study (MHAS)*. www.mhas.pop.upenn.edu/english.team.htm (accessed September 13, 2007).

Stahlberg, Ann-Charlote. 1990. "Lifecycle Income Redistribution of the Public Sector: Inter- and Intragenerational Effects." In *Generating Equality in the Welfare State: The Swedish Experience*, ed. Inga Persson. Oslo: Norwegian University Press.

———. 1995. "Women's Pensions in Sweden." *Scandinavian Journal of Social Welfare* 4: 19–27.

Stahlberg, Ann-Charlote, Marcela Cohen Birman, Agneta Kruse, and Annika Sundén. 2006. "Pension Reforms and Gender: The Case of Sweden." In *Gender and Social Security Reform—What's Fair for Women?*, ed. Neil Gilbert. New Brunswick, NJ: Transaction Publishers.

Stahlberg, Ann-Charlote, Agneta Kruse, and Annika Sundén. 2006. "Pension Design and Gender: Analyses of Developed and Developing Countries." In *Gender and Social Security Reform—What's Fair for Women?*, ed. Neil Gilbert. New Brunswick, NJ: Transaction Publishers.

Street, Debra, and Janet Wilmoth. 2001. "Social Insecurity? Women and Pensions in the U.S." In *Women, Work and Pensions: International Issues and Prospects*, ed. Jay Ginn, Debra Street, and Sara Arber. Buckingham, UK: Open University Press.

Sundén, Annika, and Brian Surette. 1998. "Gender Differences in the Allocation of Assets in Retirement Savings Plans." *American Economic Review* 88 (2): 207–11.

Superintendencia de Administradoras de Fondos de Pensiones (SAFP). 2003. *The Chilean Pension System*. Santiago, Chile: Superintendencia de Administradoras de Fondos de Pensiones.

Superintendencia de Administradoras de Fondos de Jubilaciones y Pensiones (SAFJP) and Instituto Torcuatto di Tella. 1999. "Regularidad: Proyecto de Indicadores de Control Previsional, Etapa 2." (Manuscript November). Buenos Aires, Argentina: Superintendencia de Administradoras de Fondos de Jubilaciones y Pensiones and Instituto Torcuatto di Tella.

Universidad de Chile–Santiago. 1994. *Caracterización Socioeconómica Nacional (CASEN) Household Survey*. Santiago, Chile: Department of Economics, Universidad de Chile–Santiago, for Ministerio de Planificación y Cooperación, Chile.

U.S. Census Bureau. 2001. *Gender 2000: Census 2000 Brief*. Washington, DC: U.S. Census Bureau

U.S. Government Accountability Office (GAO). 1997. *Social Security Reform: Implications for Women's Retirement Income*. GAO/HEHS-98-42. Washington, DC: U.S. Government Accountability Office.

University of Chile. 2000. *Encuesta de Ocupacion y Desocupación en el Gran Santiago 2000*. Santiago, Chile: Centro de Microdatos, Departamento de Economía.

Valdes, Salvador. 2002. *Políticas y Mercados de Pensiones: Un texto Universitario para América Latina.* Santiago, Chile: Ediciones Universidad Católica.

Whitehouse, Edward. 2000. "How Poor are the Old? A Survey of the Evidence from 44 Countries." Pension Reform Primer Working Paper Series. Washington, DC: World Bank. www.worldbank.org/pensions (accessed September 13, 2007).

———. 2003. "Guide to World Pension Systems: Eastern Europe and Central Asia." Washington, DC: World Bank.

Wong, Rebeca, and Susan Parker. 2001. "Social Security Reform in Mexico: A Gender Perspective." Paper presented at the Population Association of America Meetings, Washington, DC, April 2001; also presented at Interamerican Conference on Social Security, Fortaleza, Brazil, November 2001.

Wong, Rebeca, Monica Espinoza, and Alberto Palloni. 2007. "Adultos Mayores Mexicanes en Contexto Socioeonomico Amplio." *Salud y Envejecimiento* 49, forthcoming.

World Bank. 1997. *Chile: Poverty and Income Distribution in a High-Growth Economy 1987–1995.* Report 16377-CH. Washington, DC: World Bank.

World Bank. 2004. *Averting the Old Age Crisis: Policies to Protect the Old and Promote Growth.* Washington, DC: Oxford University Press and World Bank.

Woycicka, Irena, Agnieska Chlon-Dominczak, Irena Kotowska, and Irena Topinska. 2003. "Gender Impact of Social Security Reform in Central and Eastern Europe: Poland." in *The Gender Dimensions of Social Security Reform in Central and Eastern Europe: Case Studies of the Czech Republic, Hungary, and Poland,* ed. E. Fultz, M. Ruck, and S. Steinhiber. Budapest, Hungary: International Labor Office.

INDEX

DATE DUE